LARRY GOLDSTEIN

MW00329438

A Guide to College & University Budgeting

Foundations for Institutional Effectiveness

4th EDITION

Library of Congress Cataloging-in-Publication Data

Goldstein, Larry, 1950-
  A guide to college and university budgeting : foundations for
institutional effectiveness / by Larry Goldstein. — 4th ed.
      p. cm.
  Rev. ed. of: College & university budgeting, 2005.
  Includes bibliographical references and index.
  ISBN 978-1-56972-007-3 (pbk. : alk. paper) 1. Universities
and colleges—United States—Finance. 2. Universities and
colleges—United States—Business management. I. Goldstein,
Larry, 1950- College & university budgeting. II. Title.
  LB2342.M43 2012
  378.1'060973—dc23
                                        2012010075

NC3200

Contents

Foreword

In fall 2011, I ran into my longtime friend and colleague Larry Goldstein. In the course of our conversation, he mentioned the new edition of his book on college and university budgeting. A few weeks later, he sent me the manuscript for the fourth edition so I could have the pleasure of reviewing it in advance.

The term "budget" may have many definitions in an organization and can serve many purposes. A budget, for example, can be viewed as:

1. A planning document
2. A reflection of values and priorities of an organization
3. An indication of institutional culture
4. A sign and degree of organizational transparency
5. A manifestation of decision making in an enterprise

Of course, some people view budgeting as a mechanistic exercise based on a purely prescriptive and bureaucratic procedure. Given the complexity of the concept, every one of these perspectives has some merit.

In higher education, the concept and nature of budgets become even more confusing and multifaceted. One plausible explanation is that higher education is a political enterprise rather than an economic one. Within such a framework, budgets in colleges and universities become a mystery—perhaps because, despite the common rhetoric of transparency and openness, higher education favors opaque budgeting processes.

This is where I notice the strength of this book. The author demonstrates the organic link between planning and budgeting, making it unambiguously clear that budgets and plans represent two sides of the same coin. In other words, the budget is the financial manifestation of the university's plans. He discusses factors essential to the success of the budgeting process, including open communication with key stakeholders, clear articulation of the budget to the strategic plan, budget implementation and monitoring processes, and the role of technology.

In addition, Larry has done a very good job of introducing the concepts and variables special to higher education, which, like any enterprise, has its own unique vocabulary. His ability to illustrate complex concepts in easily understood terms makes this book a must-read for leaders who are new to this sector, even if they have held senior leadership positions in the for-profit sector.

In his book, *Honoring the Trust: Quality and Cost Containment in Higher Education*, William F. Massy states that, for-profit entities offer a fixed number of products and services with the intent of maximizing return for the investors. In the nonprofit environment, however, the organization has a fixed amount of resources and a mission to maximize value for all its stakeholders. If a corporation makes an innovative change that reduces the cost of production, it either invests in infrastructure to offer more products and services to more customers, increases profits returned to investors, passes the savings to its customers, or undertakes a combination of all three options.

By contrast, in a nonprofit organization, savings from an efficiency gain are not passed on—because there are no owners. Instead, the organization invests in other activities to add more value. For instance, if a university invests in a new information technology (IT) system or energy management project that results in cost reductions, the savings typically will not result in reduced tuition prices. Because there are limitless projects that, in theory, will maximize the value for stakeholders, the university will deploy its available resources toward those projects. Therefore, the relationship between cost and efficiency gains is more complex in universities (although this may be less true for the small number of for-profit institutions). This subtle difference may not be obvious to those coming from the corporate sector to higher education. That is one way this book can provide excellent context for them.

Even for those who have come up through the ranks in higher education, this book offers a wealth of knowledge. Most likely, they will not have been exposed to all of the concepts covered in the book—or they may have learned the concepts in a biased or incomplete fashion.

The author not only explains various types of internal budgets—namely, operating, capital, and special allocation—but also talks about the external factors that can affect those budgets, such as the federal government, state statutes, local ordinances, and the overall political and regulatory environment. He discusses how the budgeting process reflects subtle elements of the organization's culture—such as the degree of transparency and openness, institutional character, and decision-making authority—and emphasizes the starring role that budget flexibility plays in enabling a college or university to respond to challenges. The true strength of an organization—and the true test of leadership—is how one deals with such challenges during economic downturns and other financial emergencies, not just in stable situations.

Having spent more than three decades in higher education, including positions as chief financial officer of two universities, I was impressed with the book's depth and breadth of the coverage of topics pertinent to higher education budgeting. I was equally impressed by the brevity of the discussion, without any compromise on its technical rigor or quality. The author has very capably treated the subject matter in an easily understandable fashion.

I highly recommend this book to up-and-coming managers in higher education who aspire to move further up the administrative ladder, as well as to seasoned leaders looking for a comprehensive resource. Finally, for those coming to higher education from other sectors, this is a must-read.

Mohammad H. Qayoumi, Ph.D.
President
San Jose State University, San Jose, California
February 2012

Preface

The budget is an essential management tool for colleges and universities. It takes on even greater significance because of the financial distress experienced in the wake of the 2008 recession. As this fourth edition was being written, U.S. higher education was facing financial challenges not seen since the Depression. Few institutions had anticipated or prepared for economic hardships of the magnitude they encountered. Many institutions, including some considered immune to financial stress, have faced the difficult decision to curtail or eliminate programs and terminate appointments in the process. And dozens of institutions have closed since the recession began.

Nothing in this book will create additional resources for an institution. But adhering to the principles it presents can help institutions weather the current storm and better prepare for the next one. A deeper understanding of higher education budgeting will help institutions—the people working in them and the people governing them—make wiser decisions about the deployment of resources to support priorities established through an effective planning process.

Resources are scarce—and they're expected to remain that way for the foreseeable future. Higher education does not enjoy the untarnished reputation it once did, and too many other programs now compete for a significantly reduced pool of resources. It's crucial that every dollar expended provides maximum value.

The intended audience for this primer has expanded since publication of the third edition. It originally was targeted primarily to new academic administrators and faculty seeking to participate in the resource allocation process but with an informed perspective. A conscious decision has been made to retain the focus on these two groups while expanding coverage, which should appeal to boards, senior administrators, and others interested in the resource allocation process. This book should prove especially valuable to individuals who recently have accepted positions in higher education institutions after working in other industries—especially those from the for-profit sector. Its particular value to the latter group is its focus on the collegial decision-making processes prevalent in higher education.

Readers of this book should gain a better understanding of the budget process at their institutions. They will learn that the most effective budget processes are driven by plans—in particular, plans developed using open and inclusive processes. And they will realize that resource allocation decisions in higher education rarely mean a choice between good and bad options but rather between good and better options.

A Brief Overview

This book will enable readers to ask meaningful questions about the budget process on their campus. Although this book does not aim to address every possible budgeting variation one might encounter, it does identify the most important elements of the budgeting process and provides information about the ways in which internal and external factors influence the budget.

More specifically, Chapter One explains why budgeting is an important element of policy making. This introductory chapter describes the types of budgets used in higher education, which go beyond mere numbers to describe what an institution is all about. Chapter Two addresses the broader political and regulatory contexts affecting higher education, including the extensive range of federal rules and regulations that affect campuses and, in the process, consume resources. In addition, the chapter briefly explores the impact of inflation on higher education's costs and the problems this creates for those seeking to suppress tuition prices.

Chapter Three shifts the discussion from politics to the national economic climate. It discusses the growth of for-profit institutions within higher education and other major trends, such as competition, technology, sustainability, and changing student demographics.

Chapters Four and Five are different sides of the same coin. The first focuses on the revenues and resources typically available to higher education institutions, including financial aid from the federal government, while the latter concentrates on expenses and costs. Chapter Five is divided into two sections due to the differing rules applicable to financial reporting by public and independent institutions.

New to the fourth edition, Chapter Six focuses on planning and its implications for resource allocation. The chapter highlights the importance of integrating planning, resource allocation, and assessment, and it discusses the importance of broad-based participation. Chapter Seven describes the key elements of the most common budget models—formula, incremental, responsibility center, and zero-based budgeting—as well as two special-purpose budget models: initiative-based budgeting and performance-based budgeting.

Chapter Eight explores the factors that commonly influence the budget process, including institutional character, decision-making authority, transparency, and communication. In-depth coverage of the elements of the operating and capital budget cycles appears in Chapter Nine, along with the key considerations related to the budget calendar. Coverage of the capital budget cycle, for example, includes a discussion of deferred maintenance and its implications for both operating and capital budgets.

The attention then shifts to budget management. Chapter Ten addresses how to maximize budget flexibility to accommodate fluctuations in
enrollment, revenues, and expenses, while Chapter Eleven explores how
institutional policy decisions can impact the budget.

Chapter Twelve tackles the sensitive issue of budgeting under extraordinary circumstances. It discusses the difficult decisions that arise when an
institution faces severe economic challenges—whether driven by broad-based
economic catastrophe, natural disaster, or simply poor management—and
offers both short- and long-term responses to difficult financial times. This
chapter also suggests planning approaches that can help the institution
avoid retrenchment—or address it, if that becomes necessary.

The final chapter, Chapter Thirteen, highlights key points and offers advice for readers who seek to apply the principles presented in this book on
their campuses. The Appendix addresses several accounting issues relevant
to budgeting, including noncash expenses (and the related issue of funding
depreciation), financial aid (and the importance of avoiding double-counting
revenues and expenses), and the impact of differing accounting standards.

A Unique Approach

Every campus has an institutional character, culture, and operating style
that dictates how its budget is developed. The same factors also influence
which individuals—by title, role, responsibility, or personality—have the
greatest influence over the final product. In some organizations—small
independent institutions, for example—faculty voices may be heard loud
and clear throughout the budget process. In other institutions—especially
large community colleges and some research institutions—the faculty may
not be as actively involved in the budget process. Traditions are important
when dealing with something as sensitive as a budget process and everything it represents, but they should not be used as an excuse to justify
"doing what we've always done."

Effective budgeting, appropriately linked with planning and assessment,
provides a wonderful opportunity to review options and reprioritize an institution's agenda. Understanding the process for developing a budget, as
well as the role an individual can play in that process, can significantly
affect the future success of a campus.

That said, there is nothing magical about budget work. It's hard work
because the stakes are high and the choices are difficult. Nevertheless,
those who are willing to invest the time to participate in the planning
and resource allocation processes can reap significant rewards. The more
knowledgeable and informed they are, the greater those rewards will be.

Acknowledgements

I would be remiss if I didn't once again extend thanks to Richard J. Meisinger, Jr., author of the first and second editions of this book. I hope he would appreciate the fact that many of his original words and concepts appear in this edition.

Thanks also are due to the NACUBO team for their invaluable support and encouragement throughout the writing process.

- Content expertise, Sue Menditto, director, accounting policy, NACUBO
- Project management, Tadu Yimam, director, online learning, NACUBO
- Art direction provided by Kaysha Johnston, production & design manager, NACUBO
- Editor, Sandra R. Sabo, freelance consultant Zaki Ghul

One of the most welcome enhancements to this book is the foreword by Mo Qayoumi, president of San Jose State University. He undertook this effort during an incredibly busy time and while dealing with some personal challenges due to a death in his family. I am truly grateful for his efforts on my behalf.

The next group deserving special recognition is the advisory committee assembled by Tadu and Sue. The members of the committee provided invaluable guidance and suggestions to enhance the final product. In addition to Sue and Tadu, they include Craig Becker (Yeshiva University), Melody Bianchetto (University of Virginia), Patricia Charlton (College of Southern Nevada), Theresa P. Gordon (University of Idaho), Linda Kroll (University of Notre Dame), Debra Lipkey (Gallaudet University), Jack Mahoney (Rensselaer Polytechnic Institute), and John Sell (The College of Wooster).

I wish to express appreciation to individuals who have contributed significantly to my professional development. Pat Sanaghan of The Sanaghan Group has been a longtime colleague and thought partner. He has taught me a great deal about planning, including the need to engage the masses in an open, participative process. Along the same lines, special thanks go to Bob Dickeson, president emeritus of Northern Colorado University—the creator of the academic prioritization process described in these pages. Working with Bob over the last several years has been a wonderful experience, and that has afforded me the opportunity to benefit from his years of experience in higher education.

One other group must be acknowledged and thanked, although it is not possible to list these individuals by name. Still, I want to express appreciation to my current and former colleagues in higher education financial management—those on campuses as well as those working in the association community and the commercial sector providing services to higher education. I'm richer for having known you, and this is a better product because of the lessons I've learned from you.

Last, and certainly not least, I want to thank my wife, Sue, for putting up with me as I tried to complete the writing while still attending to numerous client engagements. Our recent vacation and weekend trips were made much less enjoyable for her as I woke up early each morning to work on the book. Hopefully, we can relax together a little more now that it's completed!

Larry Goldstein
Crimora, Virginia
February 2012

Historically, especially in what now is referred to as the nonprofit sector, most activities were managed on a cash basis. Activities and service levels varied based on the presence or absence of adequate resources. By the late 1800s, public administration had evolved to the point where revenues were anticipated; this information was then used to develop expenditure plans.

Budgets provided a mechanism for dealing with both known and anticipated financial problems in an organized manner. Even before adopting full accrual accounting—which measures revenues when earned (rather than when cash is collected) and expenses when incurred (rather than when paid)—budgets proved valuable in eliminating the uncertainty that comes with pure cash accounting. Given that needs always exceeded resources, the relatively recent advent of planning and budgeting helped institutions set priorities.

Why Bother with Budgeting?

Even more than many other nonprofit institutions, colleges and universities have a complex operating environment. The variety of revenue sources, the compliance requirements to which they are subject, and the nature of the restrictions attached to many of their resources make both planning and budget development challenging propositions. Still, without an effective budget process, managing a college or university from a financial perspective would be nothing less than chaos. An effective planning process leading to a clearly articulated budget provides a means of tracking revenues and expenses so that resources can be used most effectively to meet the institution's goals while still complying with external constraints.

Budgeting also enables an institution to highlight the costs of particular activities and their respective claims on resources. This exercise is especially valuable for activities supported with unrestricted resources, where there may not be a direct link between the sources of revenue allocated to the activity and the activity's expenses. It may be less necessary for some activities supported with restricted resources: If the revenues are reduced or eliminated, it usually is obvious that the activity will experience operational cutbacks or be terminated.

On the other hand, when unrestricted resources are expected to increase, the institution has an opportunity to increase the resources allocated to particular activities, undertake new activities, or simply increase amounts reserved for future use. These decisions become more evident when articulated through the budget. And they become easier to make and implement if they are guided by an effective planning process.

In short, a budget is a map that guides an institution on its journey to carry out its mission. For nearly every institution, the mission includes multiple elements, such as instruction, research, and public service. Some institutions have an additional mission element—patient care. Regardless of the specific elements of an institution's mission, an effective budget will address them all.

You can learn a great deal about an institution merely by reviewing the budget—especially if prior-year budget information is available for comparison. Comparing the projected revenues and anticipated expenses provides clues about the institution's priorities. Even a cursory review will suggest the relative importance of the mission components and will detail what revenues are anticipated and how they will be deployed in carrying out the mission.

A Range of Roles

Budgets take many forms but usually include at least two components: quantitative and narrative information. The quantitative component details the numbers that indicate the expected revenue—by category and by relative amount. It also provides the basic information about how funds will be expended. Some quantitative formats are highly aggregated, showing just the major categories of revenues (for example, tuition or governmental appropriations) and expenses (for example, instruction and public service or compensation and utilities). Others are detailed, showing individual expense categories for specific institutional units.

The narrative component provides additional information about the numbers that appear in the quantitative budget. Depending on the approach taken, the narrative may highlight the specific priorities addressed, the assumptions used in developing the budget, and the constraints that affect the numbers in the budget. It also may refer to specific goals and objectives for the institution as well as its individual units.

Budgets serve many purposes and have various roles. Specifically, the budget is:

The financial representation of the institution's plans—both strategic and operational. It is developed through iterative processes and, once finalized, presents the results of a multitude of resource allocation decisions. These decisions are not made in a vacuum. They reflect advice and guidance from the board, discussions among senior managers, and—in the most effective settings—dialogues involving the institution's various stakeholders.

Unless driven by the institution's plans, the budget will not achieve the ultimate purpose of intentionally moving the institution toward enhanced service and improved quality. Some people mistakenly believe that the budget *is the plan.* But if that's the case, the budget process represents constrained thinking because it is overly influenced by the previous budget. Starting the budget process with effective planning that identifies institutional priorities in light of current realities and past financial decisions is one step toward ensuring that resources are deployed most effectively.

A contract between management and the operating units charged with carrying out the plans. The budget indicates what resources the institution will provide to the units and, in broad terms, what the units will focus on in utilizing those resources. Like many contracts, however, it does not represent a guarantee. Effective budgets include provisions for contingencies, yet unforeseen circumstances still may prevent the institution from providing all the resources identified in the budget. Even so, both management and the units should view the budget as a shared commitment.

A forecast of the institution's financial picture at a future time. Assuming that a budget covers an annual operating cycle that coincides with the institution's fiscal year, the institution can prepare pro forma financial statements that assume all revenues and expenses will materialize as predicted. These pro forma statements depict the institution's expected financial condition at the end of the cycle. If reasonably accurate in its predictions, the institution will know what to expect. This effort also can influence the development of the budget. Performing a "what if" analysis can help avoid excessive spending that would adversely affect the institution's financial health.

Financial ratio analysis (see Chapter Six) can be used to measure the financial health of an institution. By projecting the results of the budgeted operating and capital activity—and making assumptions about investment performance—the institution can project its financial health at the end of the cycle. Most likely, the actual results will vary because of unforeseen factors and the unpredictability of financial markets. Nevertheless, operational results typically have the greatest impact on an institution's financial health. Therefore, preparing pro forma financial statements based on budgets can be beneficial to an institution that has established a goal of achieving certain financial objectives along with its programmatic objectives.

An indicator of risk tolerance. Assumptions and predictions made throughout the planning and budget development processes cover items as critical as the number of expected entering freshmen and transfer students and as mundane as the expected increase in elevator maintenance fees. Some decisions are imposed on the institution, such as increased utilities costs, while others—such as faculty salary increases—are imposed *by* the institution. The specific decisions and their impact on the institution's financial health indicate the level of risk the institution can tolerate.

The greater the risk tolerance, the smaller the contingency built into the budget. Institutions with a relatively higher tolerance for risk budget revenues aggressively and allocate most resources for expenses (including appropriate additions to reserves for future use, such as facilities maintenance). On the other hand, institutions that are less comfortable with risk are more likely to budget revenues conservatively and include contingency amounts to address revenue shortfalls or expense overruns.

Regardless of the institution's tolerance for risk, it should allocate a portion of the budget to address contingencies. This can be a mix of recurring and one-time reserves that can be used in response to unanticipated opportunities or challenges.

A political instrument. To create the budget, administrators from various units strike bargains and make trade-offs. Throughout the process, many people seek to exert their leadership to influence the ultimate distribution of resources. The final outcome reflects a series of negotiations about which activities should be funded and at what levels.

Often, multiple budget cycles overlap, making it common for negotiations in one cycle to influence other cycles. Although these negotiations rarely result in complete satisfaction for the parties involved, the process is worthwhile. The negotiations provide the opportunity to communicate needs for services and the resources required to provide them. This process can lead to a better understanding of other activities competing for the same scarce resources. Care is needed though because negotiations can be counterproductive if not properly managed. It is important that the process afford each perspective the opportunity to be heard and to receive feedback about the rationale for final decisions in a transparent manner.

Prelude to a Budget

In well-managed institutions, the budget is a manifestation of the institution's plans and reflects the relative priorities assigned to different activities. It also takes into consideration all constituents' needs and interests. Because planning must precede budget development, many key decisions already will have been made before the budget cycle begins.

Planning is not about choosing between good and bad ideas. It's about choosing between good and better ideas. Both the planning process and the budget process should have the same ultimate objective: the most effective deployment of resources to support the institution's overall vision and the priorities that will lead to attaining that vision.

That's why an institution should decide its priorities before beginning the budget process in earnest. Individual allocation decisions should grow from the decisions made throughout the planning process. Unfortunately, too few higher education institutions use effective planning mechanisms. And many of those that engage in planning do not use it to intentionally guide the resource allocation process.

In too many instances, institutions rely excessively on incremental budgeting—adjusting the prior year's budget by a fixed percentage to address changes in available resources. While reasonable for addressing portions of the budget, this approach is often used to excess, which leaves the institution unable to achieve enhanced results, build on areas of identified strength, or successfully pursue its mission and attain its vision.

Purely incremental approaches assume that the way resources currently are deployed is the most effective distribution, that all units have approximately equal needs for additional resources, and that maintaining the status quo is in the institution's best interests. Incremental processes do not lead to success because it is highly unlikely that the current budget—the starting point—is allocated in the most optimal manner. Activities that might flourish with increased resources remain underfunded, while others that may have outlived their usefulness or value to the institution continue to consume resources.

Two factors may help explain the continued popularity of incremental approaches—despite the fact that regional accreditation agencies identify the linkage of resource allocation to planning as evidence of institutional effectiveness. First, incremental budgeting is deemed to be fair: All units receive the same relative percentage of increased resources (or reductions in times of contraction). Second, it is efficient because it provides a starting point and a fixed percentage for adjustments.

The presumed fairness and efficiency, however, come at the expense of effectiveness. A system that perpetuates embedded inequities cannot be deemed fair. Instead, high-performing units should be rewarded with increased resources and spared from cuts. Similarly, activities with the greatest potential to contribute to—or enhance—the institution's success should receive relatively more resources than units that do not contribute to institutional success or otherwise underperform relative to others within the institution.

The bottom line is that incremental budgeting is efficient, but not necessarily effective, because it ignores the results of planning—which should have identified priority areas. Without question, the most successful approach to budgeting starts with an effective plan—one developed with extensive input from all institutional stakeholders—and develops the budget based on the decisions reflected in the plan.

Types of Budgets

At the highest level, budgets focus on the resources higher education needs for programmatic success: dollars, positions, space, technology, and equipment. Most budgets focus on dollars, because money is the easiest resource to measure and monitor. But budgets also focus on resource allocation decisions. For example, the number of faculty positions is a resource that is estimated based on needs and objectives. For example, the number of faculty positions (or lines) assigned to a given unit translates into salaries and benefits—represented by dollars—for those positions. In turn, space, technology, and equipment will be affected by decisions involving positions.

Higher education institutions use different budgets for a variety of purposes. As its name suggests, the operating budget identifies all revenues and other resources available to support operations—both those that result from various service efforts (for example, tuition and patient charges) and those derived from other sources (for example, governmental appropriations and gifts). It addresses the various elements of the institution's mission (for example, instruction and research) and also focuses on supporting and ancillary activities, such as libraries and intercollegiate athletics.

Operating revenues either finance the current expenses or contribute to institutional reserves—a form of savings. The vast majority of revenues received during a given period will be expended on operations and related activities during that period. Any remaining unexpended resources will be added to reserves—resources set aside for specific purposes, typically for use in the future. In some cases, however, reserves merely serve as a cushion against future financial problems.

In addition to revenues and reserves, operating budgets present the day-to-day expenses incurred by the institution as it carries out its mission. Colleges and universities incur a wide variety of expenses. Some, such as salaries and wages, make up a significant percentage of the budget. Others may be relatively small and vary significantly based on the character of the institution. For instance, maintenance costs for residence halls typically do not represent a significant expense for community colleges.

Expenses in an operating budget may be displayed in either of two broad categories: natural classification or functional classification (sometimes called programmatic classification). *Natural classification* refers to expenses identified by type rather than purpose, such as salaries, benefits, travel, and supplies. Though valuable for many purposes, a budget prepared using the natural classification approach provides little information about the activities being conducted. For instance, the natural classification budget for a consulting firm or a health care organization might look very similar to one prepared for a research institution because both entities are labor-intensive.

A budget by functional category would be more valuable as an aid to understanding what is taking place.

Functional classification organizes expenses by the nature of the activity the expense supports. Examples of functional categories for a college or university include instruction, public service, and academic support. The instruction function includes various natural-class expenses, such as salaries, employee benefits, supplies, and travel. Similar types of expenses would be incurred in the other functional categories.

A matrix displaying natural-class expenses in functional categories is a useful representation of an operating budget's expense side. It indicates the relative investments by functional category and the proportional amount of types of expenses incurred to achieve the multiple programmatic objectives.

Figure 1-1 Sample University Expense Matrix Illustrating Expenses by Natural and Functional Category

Operating Expenses	Compensation	Services & Supplies	Utilities	Depreciation	Scholarships & Fellowships	Total
Instruction	$90,774,000	$14,903,000	$792,000	$1,912,000	$275,000	**$108,656,000**
Research	51,719,000	22,180,000	998,000	1,441,000	236,000	**76,574,000**
Public Service	27,531,000	12,399,000	892,000	1,329,000	14,000	**42,165,000**
Academic Support	22,231,000	5,851,000	798,000	1,848,000		**30,728,000**
Student Services	10,457,000	5,165,000	189,000	490,000	6,000	**16,307,000**
Institutional Support	13,480,000	4,453,000	184,000	276,000		**18,393,000**
Operation & Maintenance of Plant	11,562,000	9,365,000	3,737,000	6,305,000		**30,969,000**
Student Financial Aid	1,000	109,000			4,021,000	**4,131,000**
Auxiliary Services	17,957,000	25,008,000	3,454,000	6,464,000		**52,883,000**
Total Expenses	**$245,712,000**	**$99,433,000**	**$11,044,000**	**$20,065,000**	**$4,552,000**	**$380,806,000**

A capital budget maps out the finances for construction or other acquisition plans related to physical facilities and infrastructure on a campus. It also details the sources and uses of funds for renovating or renewing existing facilities. As with the operating budget, a capital budget addresses inflows and outflows—either expenses or additions to asset balances. The revenues can come from various sources, including tuition and fees, governmental appropriations, and gifts.

In addition to revenues, financing for facilities comes from reserves and borrowing arrangements. *Reserves* are funds that have accumulated through savings or have been set aside as part of the operating budget. Institutions often set aside a certain portion of the annual operating budget to cover costs that will be incurred in a future period. This practice is typical for auxiliary enterprise units (which should be self-supporting). For example, residence hall systems typically rely on borrowed funds to finance new construction. It is a fairly standard requirement of bond covenants that a certain portion of annual system revenues be set aside for facilities maintenance, such as carpet replacement, painting, and roof repairs. These funds are maintained in a reserve and invested until they are needed.

Borrowed funds are either short-term construction loans or long-term bonds that finance the acquisition or construction costs for new facilities, major equipment, or infrastructure upgrades or additions. The long-term debt serves the same purpose as a home mortgage for an individual. Colleges and universities frequently issue tax-exempt bonds to fund capital expansion. For some public institutions, the state issues the bonds or provides the resources needed to repay the bonds as they come due.

Many institutions that issue their own debt have established complex financing arrangements to support their capital expansion programs. These usually are supported by board-approved debt plans. Variable-rate debt is a staple among many financing choices to obtain resources needed for longer periods. A number of institutions have relied on various forms of short-term debt to finance construction projects until the institution is ready to convert the obligation to long-term debt.

Internal banking arrangements have become popular in recent years. With an internal bank, the institution issues long-term debt and redistributes the proceeds as needed throughout the institution. The various units receiving the proceeds are then assessed principal and interest charges to generate the resources needed to compensate and repay the bondholders who purchased the institution's long-term debt.

Expenditures appearing in a capital budget include construction costs that will be capitalized as well as other costs that—because they cannot be capitalized—will be recognized as expenses during the year they are incurred. (Capitalized costs relate to an asset that will provide benefits beyond one year.)

Both operating and capital budgets can be developed for the institution as a whole or for subsets of the institution. For instance, a capital budget might apply to an individual project, such as construction of a particular building, or it can address all currently approved capital projects for a given period. Similarly, operating budgets can address the complete range of activities for the institution, or they can simply cover activities within a department or a single programmatic area, such as instruction or student affairs.

Several variations of budgets address specific situations. For instance, some institutions prepare special budgets focused only on restricted funds. *Restricted budgets* indicate resources provided by external parties that carry stipulations about how they must be expended. Examples include gifts provided to acquire library books and income from an endowment established to fund scholarships for undergraduate students from a particular locale. Another example is a grant from a governmental entity that must be expended for specific purposes.

Special-purpose budgets must be clearly labeled and explained to avoid confusion about what they represent.

Subject to Revision

Even the best of planning processes simply cannot anticipate some events and developments, so all budgets are subject to revision. In fact, the ink on the latest budget document probably will not be dry before circumstances dictate that adjustments be made.

In most cases, the budget for a given cycle begins with the budget from the current or most recently completed cycle. Presumably, the starting point reflects the cumulative impact of all revisions to the previous budget other than temporary situations. Even so, the budget will continue to change over time. That's why the budget process and the budget itself must be flexible enough to respond to these changes (see Chapter Ten).

Apart from the unpredictability of some expense categories, revenues can vary widely from one year to the next. All institutions have uncertainty regarding the amount of revenue that some sources will generate (for example, investment income). Enrollment unpredictability can be an even greater concern.

For a tuition-dependent institution—one in which 85 percent or more of the revenue comes from tuition and required fees—a relatively small decrease in enrollment can substantially affect the pool of available resources. And this can happen without materially altering the level of expenses that will be incurred. For example, when the freshman class entering a small high-priced institution falls a few dozen students short of the number budgeted, the impact on revenues can approach a half-million dollars. Yet those students may be spread throughout the curriculum in such a way that the same number of faculty will be needed. In this scenario, the reduced enrollment may not bring any cost savings. This is one factor that encourages institutions to diversify their revenue stream.

Different institutions address the unpredictability of revenues in different ways. For institutions that have budgeted revenues conservatively, positive net financial results may lead to increased allocations of resources for use in the current period. Similarly, institutions that include expense contingencies in the budget periodically will make adjustments to reallocate available resources from the contingency line to the expense category that has experienced the cost overrun. This enables the institution to properly reflect its utilization of resources. In contrast, charging expenses directly to the contingency budget will understate the expense category that experienced the overrun. Moreover, if the situation is likely to continue, the starting point for the subsequent budget will not provide a true picture of resource needs.

The number of budget adjustments tends to be lower for conservative institutions compared to those that budget more aggressively. Aggressive budgeters often need to make more adjustments because they are more likely to experience revenue shortfalls and expense overruns in specific categories. With luck, the net impact of the shortfalls and overruns will not create an overall deficit situation, but it is an increased possibility for institutions that rely on aggressive budget assumptions.

Key Points

- A budget is a map, expressed in financial terms, guiding an institution on a journey as it carries out its mission. A budget is not a plan; it is a product of the planning process.

- Budgeting is a form of resource allocation. Effective institutions integrate resource allocation with planning and assessment. Plans determine what will be done, while budgets dictate the level of resources to be deployed in executing the plans.

- Operating budgets provide details on anticipated revenues and on investments needed to carry out the institution's day-to-day activities. A capital budget provides financial details on the institution's short-term and long-term plans related to physical facilities and infrastructure.

Various economic, political, and regulatory developments influence ⌐ stitution's budget. Most are beyond the control of individual institutions or even the national higher education community. Accordingly, budgeters must anticipate changes in economic and political conditions that may affect the amount of revenues available and, of equal importance, the expenses the institution may have to bear. Unless an institution's budget can withstand the pressures created by external forces, its survival may be in jeopardy.

Beginning in the 1990s, economic changes have significantly affected institutions of higher education. In many respects, a sea change in the nation's support for higher education has accompanied the economic turmoil. Higher education no longer enjoys the high ranking on national, state, and local societal agendas that it once did. Other sectors now capture resources previously directed to higher education, especially by governments. Whether the focus is instead on security, K-12 education, health care, or general social service programs, higher education no longer is viewed as a top priority. Part of this shift stems from a change in perception. Instead of viewing higher education as a public good, many now see it as a private benefit.

In today's environment, higher education must defend itself continuously against criticism from numerous quarters. In years past, it was enough to highlight the economic value of a college education or point to the discoveries growing out of campus-based research. Such arguments no longer sway a nation that no longer focuses on an ability to pay. The issue has shifted to a *willingness* to pay. As college prices have escalated—at rates greater than the Consumer Price Index (CPI) in most years—both the federal government and the general population have questioned whether higher education is being managed effectively.

As of 2012, higher education was coming off the worst economic period since the Depression. Although inflation has been held in check, campuses still are experiencing cost increases in critical areas. At the same time, various revenue sources are depressed, with nothing to suggest that things will turn around in the short run. In fact, even prestigious institutions have suspended programs, eliminated positions, or resorted to other cost-cutting measures that have dramatic effects on program delivery. A climate like this requires careful examination of external factors.

The Political Climate

Higher education leaders have plenty of issues to keep them awake at night, with the U.S. Congress often providing the impetus. In recent years, for example, congressional (or federal agency) initiatives have focused on higher education issues as diverse as college costs and affordability, the size of higher education endowments and annual endowment spending, unfair competition with the private sector by colleges and universities, pollution emissions from boilers powered by certain types of energy, and protection against identify theft.

One large federal initiative related to higher education began early in the Obama administration with a call for the United States to have the highest proportion of students graduating from college in the world by 2020. To support this objective, the Obama administration has proposed new initiatives to raise higher education attainment and student outcomes, as well as encourage colleges and universities to keep tuition affordable. As the country's political winds shift due to party changes in the White House and Congress, different approaches to influencing higher education will likely receive favor while others will fall by the wayside. What is certain, however, is that we have not seen the last of federal government efforts focused on improving higher education's effectiveness or challenging it to become more efficient.

In fact, the Department of Education has continued pressuring institutions to justify tuition increases that exceed what it believes to be reasonable. As reported by The College Board, the fiscal year 2012 average tuition increase for in-state students was 8.3 percent at public four-year institutions and 8.7 percent at in-state public two-year institutions.[1] The comparable numbers for out-of-state students at four-year public institutions was 5.7 percent and 4.5 percent for students at four-year independent institutions.[2] What makes this troubling for those monitoring higher education's performance is the fact that inflation averaged 1.6 percent during 2010, when tuition prices were being set for 2012.[3]

Without question, a reduction in appropriations from the states has contributed to tuition increases at public institutions whose costs continue to increase partially because of increased enrollment. Decreased endowment income, much of it related to the subprime mortgage market meltdown, has placed more pressure on tuition as well. The situation raises a legitimate question: How much endowment is enough? Various stakeholders have asked higher education institutions to increase spending from endowments rather than raise tuition. Some institutions responded with various initiatives aimed at holding tuition increases to a minimum, but endowments still remain an attractive target to various critics of higher education's financial structure. It's highly likely that the pressure will resume when endowments return to previous levels.

Although effective planning and cost management can accommodate steadily increasing prices, most institutional budgets cannot withstand major fluctuations over short periods. Furthermore, exceptional cost increases in any category can wreak havoc on even a well-managed budget. For instance, colleges and universities continually face the prospect of replacing expensive instructional and research equipment as it becomes obsolete. Unless institutions have funded depreciation and maintained reserves for this purpose (see Appendix), the impact from these purchases will be a significant charge on the current budget and may have significant cash-flow impacts as well. Some exceptional situations may even force a college or university into a serious financial crisis.

Tracking Cost
Increases

Costs incurred in higher education do not mirror costs used to track inflation in the general economy. That's why many in higher education rely on the Higher Education Price Index (HEPI) as an alternative to the more popular Consumer Price Index (CPI). The CPI is deemed too general and not representative of the types of purchases made by higher education institutions; the HEPI cost components include faculty salaries, administrative salaries, clerical salaries, service employee salaries, fringe benefits, miscellaneous services, supplies and materials, and utilities.[4]

The HEPI has attracted critics, however, and it may no longer represent the accepted standard for higher education price changes. One reason HEPI has not enjoyed universal acceptance stems from the fact that it was developed in the private sector. Also, questions have arisen about the validity of the method used to calculate the index.

Another commonly used index is the CPI-U–a variation of the CPI based on goods and services purchased by the typical urban consumer. Some argue that, because HEPI and the CPI-U have not differed dramatically for some brief periods, the CPI-U is a reasonable choice. Others contend that significant variances can occur over time. As a result, efforts continue to identify a reliable index for use by higher education.

The State Higher Education Executive Officers (SHEEO) organization has attempted to bridge the gap between the HEPI and the CPI-U by offering the Higher Education Cost Adjustment (HECA). The HECA is developed by weighting and combining two federally developed and maintained indexes–the Employment Cost Index (75 percent) and the Gross Domestic Product Implicit Price Deflator (25 percent).[5]

Impact of Federal Regulation and Social Programs*

A portion of the cost of doing business in any industry can be attributed to informal social pressures and government mandates in a number of areas: personal security and safety, participation and due process, public information,

---

*This section is based largely on Howard Bowen, *The Costs of Higher Education: How Much Do Colleges and Universities Spend per Student and How Much Should They Spend?* (San Francisco: Jossey-Bass, 1980).

and environmental projection, to name a few. In addition to these universal pressures, colleges and universities experience costs unique to their operations, such as protection of students' privacy and federal financial aid programs.

Overall, commercial entities have an advantage in dealing with socially imposed costs. First, many regulations do not apply to commercial entities because they do not typically receive federal funding. In addition, when they are subject to external mandates that increase operating costs, commercial entities can pass these costs along to their custovmers. While independent institutions have control of their tuition, this is not always the case for public institutions. Frequently, a state agency or the legislature has the authority to set tuition at public institutions. When institutions are unable to raise tuition to offset the costs of mandated programs, the only option is to cut back in other areas—either in the primary programs of instruction, research, and public service or in a support activity.

At What Cost?

Federal regulations and mandated social programs touch all aspects of institutional operations, from athletics to the care of laboratory animals. It has proven difficult, if not impossible, to isolate the true cost of externally imposed regulations and guidelines. A primary reason is that compliance with the mandates often cannot be separated from the routine operations of the institution. Another reason is that colleges and universities frequently support the objectives of imposed regulations and programs, and would initiate similar actions on their own even without the requirements.

Consider the following factors when assessing the impact of federal regulation and social pressures:

- The adoption of programs can increase or decrease costs. For example, a mandated staff training program may lead to greater employee morale and improved productivity, thereby reducing operating costs.

- Socially imposed programs have two types of costs: the cost of program operations and the cost associated with compliance (for example, reporting). In many cases, the concern about program cost is focused on the compliance aspects rather than the substance of the program.

- How costs are counted and when they must be incurred introduce another set of issues. The overall cost of a program may not be significant when measured over time. Too often, however, the mandate requires significant up-front investments that become a burden on a single year's budget.

- The implementation of some programs may not increase aggregate expenses but may force a shift in priorities. For instance, resources once earmarked for library acquisitions may be diverted to cover safety and security mandates.

To illustrate the range of issues campuses must address, here are some of the mandates and requirements applicable to higher education:

Personal security and safety. Occupational Safety and Health Act of 1970 (OSHA) establishes employee safety and working condition standards. Other federal laws provide legislation on radiation safety and the protection of human and animal subjects used in research and teaching. The Campus Security Act of 1990, including the Campus Sexual Assault Victims Bill of Rights and the Campus Sex Crimes Prevention Act, and 1999 Department of Education regulations mandating the reporting of campus crime statistics.

Retirement. The Social Security Act of 1935 as amended, addresses retirement, pensions, survivors benefits, disability insurance, unemployment compensation, and health insurance. The Employment Retirement Income Security Act of 1974 (ERISA) provides safeguards for employees participating in pensions offered by independent institutions.

Labor relations. Major laws include the National Labor Relations Act of 1935, establishing the rules applicable to collective bargaining and employee organizing; the Fair Labor Standards Act of 1938, establishing minimum wage levels, maximum work hours, and overtime compensation rules; and the Equal Pay Act of 1963, mandating that employees doing similar tasks must receive equal pay regardless of sex.

Personal opportunity. Although various courts have reduced protections in some areas related to affirmative action, guidelines remain in force through federal regulations and laws. These include Executive Order 11246 of 1965, as amended in 1967, prohibiting discrimination on the basis of sex; the Employment Act of 1967, prohibiting discrimination on the basis of age; Title VII of the Civil Rights Act of 1964, as amended by the Equal Employment Opportunity Act of 1972, prohibiting discrimination on the basis of sex, race, creed, or national origin; Title IX of the Educational Amendments of 1972, prohibiting discrimination on the basis of sex in educational policies, facilities, programs, and employment practices; student financial aid programs rules, which impose significant administrative burdens and may require institutional contributions; and Internal Revenue Service regulations concerning discrimination in favor of highly compensated individuals and in student admissions.

Participation, openness, due process, and privacy. The guiding legislation includes the First Amendment to the Constitution; the National Labor Relations Act of 1935; and the Family Educational Rights and Privacy Act of 1974 (FERPA, or the Buckley Amendment), dealing with the management of records and the release of information. The Gramm-Leach-Bliley Act, aimed at financial institutions, imposes requirements to protect the privacy of consumers engaging in financial transactions. Regulations commonly known as the Red Flags Rule require institutions to have a protection program designed to detect warning signs (or "red flags") of identify theft in their daily operations. Terrorist actions and threats have somewhat clouded privacy issues, with campuses frequently caught in the middle in terms of complying with FERPA while responding to requests for information from federal agencies.

Public information. Requests for information primarily relate to consumer protection, fund-raising, enforcement of government programs, general statistical needs of society, national security, and the general public's demands for accountability. For example, the Office of Management and Budget (OMB) must clear all surveys funded under federal grants; OMB Circular A-21 dictates procedures for calculating indirect or facilities and administrative (F&A) cost rates applicable to sponsored activities; federally funded student financial aid participation requires verification and audit reports; and the Department of Education's National Center for Education Statistics Integrated Postsecondary Education Data System (IPEDS) collects data from institutions annually. The Student and Exchange Visitor Information System (SEVIS), which grew out of the events of September 11, 2001, requires all colleges and universities to provide information on international students, scholars, and other visitors.

Environmental protection. Increasingly, pollution control requirements, restrictions on research involving hazardous materials and recombinant DNA, and vandalism and the problems of neighborhood deterioration call for action by colleges and universities. The Environmental Protection Agency (EPA), for instance, assesses fines under the Resource Conservation and Recovery Act, which also mandates specific safety steps related to the treatment of hazardous waste; the Toxic Substances Control Act mandates storage and usage procedures for industrial chemicals.

Disabilities. The Americans with Disabilities Act (ADA) of 1990 specifies how to make programs and facilities accessible to people with disabilities and requires employers to make those accommodations in the areas of employment, education, and commercial activities. This alone has had staggering implications for campuses, which have invested in technology and facilities for students and employees with special needs. As an example, supporting just one hearing-impaired, full-time student can equal the cost of a full-time employee.

Shared costs in federal grants and contracts. Institutions are expected to absorb some costs associated with conducting research sponsored through federal grants and contracts. Cost sharing may involve matching on individual grants and contracts. Especially frustrating to campuses is the federal government's complex approach to the reimbursement of F&A costs related to sponsored programs, as outlined in OMB Circular A-21. In theory, the calculation mandated under A-21 should support a negotiation designed to ensure the government and the institution pay their respective fair shares of the direct and indirect costs of sponsored projects. The federal government, however, has unilaterally disallowed some cost categories and imposed seemingly arbitrary caps on others. These actions force campuses to bear an increasingly larger share of the F&A costs of conducting research.

At the same time, the government has imposed additional requirements that increase the amount of unreimbursed costs by incorporating provisions of the Cost Accounting Standards Board (CASB) in A-21. Many of the CASB standards, initially designed to address issues in the for-profit defense contracting industry, do not recognize the nonprofit approach taken by colleges and universities. One particularly burdensome requirement applies to institutions that receive the largest amount of federally sponsored support. These institutions must make a comprehensive filing with the federal government—the DS-2 Disclosure Statement—describing their accounting practices in significant detail. If they subsequently change anything addressed in the disclosure statement, they must justify the change to the government.

Although accountability for the use of taxpayer funds is appropriate and necessary, some requirements are excessive and impose significant additional costs on institutions. For instance, the receipt of grant and contract funds comes with strict accounting requirements, which affect both direct project expenses and the institution's method for claiming project-related indirect costs. Cumbersome processes, referred to as effort reporting, require faculty, staff, and graduate students to document the time they spend on sponsored projects. The institution must have a methodology to ensure each project is charged only the appropriate salary for the amount of time spent by those working on the project.

Equally daunting are regulations related to federal financial aid programs that provide grant, loan, or work-study funds to students. The rules specify how and when funds may be disbursed, the methodology for providing refunds to the federal programs when students withdraw before the end of a term, and the collection procedures that must be used to recover amounts loaned. These complex regulations change regularly, making it difficult to remain in compliance. As is the case with sponsored programs funding, however, the benefits of federal financial aid funds far outweigh the costs of compliance and the negative impact on institutional flexibility. In fact, few institutions could survive if their students did not participate in the federal student aid programs.

Audit standards and mandated management practices. Institutions receiving federal support in the form of student financial aid or sponsored grants and contracts are subject to rules promulgated by the sponsoring federal agencies as well as OMB. OMB Circular A-110 specifies uniform administrative requirements applicable to all federal programs. OMB Circular A-133, the single-audit standard, specifies the requirements for audits of federally funded programs and activities.

In theory, colleges and universities should undergo only one annual federal financial audit. All federal agencies are supposed to rely on that audit to ensure proper management of their resources. In practice, however, many federal agencies go beyond the requirements of A-133 and conduct their own audits.

Special costs of teaching hospitals and clinics. Although primarily targeted to hospitals and physicians serving the general public, the Health Insurance Portability and Accountability Act (HIPAA) imposes significant burdens on higher education student health and counseling clinics, which must ensure the privacy and security of patient information. In addition, institutions with teaching hospitals and clinics are subject to restrictions and guidelines governing patient care review, patient privacy, accreditation and licensure, accounting procedures, control and care of drugs and blood, use of radiation, and use of human and animal subjects for research purposes.

Higher education is unlikely to receive relief from all of these regulatory mandates anytime soon. As the federal government continues investing significant amounts in postsecondary education, it also will seek assurances about the effectiveness of institutional operations.

Issues Unique to Public Institutions

In addition to the federal regulations affecting all higher education institutions, public institutions must comply with regulations imposed by state agencies and departments. Here are a few of the regulations that typically affect only public colleges and universities:

Formula allocation procedures. In general, budget formulas guide institutions in developing their funding requests. Formulas are intended to simplify what otherwise would be a complex process for determining the level of support required to operate an institution. The formulas, however, do not represent how campuses actually operate. In fact, they are nothing more than a shorthand to ease the difficult process of allocating scarce resources. It is highly unlikely that the formula would be used to make allocation decisions within the institution.

The restrictiveness of formula allocation procedures stems not from their use as a means to generate budget requests but from the perception of formulas as an implicit or explicit commitment of how funds will be used. The more that state-level decision makers perceive the formula as an instrument of accountability—as opposed to a tool for allocating resources—the more complex it becomes to respond to the variety of activities taking place on campus. In this way, formulas can lead to a more restrictive budgetary environment.

Enrollment ceilings. To control institutional demands for financial support, some states have imposed enrollment ceilings on colleges and universities. The state usually agrees to support instructional and other costs up to the level required to serve the target enrollment. That leaves institutions to absorb the excess costs of educating students at levels beyond the target—or simply decide not to admit those students. A backlash to this approach has led many states to replace enrollment ceilings with appropriation formulas, which are adjusted to manage the state's financial commitment. The burden still falls on the campus to find resources to finance its operations, but the state does not become the target of an unhappy population.

Some states employ enrollment thresholds when making their appropriations. The state establishes a bandwidth for enrollment projections of, for example, plus or minus two percent of a specified target. If actual enrollments fall within the four percent range, the appropriation remains unchanged. If enrollments exceed the projection by more than two percent, the state provides funds for the additional enrollment. Similarly, if enrollment is lower than the floor of the bandwidth, the institution receives less funding. In this example, the institution would cover any funding deficiency caused by enrollments exceeding the projection by less than two percent and retain the full appropriation if enrollments are less than two percent below the projection.

Appropriations bill language. The contents of the state appropriations bill may restrict an institution's flexibility. Some states include all institutional resources in the appropriation—even resources that do not come from taxpayers. Other states appropriate only the resources provided directly by the state. In general, the fewer items addressed in the appropriations bill, the more control the institution has over its resources.

Many states use the appropriations bill to regulate activity within colleges and universities. This approach can be troublesome because, unlike the more typical process for establishing state regulations—which usually involves department and agency staff, appropriation bills tend to be developed by legislators and their staff. Without the expertise of staff from departments and agencies, it is possible, if not probable, that the bill will have impacts beyond what the legislature anticipated. Items that might be addressed in this manner include faculty productivity, student-faculty ratios, travel, intercollegiate athletics, campus security, technology standards, and distance education. Serious problems may arise with this oversight mechanism, because states usually don't have provisions to waive legislation.

State agency staff. Many state agencies and departments directly influence daily operations on public college and university campuses. State agencies, for example, often draft statewide plans for higher education, review new and existing academic programs, look over budget requests, and have a say on capital projects. In addition, staff members in various state legislative and executive offices influence the development of policies affecting campuses and, in some states, wield tremendous power over financial matters affecting higher education.

Position control. States commonly control the number of authorized employee positions at public institutions. Some grant campuses a great deal of latitude to determine the mix of employees, setting an overall position maximum and leaving the detailed decision making to the institutions. Provided they don't exceed the maximum at any point during the year, the institutions can hire as needed. Other states attempt to control only full-time employment and leave institutions with the flexibility to rely on part-time employees or independent contractors for some services.

Still other states prescribe the number and types of employees a campus may employ in a given period. This approach limits the way in which salaries and wages are spent and may prevent the institution from optimally deploying staff and faculty resources.

Year-end balances. It is not unusual for colleges and universities to spend a disproportionate amount of their annual budgets in the latter part of the fiscal year. In many states, this flurry of activity is driven by a requirement to revert unexpended funds to the state treasury at year-end. Unfortunately, such "budget balance sweeping activity" may lead to purchasing unneeded materials and supplies to avoid returning funds. It's usually based on the thinking that unexpended funds may lead to future budget reductions, because legislators will believe the budget was too generous.

The overall goal should be to expend resources for what is necessary, when it is needed. A more rational policy allows unspent funds to be carried forward from one fiscal year to the next; this policy reflects the reality that the timing of an expenditure may be as critical as the expense itself. When carryover is allowed, institutions and their departments no longer feel obliged to spend every dollar just to avoid the appearance of having more resources than needed.

Some institutions operating in states that allow carryforward of funds don't extend the same flexibility to their own units. In doing this, the institution essentially encourages units to spend unwisely, to avoid losing funds in future budgets. Admittedly, managing the budgets to allow carryforward is difficult and time-consuming, but it usually leads to improved effectiveness. Institutions that invest the effort to manage the carryforward process will achieve better operating results and more effective resource utilization.

In general, states rely on controls rather than incentives to ensure that funds are expended appropriately. A common method for distributing appropriated resources is the allotment process. Essentially, this rationing process makes appropriated funds available to institutions on an established schedule, such as monthly or quarterly. The more frequent the allotments, the greater flexibility institutions enjoy. Because purchasing commitments usually require having the funds on hand, receiving less frequent allotments may force a campus to postpone some purchases.

Salary savings targets. A few states rely on a management device intended to force the early return of a portion of an institution's appropriation. Such programs are known by various names, including salary savings, budgetary savings, turnover savings, vacancy savings, and forced savings. State agencies, including public colleges and universities, are expected to return a specified portion of their total appropriations, usually expressed as a percentage of salaries and wages. The practice is most prevalent in states that do not allow carryover of unspent funds as well as in states that budget personnel costs using a line-item approach.

States created these programs when they began focusing on unspent amounts at year-end related to position vacancies at agencies and institutions. This approach can be problematic for colleges and universities, because it often takes a long time to recruit faculty, especially at senior levels. By specifying savings targets and requiring the return of the funds throughout the year rather than at year-end, some states can increase appropriations in a given year and accelerate the distribution of those funds. In other cases, however, states use such programs to reduce the level of support provided to higher education.

Salary savings programs do not generate new resources but shift existing resources. They merely recognize that not all compensation can be spent in a given period. Rather than allow state agencies and institutions to make judgments about how to use the savings, the states capture the savings and then use them to fund specific initiatives or increase contingency reserves.

In most cases, an institution of higher education achieves the specified target by either holding back enough resources from the appropriation or passing the savings target on, pro rata, to all campus units receiving state funding. The first approach ensures the institution will meet its savings target, but it shields the units most likely to generate salary savings through turnover. It also enables units to retain the savings from position vacancies and use them for internal activities that may reflect the highest institutional priorities. The second approach ensures that individual units do not benefit from savings at the expense of other institutional priorities. On the other hand, distributing the target among all units can place a large burden on the smaller ones, which may not experience the turnover needed to generate the required savings.

A third approach combines the first two. Rather than meet the target completely from central resources or distribute it to all units pro rata, the administration assigns the majority of the target to the major budget units and allows them to determine how their departments will meet the target. Some administrators assign variable targets to their departments, thereby shielding the highest-priority areas, while others distribute the target pro rata to all departments within the major budget unit. Shortfalls arising when departments are unable to meet the target due to a lack of turnover are addressed on a case-by-case basis.

Topics of Discussion

Issues of greatest importance will vary by institution and by state. Here's just a sample of what state-level officials and campus representatives might discuss during their interactions:

- Funding formulas
- Budget review practices
- State appropriations—both operating and capital
- Tuition and fee policies
- Auxiliary enterprise policies, especially as they relate to competition with the private sector
- Continuing education, evening programs, and summer programs
- Distance education
- Acceptance by public four-year institutions of credits for courses taken at public two-year institutions
- Time to degree
- Research policies and funding
- Technology transfer
- Economic development
- Relative importance of athletics and whether it can be subsidized with educational and general revenues
- Faculty workload standards
- Enrollment ceilings and thresholds
- New facilities needs
- Deferred maintenance
- Debt policies
- Investment policies
- Procurement policies
- Travel policies

Relationship between state policy makers and higher education institutions.

The operating environment in public higher education varies tremendously from state to state. Some states rely on a central system office to oversee all public institutions. In other states, individual campuses are freestanding entities not included in a state system. Still others use a combination: Some campuses are part of a system, while others operate as freestanding entities with their own governing boards. As another option, states may rely on the use of a coordinating body in place of a central system office; the coordinating agency serves as an interface between the executive and legislative branches and the individual campuses.

Regardless of the organizational model, public institutions must ensure that key decision makers in their state have an in-depth understanding of the issues colleges and universities confront. Even when a state system or coordinating agency advocates on their behalf, campus officials must leverage opportunities to interact directly with state executive and legislative staff as well as with staff from state agencies that influence higher education.

Formal opportunities for interaction occur on a semi-regular basis, for example, at legislative budget hearings or capital project review hearings. Although important, such formal interactions may carry less overall significance than the informal contact that occurs from time to time—for example, at college athletic events. The informal exchanges between campus representatives and state-level decision makers at sporting events provide the opportunity to share information and advocate for specific decisions that will provide the maximum benefit to the institution.

Key
Points

- Higher education institutions are subject to many external mandates that affect how they conduct their operating and capital activities. The Obama college-completion initiative is just one example; it's having a tremendous impact on higher education, particularly community colleges.

- The extensive range of issues emanating from the federal government addresses topics as diverse as unfair competition between institutions and the private sector, protection against identity theft, and whether higher education endowments should be subject to taxation.

- In addition to the above issues affecting all colleges and universities, institutions receiving state support are affected by an additional set of laws, regulations, and policies. They vary from state to state but address issues as diverse as enrollment ceilings, staffing levels, and the reversion or carryforward of year-end budget balances.

The economies of all institutions are linked with the national economy, which is increasingly connected to the world economy.

Before 2008, the U.S. economy was strong, savings levels were up, financial markets were performing at all-time highs, and national productivity was rising comfortably each year. Except for continuing concerns about tuition prices, which surfaced initially during the 1990s, higher education was experiencing a relatively comfortable period as well. Enrollments were up and endowments were growing, thanks to investment performance and significantly increased giving levels. And public support for higher education remained relatively strong.

The U.S. economic environment changed dramatically in the wake of the recession that began in 2008. The federal budget deficit is at record levels, the trade deficit grows larger each year, and the federal debt ceiling continues to break records. Despite modest signs of recovery, markets and indexes remain far below prerecession levels. Financial markets are unsettled, and the United States continues to spend heavily on defense. Resources diverted to pay for defense, security, or interest on the national debt mean fewer resources available to support higher education research or student financial aid.

Revenues represent only one side of the equation. Costs are a significant consideration as well. Quite simply, delivering quality education is expensive. As of 2010, the United States had just under 4,500 degree-granting institutions,[6] including public, independent, and for-profit institutions. For fiscal year 2009, aggregate expenditure data show total expenditures of $273 billion (public institutions),[7] $141 billion (independent institutions),[8] and $16 billion (for-profit institutions)[9] for a total of $430 billion. This represents slightly more than 3 percent of the U.S. Gross Domestic Product (GDP) for 2009 of $13,939 billion.[10] These funds were expended in support of 19.1 million students enrolled in full-time and part-time degree programs.[11] Off-campus extension, noncredit continuing education, and community service programs reached many more.

The same economic and political pressures that affect major social programs also affect higher education. Exacerbating the impact of these cost pressures are reduced federal aid and reduced state support as policy makers seek to manage deficits triggered by the recession. The most significant cost categories for colleges and universities are summarized in the following sections.

Human Resources

Higher education institutions employed 3.7 million individuals during fall 2009,[12] just under two-thirds of whom were full time. Of the total employment, the largest single category is faculty, amounting to 1.4 million employees.[13]

The next largest category, consisting of 941,000 employees and identified as nonprofessionals in the U.S. Department of Education's data collection, includes clerical personnel, custodians, skilled trades, and a variety of other job classifications.[14] The remaining positions fall into various nonfaculty professional categories, including accountants, planners, institutional researchers, and senior administrators (for example, presidents, chancellors, and provosts).

In this labor-intensive industry, compensation—encompassing salaries, wages, and benefits—represents the largest single expense category. Current staffing models result in some campuses spending as much as 70 percent of their total budgets on compensation. What's more, the educational model does not lend itself to dramatic gains in productivity, which higher education defines as increases in the value of services without corresponding increases in costs.

Some service industries—particularly financial services—have employed technology to achieve significant gains in productivity without raising overall costs. In contrast, technology provides only marginal improvement in productivity within higher education. Certainly, instructional technology can dramatically increase the number of students taught by a single faculty member, via either large lectures enhanced by technology or Web-based instruction. But for the most part, low student-faculty ratios are still believed to produce the most effective outcomes. A true gain in productivity requires the quality of the service to remain high while output levels increase; thus, larger classes will increase a faculty member's productivity only if the quality of instruction can be maintained.

With such a large proportion of costs being personnel related, achieving significant economies depends upon controlling salaries or benefits. When revenues remain flat or decline, average compensation or the number of employees must decline—or deficits will develop. Institutions that anticipate financial difficulties and plan accordingly will have more options than institutions that do not manage their finances effectively. Planning for possible personnel actions before a financial crisis erupts enables the institution to make informed decisions without the heightened pressure of the moment. (See Chapter Twelve on responding to extraordinary financial circumstances.)

Even when plans have been developed in advance, serious financial difficulties may call for staffing reductions. These may be accomplished through normal attrition (for example, retirements and resignations), enabling an institution to avoid involuntary terminations when relatively small savings are needed. If large-scale savings are needed, involuntary personnel actions are inevitable. Be aware that cutting faculty and staff positions will dramatically affect morale—especially if done over a short period. Moreover, rapid workforce reductions are difficult to accomplish in higher education because of tenure and contracts.

With the U.S. economy remaining relatively weak and their investment portfolios still staggering from the 2008 recession, members of the baby boom generation who are approaching traditional retirement age may elect to postpone retirement. That means many tenured faculty and other employees will stay on the job so they can rebuild their retirement savings programs and continue receiving benefits.

Some benefits provide current protection for employees or their families. These include workers' compensation; health, life, and disability insurance; and unemployment compensation. Other benefits provide protection for the employee once he or she retires. This category includes Social Security, pensions, and postretirement benefits, such as health insurance. The cumulative investment in these benefits is substantial and continues to grow dramatically.

Institutions, particularly independent ones, used to bear the full cost of most benefits, but today employees commonly share the cost of health insurance premiums. Similarly, many institutions have converted their pension plans from defined-benefit—under which the institution was obligated to contribute enough funds to guarantee a specified level of retirement benefits based on age and service—to defined-contribution. The latter approach specifies the amount of current contribution required of the employer but does not guarantee a specific level of benefit.

These changes, coupled with the increasing popularity of retirement savings options for individuals, have resulted in many employees participating to the maximum extent possible in individual retirement accounts, 401(k) (income deferral) plans, and 403(b) (tax-sheltered annuity) plans.

Facilities Maintenance

Most institutions invested heavily in facilities to accommodate increased enrollments during the 1960s, 1970s, and 1980s. More recently, many institutions focused on physical plant improvements as a strategy for enhancing their competitiveness in student and faculty recruitment. They upgraded residence halls, recreational facilities, research facilities, and classroom facilities.

The 2008 economic downturn, however, dramatically curtailed investment in new facilities. In fact, many campuses struggled to complete projects undertaken before the downturn and abandoned other projects completely, causing the institutions to experience a loss on their investments.

Although there never is a good time to experience financial problems, the 2008 recession may have come at the worst possible time for educational facilities. Buildings constructed during the second half of the 20th century are nearing the end of their useful lives and, therefore, require disproportionately high investments in repairs and maintenance. Even relatively new construction, if not maintained properly, can lead to increases in operating costs.

This situation is particularly acute because many campuses routinely postpone needed maintenance to meet their budget numbers. Because the average person can't see many facets of facilities maintenance, senior administrators often elect to postpone needed investments. The problems then compound: Facilities not being maintained adequately today will cost more to operate tomorrow and deteriorate more rapidly. In addition, research demonstrates that facilities that have fallen into disrepair can adversely affect student recruitment and retention.*

While some institutions make no provisions for maintaining facilities, others have established policies that prohibit the addition of new facilities unless adequate resources exist to maintain them. This approach will help address future maintenance needs, but it does nothing for the current backlog. There are no recognized standards for the amount to invest in ongoing facilities maintenance, although institutions that annually invest 1.5 to 2 percent of a facility's replacement value in routine repair and maintenance should be well positioned to avoid serious problems.

Facilities may require upgrading to accommodate new technologies. With the ubiquity of technology throughout an institution's operations, nearly every campus facility must be connected to the Internet through hard wiring or wireless technology. And every classroom must accommodate technology used in support of instructional activities. Adding technological capabilities represents a significant cost, but without these investments, institutions will have trouble meeting the demands of faculty and students.

Ancillary costs—utilities, in particular—account for another substantial expense for institutions. Many institutions incur facilities costs around the clock, as they provide services through auxiliary units that serve students 24 hours per day.

Performance contracting offers one means of potentially reducing utilities costs. It involves partnering with energy conservation firms, which are compensated based on savings they achieve through reduced energy costs. Another tactic is using long-term debt to finance energy conservation investments. With relatively low interest rates, an institution with sufficient debt capacity and access to the requisite expertise in energy conservation can achieve significant ongoing savings with a relatively small investment.

Technology

As society depends more on technology, institutions must keep pace—to meet their own needs and to teach the most current technologies. To boost their

---

* For further information, see Gary L. Reynolds & David Cain, *Final Report on the Impact of Facilities on the Recruitment and Retention of Students* (Alexandria, VA: APPA: The Association of Higher Education Facilities Officers, 2006).

efficiency, institutions have invested heavily in administrative software and technologies that bring increased capabilities. In fact, technology is the second fastest growing expense category in higher education. To maintain and gain maximum benefit from the technology, institutions often must increase their investment in personnel as well.

Obtaining reliable data for technology expenditures proves difficult because much of the investment comes from decentralized budgets. In general, approximately 5 to 8 percent of total campus spending is devoted to various forms of IT. Academic computing—devoted primarily to instructional technology and research—consumes approximately one-third of the total technology investment. Whether considered in terms of the costs of implementing administrative applications, such as enterprise resource planning (ERP) systems that can cost tens of millions of dollars, or the introduction of technology into the classroom, technology is expensive. The most modern systems, use a standard architecture to address a multitude of functional applications. These easy-to-use systems also can be customized to include embedded controls and edits, which can prevent inadvertent noncompliant actions.

Since 2000, EDUCAUSE—the higher education association focused on technology and related issues—has conducted an annual survey of its members to identify the most challenging technology issues they face. With the exception of 2008, when it dropped to third place, IT funding has ranked first or second on that list.[15]

That ranking isn't surprising, because technology represents a moving target. No sooner had institutions wired all their facilities than wireless access became the standard. And as soon as campuses invested in wireless access, they had to start exploring ways to employ mobile technology in the classroom.

Technology has multiple facets with varying cost patterns. Hardware costs, for example, have declined significantly over time; almost any item—whether a handheld computer or a cell phone—costs less today than it did a year or two ago. Yet when a computer wears out or becomes obsolete, users seek a faster and more powerful model with increased functionality—and a higher cost. Similarly, new software has more features but also a higher price tag.

The power of today's applications and tools means that institutions need more sophisticated staff in IT operations, including network administrators, systems analysts, help-desk support personnel, database administrators, and curriculum designers. Beyond staff working directly in IT units, staff in other areas (for example, accounting, human resources, and facilities) must possess as much technology knowledge as functional area expertise. An accountant, for instance, must be able to understand the principles of cost analysis as well as manipulate data using sophisticated Excel features. An architect must be capable of employing computer-aided design techniques when developing the layout for space renewal as part of a building renovation.

On the administrative side, apart from expensive ERPs and their continuing upgrades and new releases, many of the regulatory burdens placed on institutions trigger increased technology investments. These could include adding new applications or enhancing security and privacy measures in response to threats from hackers.

Increased investments in technology also drive up tangential costs. As an example, as various administrative operating units on campus rely more heavily on technology, they must invest in training current staff. In many instances, job demands also require the recruitment of new staff with different expertise. Whether for the accounting office or facilities management, staff must have more sophisticated—and, therefore, more expensive—skill sets than before.

Technology for academic purposes is likely to increase dramatically, especially in the area of Web-enabled distance education. Based on 2010 data, more than 5.6 million students reported taking at least one online course.[16] Online enrollment has grown to 29.3 percent of total enrollment.[17] More than 43 percent of chief academic officers who responded to one survey indicated that online learning will become increasingly important to their institution during the next few years.[18]

The Numbers for For-Profits

Between 2000 and 2010, the number of for-profit educational institutions grew to 1,199,[19] accounting for about one-quarter of all degree-granting institutions. This 67 percent increase occurred even as 79 for-profit educational institutions closed, compared to 59 independent institutions and one public institution.[20]

Enrollment data, available through fall 2009, show that the for-profit sector enrolled 1.9 million students, or 9 percent of the total enrollment of 20.4 million students.[21] Ten years previously, for-profits enrolled 450,000 students, representing less than 3 percent of total enrollment of 15.3 million students.[22]

Financial indicators for the for-profit sector tell an interesting story of profitability. Their total revenues for fiscal year 2009 reached $19.4 million,[23] representing 6.4 percent of the industry total of $355.5 billion, which includes $267 billion for public institutions[24] and $69.1 billion for independent institutions.[25] The corresponding numbers for expenditures were only $16.4 million,[26] amounting to 3.9 percent of the industry total of $430 billion, which includes $273 billion for public institutions[27] and $141 billion for independent institutions.[28]

Competition

Higher education competes for both students and faculty. Attracting students may lead to tuition discounting—using institutional resources to award merit scholarships that encourage students to enroll. Essentially, the institution sets tuition at a higher level to generate revenues, which can fund scholarships for students who possess particular academic, athletic, or artistic talents deemed desirable by the institution in terms of the student body's diversity. Students also may receive aid simply because of the amount of revenue they represent beyond the discount received. (See Chapter Four for a detailed discussion of tuition and financial aid, especially aid funded by public support.)

One hidden cost of higher education is the amount of foregone revenue represented by institutional financial aid provided through tuition discounting. Managing tuition discounting—both through pricing and institutional aid—is somewhat of an art. The goal is to recruit the most desirable student body while maximizing net tuition revenue.

Competition for faculty also has intensified. Historically, this issue was limited to research institutions, but it has expanded to other institutional categories as well. The investment required to attract a highly successful researcher can reach millions of dollars in terms of one-time and continuing investments.

The one-time investments tend to focus on facilities and related costs. Eminent researchers, for example, require significant amounts of space to accommodate

Figure 3-1 Change in Number of Degree-Granting Institutions between 1990 and 2010

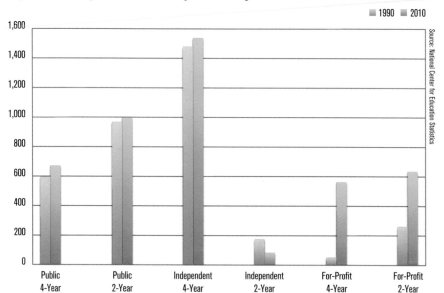

Source: National Center for Education Statistics

the staff and equipment needed to support their research. This translates into significant facilities renovations when those faculty accept an offer.

Then there are the ongoing costs for personnel. When a high-profile researcher leaves an institution, he or she usually brings research staff and graduate students to the new institution, which then must provide compensation and benefits. The prestige gained by having a high caliber of faculty on campus makes this effort a good investment. Still, the costs can strain an already challenged budget.

Sustainability

Like many industries, higher education faces pressures related to going "green." Yet while other industries hear from special interest groups, probably few of them have higher education's built-in, vocal constituency. Students, who have a formal voice in the way activities are conducted on their campuses, champion sustainability—through ecological, social, and economic means—as a way to protect the future of the planet.

Economic sustainability often translates into providing a "living wage" for employees of the institution and the companies with which it does business. Living wage—defined as the minimum hourly income required to meet basic needs—varies by locale but is significantly higher than the federal minimum wage. The concept extends to purchasing commodities for sale in bookstores or for use on campus; for example, purchases of clothing or athletic shoes should not involve vendors that ignore child labor laws or operate sweatshops.

Social sustainability refers to the way an institution coexists or interacts with its community neighbors. An institution, for example, may invest in the local economy for housing, transportation, or neighborhood beautification. Socially responsible investing is another facet of this issue. Most higher education institutions have implemented policies that dictate the types of investments that will not be utilized for the endowment. Such policies and practices, which make sense from a societal perspective, might reduce revenues or increase operational costs.

Issues related to *ecological sustainability* prompted the creation of the American College and University Presidents' Climate Commitment. This initiative has resulted in more than 670 institutions signing on to a series of actions intended to have a positive impact on global warming.[29]

By signing the commitment, an institution agrees to conduct an inventory of greenhouse gas emissions and develop an action plan for becoming climate neutral. The institution also must choose at least two specific actions while the plan is being developed. For example:

- Establish a policy that new campus construction will achieve the Silver level of the Leadership in Energy Efficiency and Design (LEED) designation.

- Purchase at least 15 percent of the institution's electricity consumption from renewable sources.

- Encourage the use of and provide access to public transportation for all faculty, staff, students, and visitors to campus.[30]

Unprepared Students

One difficult-to-measure cost relates to the students who arrive at college unprepared to do the work required to earn a degree. Students lacking the core skills necessary to perform at a college level, as well as those who do not have sufficient command of the English language, translate into extra learning labs, increased office hours for faculty, and tutoring services on campuses.

No matter how an institution addresses this problem, the costs are significant. After assessing students' preparedness for college, some institutions slot them into remedial classes. In other situations, especially at public four-year institutions, state policy precludes offering remedial classes. Problems also may arise with student financial aid, because some courses do not count toward participation requirements established for federal student aid programs.

Changing Demographics

Historically, higher education has primarily served the traditional college-age population of 18- to 24-year-olds. Nontraditional students, however, now represent a sizable percentage of enrollments—not just for two-year institutions, where they have always been a significant factor, but for four-year institutions as well.

Enrollments have risen steadily in recent years—a trend expected to continue for the foreseeable future. Based on U.S. Department of Education data, enrollment in all categories totaled 20.4 million in fall 2009 and will continue to grow steadily, reaching 23 million students by 2020.[31] The enrollment growth will be slightly disproportionately weighted toward nontraditional students. They will increase from 39.7 percent of the total student population in 2009 to nearly 42 percent in 2020, assuming the projected patterns are accurate.[32]

The projections regarding traditional students are based upon current enrollments in elementary and secondary schools, so they are considered reasonably accurate. The population of nontraditional students, however, holds significant potential for positive fluctuations for two reasons. First, the size of the potential nontraditional student population is substantially larger as a percentage of the total population. Second, and possibly more important, employers increasingly view advanced education as a requirement for meaningful employment. Although not all nontraditional students pursue degrees, more of them will seek advanced training and education.

An alternative way to examine these data is by sector. Degree-granting institutions enrolled 20.4 million students during fall 2009.[33] Of this number, 14.8 million students attended public institutions,[34] 3.8 million students attended independent institutions,[35] and 1.9 million students attended for-profit institutions.[36]

Changing demographics will affect different regions and types of institutions in different ways. Most institutions recruit on a regional basis. Therefore, trends among high school graduates often point to what may happen at the college level. A range of factors has caused the number of annual high school graduates to vary by region. Of greatest significance is the general population migration from the North to the South and West. The South continues to have the largest number of high school graduates annually, followed by the West. The Midwest and Northeast not only lag in terms of the number of graduates per year but also will see the gaps grow larger by 2022.[37]

Specifically, the South is expected to gain more than 120,000 graduates annually, climbing to 1.25 million by 2022.[38] The West will reach 840,000 graduates by 2022—an increase of more than 38,000.[39] The biggest drop will occur in the Northeast, which will drop to about 543,000 graduates in 2022—a decline of more than 72,000 graduates.[40] Finally, the Midwest pool of graduates

Figure 3-2 Projected Enrollment Increases from 2009 to 2020

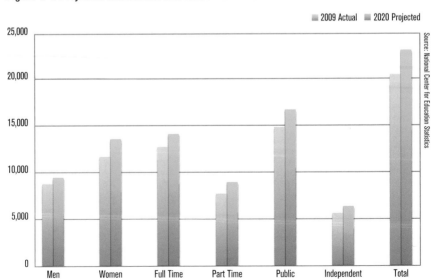

Source: National Center for Education Statistics

will decrease by slightly more than 49,000 students, reaching a low of 720,000 by 2022.[41] In those regions, institutions that are tuition dependent and attract one type of student—such as traditional day students or students interested in just a few areas of study—may face an enrollment challenge.

Given these changing demographics, colleges and universities will continue to engage in intense competition for students—especially within regions with declining school-age populations. Even institutions not seeking to increase enrollments will attempt to improve the overall quality of their student bodies by aggressively pursuing transfer students, shifting to Web delivery for many programs and courses, and offering classes at times convenient to more students. They're also likely to increase the amounts invested in institutional student aid.

The International Scene

Although they still represent a relatively small percentage of the total student population in the United States, international students make a difference—especially for some institutions. Total international student participation fluctuated between 3.2 percent and 3.7 percent between 2001 and 2011.[42] For academic year 2011, the number grew to 723,000 students, representing a 4.7 percent increase over the previous year.[43]

China and India remain the largest exporters of students to the United States. Together, they provide more than one-third of all international students studying in the United States, with 157,000 and 104,000 students, respectively.[44] The vast majority of international students enroll in traditional degree programs: Just under 91 percent of them pursue a baccalaureate or graduate degree.[45]

On the flipside, a number of U.S. students opt to pursue education internationally. In general, they take a different approach than their international counterparts. Data for academic year 2010 indicate that nearly 271,000 U.S. students chose to study abroad, representing a 3.9 percent increase over the previous year.[46] But U.S. students studying overseas engage primarily in short-term study; only 4 percent of them spent as much as a full academic year away.[47] Those abroad for the equivalent of a semester represented 39 percent of U.S. students studying in other countries, while those engaged in a short-term program (in other words, summer or eight weeks or less) represented the majority at 57 percent.[48]

Shifts in Federal Funding

The manner in which the federal government funds social programs in general, and higher education in particular, will greatly affect the revenues of institutions for the near future. On a relative basis, the U.S. government will direct fewer federal dollars toward higher education in the future because of deep-rooted changes in funding philosophy and growing competition from other sectors. In addition to the increased demands on Social Security and Medicare as the baby boom generation retires, for example, the federal budget must accommodate defense spending and servicing the growing national debt.

Examining the federal role in higher education raises the questions of who benefits from and who should pay for higher education. Increasingly, policy makers believe that the balance of benefits has shifted from society as a whole to the individuals receiving the education. Many believe that the current system of higher education is overbuilt—even though public institutions turn many students away because of resource limitations. A major aspect of the debate over who should pay is determining the proper balance between students and their families and the federal, state, and local governments.

Before World War II, states largely provided subsidies to public higher education resulting in low tuition; independent institutions received few public funds in the form of institutional aid. After World War II and the G.I. Bill of Rights of 1944, the federal government began providing massive sums to institutions and students. Both public and independent institutions benefited from this law and the funds it made available.

The balance was altered in the early 1950s when the Korean Conflict G.I. Bill awarded funds for college directly to veterans rather than the institutions. But the federal government broadened its support for higher education in 1958 with the National Defense Education Act, which provided funds to institutions as well as to students, particularly graduate students. Beginning in the late 1950s and continuing throughout much of the 1960s, the federal government provided substantial amounts of funding for facilities, equipment, libraries, research, and training.

Federal funding shifted again, from institutional support to student financial aid, following enactment of the 1965 Higher Education Act. The 1972 amendments to that legislation established the policy of basing federal student assistance programs on individual student need.

Federal funds are divided between student financial aid and support of research through grants and contracts; student financial aid represents a slightly larger share of the total. During federal fiscal year 2009, direct support to postsecondary education from the federal government totaled just under $67 billion.[49] Of this amount, $30.3 billion (45 percent) supported research conducted by colleges and universities.[50] The remainder, $36.4 billion (55 percent) was for various student financial aid programs.[51] (These figures do not include tax credits related to the Hope Scholarship or Lifetime Learning Credits Programs. Programs like these represent indirect federal support of higher education because the amounts are provided in the form of tax deductions or credits rather than direct funding.) It is important to note that federal support for higher education does not favor either public institutions or independent institutions. The federal government has pointedly avoided favoring one sector over the other.

Originally, the philosophy guiding federal support of higher education focused on enhancing access through student aid. Over time, the concept of access broadened to include not just low-income individuals but also the middle class. For many years, higher education was viewed as the primary driver of social mobility. As a result, federal support in the form of student assistance helped achieve societal goals by providing enhanced access to education.

As noted above, the U.S. student population has changed to include more part-time and adult students, including online learners, who seek college training while supporting families and maintaining jobs. Many of these students prefer a community college, where they can pursue education without sacrificing full-time employment. In addition, an increasing number of individuals are returning to college for recertification, to upgrade their professional skills, or to pursue training for an entirely new career.

For these and other budgetary reasons, the relationship between the federal government and higher education continues to evolve. The federal government now bears less of the overall burden of supporting students in pursuit of advanced education, with states and individual consumers of higher education (and their families) expected to bear a greater share of the costs. One example of this is the striking shift in financial aid from grants to loans. Another is the attention given to community service as a way for students to be relieved of the responsibility to repay federal loans.

State and Local Factors

Not too long ago, state and local government represented the highest single contributor of revenues to higher education. Then a major shift occurred. Although state and local government support continues to dwarf federal contributions to higher education revenues, even they have been overtaken by tuition and fees.

Of the $336.5 billion of revenue received by all public and independent institutions during fiscal year 2009, tuition and fees represented $105.5 billion (31 percent).[52] The next largest source was state and local government providing appropriations, grants, and contracts amounting to $97.1 billion (29 percent).[53] Coming in a distant third was the federal government, with appropriations, grants, and contracts totaling $61.9 billion (18 percent).[54] The remainder came from various sources, including auxiliary enterprises, endowment income, sales and services of educational activities, health care, gifts, and miscellaneous. (Note: The Federal contribution during fiscal year 2009 included significant amounts of stimulus funds, although the exact amount cannot be determined.)

Generally, the stronger the competition for resources in a state, the smaller the share allocated to any one social service. When states struggle financially, higher education's priority for state funding typically declines. Nothing suggests that this situation will change. In fact, other programs will likely place greater demands on limited state resources, resulting in further cuts to higher education support. Moreover, as the federal government increasingly shifts the burden for various social services to the states, relatively lower-priority services—including higher education—will receive smaller shares of state and local resources.

Another determinant of appropriations is the nature of a state's higher education structure. A system comprising many community colleges is considerably less expensive to operate than one with a comparable number of institutions but more at the four-year level. Similarly, a system with multiple research institutions will have higher operating costs than one with only one research institution and several comprehensive institutions. Some states, particularly those in the Northeast, traditionally have a strong independent sector and depend on those institutions to enroll large numbers of students who otherwise would attend public institutions. A few states, such as New Jersey, experience a considerable out-migration of potential students and allocate relatively fewer resources to higher education. Some states, such as Maryland, base their contributions to the independent sector on the level of support for public colleges and universities.

Other state and local economic and political factors influence the financial fortunes of individual institutions. For example, the cost of energy and labor generally is lower in the Sunbelt than in the Northeast. Housing typically costs more in metropolitan areas than in rural areas, which factors into the salary structure for faculty and staff as well as the housing rates charged to students. State and local regulations, which often mirror federal programs, can increase an institution's costs in areas, such as workers' compensation, safety codes, public health standards, occupational health and safety programs, unemployment compensation, and retirement programs.

Key
Points

- Higher education is subject to the same economic forces as businesses and private individuals. The recession that began in 2008 took a major toll on all institutions, leaving a changed landscape. Reduced public support for higher education characterizes the "new normal."

- Higher education represents a major industry, whether considered in terms of the number of institutions, the magnitude of annual expenditures, or the number of employees. For-profit institutions have become a significant segment, now numbering just under 1,200 institutions serving 1.9 million students (just under 10 percent of all students attending degree-granting institutions).

- The most significant cost drivers for colleges and universities are competition for students, human resources, sustainability, facilities, and technology.

- The federal government, a significant source of financial aid, has shifted away from direct aid to institutions in favor of aid to students.

Institutions in both the public and the independent sectors of higher education rely on a variety of sources for financial support. Although the sources are similar, the relative reliance on a particular source depends on the institution's character. Independent institutions, for example, count more on student tuition and fees than do public institutions, which receive state appropriations. Large research-oriented universities in both sectors receive a greater percentage of revenues from sponsors than would a comprehensive institution. And institutions with medical centers typically generate significant revenues from patient care, either directly or through a physician practice plan that provides support to the medical school.

Every institution participating in Title IV federal student financial aid programs must submit an annual survey about their revenues, expenses, staffing levels, and various factors related to tuition and financial aid. The data presented below refer to fiscal year 2009 and are drawn primarily from the database housing the information collected annually, IPEDS.

Tuition and Fees

Tuition refers to the price of an instructional service rendered to students. Unlike most prices, tuition is designed to recover only a portion of the costs incurred in providing the service.

Most institutions operate under the following revenue equation: Cost – Subsidy = Price. This differs markedly from the commercial for-profit model, which uses the following equation: Price – Cost = Profit. Cost is only one factor an institution takes into consideration when setting its tuition and fee levels. Other factors include:

- Tuition at peer institutions
- Other revenues—especially state appropriation for public institutions—and the need to balance the budget
- Student financial aid needs and available resources
- Tradition or philosophy of the institution (or state system)
- General economic conditions

In addition to tuition, institutions also charge students mandatory fees to cover non-academic services, such as intercollegiate athletics and other student recreational activities, laboratory usage, health insurance or health services, and debt service. Setting the total tuition and fee price requires an understanding of the institution's market position and the elasticity of student demand. Demand elasticity dictates that when prices are higher, fewer students seek admission compared to when prices are lower. Some institutions, such as the Ivy League universities, do not worry about reduced demand when they raise prices because they already turn away substantial numbers of well-qualified students. On the other hand, institutions with regional audiences may find that they have less flexibility when it comes to setting tuition—especially if comparable institutions exist within the same region.

To remain competitive, institutions must be sensitive to their peers' net student charges (Tuition + Fees – Institutional Student Aid = Net Student Charges). For this reason, institutions pay close attention to tuition pricing and student financial aid at peer institutions. They must take care not to share information related to specific students or general information before it's available to the public because doing so could lead to allegations of price fixing.

Institutions use different standards to detemine tuition levels. Tuition is set by calculating the amount of revenue needed to balance the budget within the constraints of their overall philosophy and market position. The economic conditions prevailing when the budget is prepared come into play as well. When costs increase rapidly—or when other revenues decline precipitously— tuition and fee charges will rise markedly. At the same time, the institution must weigh the ability and willingness of prospective students and their families to pay higher tuition.

At some institutions, traditions govern the setting of tuition levels. For many years, for instance, the California public higher education system had a policy of not charging tuition and maintaining low student fees. When the state encountered economic difficulties in the early 1990s, the system abandoned the policy and dramatically increased fees to provide revenues that helped compensate for the loss of state appropriations.

A number of independent and public institutions have attempted to increase support to low-income students. For instance, many independent institutions follow a "need-blind" admission process that doesn't consider a student's ability to pay until the admission decision has been made. Then the institution provides sufficient financial assistance to enable the student to attend regardless of financial resources.

Some institutions set tuition at a fixed percentage of the estimated annual cost of education. Virginia used this policy for many years until the economic downturn of the 1990s. When state appropriations failed to keep pace with the growth of institutional costs, tuition rates had to be increased to the point that the revenue exceeded the specified proportion of the annual cost of education.

Setting tuition in the public sector often is more complicated and indirect than in the private sector. The same factors apply—but with the added drama of political considerations. Depending on the state's budget process, for example, an institution may have to delay setting tuition rates until the legislature has determined its appropriation and the governor or state-level

Student Financial Need

To determine aid eligibility, all institutions must use the Free Application for Federal Student Aid (FAFSA) provided by the U.S. government. FAFSA must be used to determine eligibility for federally administered aid programs, such as Pell Grants and Stafford Loans. In addition, some institutions use the fee-based College Scholarship Service (CSS) Financial Aid Profile available through the College Board to determine eligibility for institutionally funded aid. Although both determine financial need, they rely on different methodologies.

Of the two, FAFSA generally determines higher need levels because of the following factors:

- FAFSA does not take into consideration home equity as a resource.

- CSS assumes a minimum level of contribution from the student, while FAFSA assumes that students may not contribute anything.

- CSS is tied to the Consumer Price Index (CPI), while FAFSA relies on estimated living allowances which do not track changes in the CPI.[55]

In seeking to attract certain categories of students, some institutions modify the federal government's formula to reduce the expected family contribution. Others have revised their overall approaches to determining the amount of institutional aid that a student is eligible to receive in the form of grants so that it can be substituted for need that otherwise would be met through loans.

oversight board has approved it. This situation proves problematic during difficult financial times, when legislatures and governors often have difficulty agreeing on the budget. Absent a budget agreement and thus an appropriation, the institution delays adjusting tuition for the fall semester and follows with a sizable increase for the second semester.

Some states take the tuition decision out of the institutions' hands completely; they set tuition either at the system level or through a state agency (or even the legislature). In states that allow institutions to establish tuition rates directly, the process is similar to what occurs in the private sector—with one major exception. While available endowment income or other investment returns may significantly influence tuition levels at independent institutions, this influence pales in comparison to the effect of state appropriations on tuition levels at public institutions.

Fees on the other hand, are set based on the actual costs of the special activity or service. Some fees—notably technology fees—are not necessarily linked to the cost of service. Rarely does the fee come close to covering the full cost of providing technology services to students, but it helps provide resources to maintain or enhance those services.

Institutions with a strong commitment to student aid, such as those that provide considerable amounts of institutional aid, typically use a portion of the revenue generated through increased tuition, combined with other revenue sources, to fund additional aid. If they did not adopt this strategy, institutions might risk pricing themselves out of their traditional student markets. In addition, if they are committed to providing student aid to those who qualify and demonstrate a need, the institutions need the additional resources to sustain their commitment.

- **Independent institutions:** Tuition and fees represented 40.2 percent of total revenues (exclusive of investment gains/losses) at independent four-year institutions and 62.4 percent at independent two-year institutions.[56] The combined value of tuition and fees typically represents a smaller percentage of revenues for independent institutions than was the case during fiscal year 2009. Although the actual amounts are higher than normal, they look more significant because the substantial investment losses for the year are excluded from the percentage calculations. Fiscal year 2009, the first full year of the 2008 recession's impact on financial markets, resulted in substantial negative investment income. As reported in the "2009 NACUBO -Commonfund Study of Endowments," the average return on endowments for the year was -18.7 percent—the worst performance in the study's nearly 40-year history.[57] This was significantly worse than the impact during fiscal year 2008, when the losses produced a -3 percent net return.[58] On a more positive note, markets had gained some stability during fiscal year 2011, when the endowment study reported average returns of 19.2 percent.[59]

- **Public institutions:** Tuition and fee revenue represented 19.2 percent of total revenues (exclusive of investment gains/losses) at public four-year institutions and 16.6 percent of total revenues at public two-year institutions.[60]

Government Funding

Both public and independent institutions receive funding from federal, state, and local governments in the form of appropriations as well as grants and contracts. Grants are awarded on a competitive basis, and the federal government does not differentiate between public and independent institutions when making awards.

Most grants include funds for direct and indirect costs, or F&A. Direct costs represent the expenses incurred by the institution in undertaking the activities being supported by the grant or contract. These funds must be used exclusively for the purposes specified in the award. Typical direct costs include the salary and benefits for the principal investigator, graduate assistants, and technicians assigned to the project; supplies; travel; and any other operating expenses authorized under the award.

The portion of the award related to indirect costs typically is calculated as a percentage of direct costs. The indirect costs are the institutional expenses that are not directly related to the specific project but provide necessary support. Examples include utilities, operating expenses of various units that support the project's business aspects (such as the accounting and payroll offices), and the cost of maintaining the space in which the project is conducted.

The federal government also provides direct appropriations to both public and independent institutions. Appropriations usually are provided through the legislative process rather than awarded as a grant or contract. They focus on various activities and programs, such as libraries, cooperative education, land-grant and extension services, international education, and vocational education.

- **Independent institutions:** Revenue from federal sources, including appropriations, grants, and contracts, represented 15.8 percent of the total revenues (exclusive of investment gains/losses) of independent four-year institutions and 12.3 percent of total revenues for independent two-year institutions.[61] State governments provided 1.4 percent of revenues for independent four-year institutions and 4.2 percent for independent two-year institutions.[62] Local governments accounted for 0.4 percent of revenues for independent four-year institutions and 0.2 percent for independent two-year institutions.[63]

  A number of states contract with independent colleges and universities for a wide variety of instructional services. Many of these arrangements involve purchasing student spaces in specialized programs, such as health sciences. Some states support the acquisition of new facilities at independent institutions through special state grants or by allowing the institutions to issue tax-exempt debt through state or local authorities.

  A small number of states provide direct support to independent institutions in the form of contracts based on the full-time-equivalent (FTE) enrollment of in-state students. Others appropriate funds to independent colleges and universities for capitation grants. For example, in fiscal year 2012, the New York legislature provided more than $35 million in Bundy Aid to independent institutions.[64] These funds aim to "maximize the total postsecondary educational resources of New York State; promote and foster the diversity of educational options in New York State; and provide increased access to these programs by assisting institutions to minimize tuition increases."[65]

- **Public institutions:** Revenues from federal sources, including appropriations, grants, and contracts, represented 14.4 percent of total revenues (exclusive of investment gains/losses) for public four-year institutions and 16.5 percent of revenues for public two-year institutions.[66] State governments provided 25.7 percent of revenues for public four-year institutions and 34.6 percent for public two-year institutions.[67] Local governments accounted for 4.3 percent of revenues for public four-year institutions and 19.8 percent for public two-year institutions.[68]

Three-quarters of the total resources of public two-year institutions come from state and local sources. The largest percentage of local resources are devoted to public two-year institutions, because many community colleges are organized as part of a city or county. State and local appropriations provide resources to cover operating expenses, capital construction, and debt service.

The combined value of state and local capital appropriations for public four-year institutions represented 2.2 percent of revenues, while the percentage was 4.1 percent for public two-year institutions.[69]

Private Funding

Sources of private funding include foundations, corporations, churches, community groups, and individuals—such as alumni, members of the institution's governing board, and interested citizens. The resources can range from gifts, grants, and bequests to contributed services and contracts in support of research.

Corporate and foundation sponsors typically provide funds for both direct and indirect costs. Unlike the government, however, most private sponsors rely on a relatively low fixed rate of reimbursement. Additionally, many private sponsors limit their support to current operating expenses and will not provide support for equipment.

State laws often prohibit public institutions from engaging directly in fund-raising activities. In response, they have created foundations to pursue private support and facilitate activities that, though appropriate, may violate guidelines for the use of state funds or be subject to cumbersome processes. Typically, these foundations both raise and manage funds in support of the public college or university. (The majority of the discussion below related to independent institutions applies to public institutions with affiliated foundations.)

In some cases, the public institution's governing board also governs the affiliated foundation. In this arrangement, the foundation operates almost like a department of the institution, with the central administration making all financial decisions. Budgeting is easier in this situation, because the institution controls the foundation's resources.

In other situations, however, the foundation operates independently of the institution. In these cases, the institution typically requests specific support from the foundation but isn't assured of receiving it; the foundation may have established different priorities for its support. Although foundations rarely decline a request from the institution, some notable instances of friction have erupted. In a few cases, a public institution and its affiliated foundation found themselves involved in a lawsuit. And in rare instances, institutions have withdrawn a foundation's right to use the institution's name in its fund-raising activities.

Compared to public institutions, independent ones depend more heavily on gifts to provide a significant portion of each year's budget. Gifts, whether restricted or unrestricted, may be directed for use in the current period or established as endowments to provide ongoing support through the investment income they generate. Although institutions value all gifts, unrestricted gifts provide the greatest flexibility; they can be spent for any institutional purpose, including current operating expenses, student aid, capital construction, and payment of debt service.

Restricted gifts carry stipulations specifying when and for what they can be used. Restricted gifts are often directed toward purposes the institution might otherwise undertake with its own resources; this frees the institution's resources to fund other activities that may not be as well supported. Restricted gifts provide budget relief by allowing the institution to redirect resources to other areas of demand.

Although institutions depend on gift support to varying degrees in their budget strategies, these revenues are not as reliable as some other sources. In years of economic downturn, for instance, personal and corporate giving often declines. Similarly, foundations may shift priorities away from higher education and divert their support to other social programs. A growing trend among foundations and even individual donors is to attach increased accountability and performance measures to their support.

Furthermore, philanthropic and corporate giving remains sensitive to changes in tax laws. Even events on campus can affect the level of giving—both positively and negatively—by alumni and local supporters. The greater the reliance on private support, the more an institution needs contingency funding in its budget to protect against shortfalls.

- **Independent institutions:** Revenues from private sources represented 13.3 percent of total revenues (exclusive of investment gains/losses) for independent four-year institutions and 9.6 percent for independent two-year institutions.[70]

  Some independent institutions are subsidized by religious organizations through either direct financial support or contributed services (teaching, for example) of members of the religious order. Some institutions pay the teaching members of the religious order salaries equal to those of lay teachers, and the order returns the salaries as a gift to the college or university.

- **Public institutions:** Revenues from private sources represented 4 percent of resources for public four-year institutions and 1.3 percent for public two-year institutions.[71] (It is important to note that the above percentages do not reflect the private support that was provided to affiliated foundations supporting public institutions. This is a significant amount for many public institutions but is not reported to IPEDS.)

Auxiliary Enterprises Sales and Services

Colleges and universities receive revenue from the sale of noninstructional educational products and services as well as from auxiliary enterprises. Educational activities might include laboratory and other testing services, demonstration schools, dairy creameries, hotels, theaters, and numerous other academic activities that, through instruction, create goods or services for sale to the general public. Teaching hospitals, outpatient clinics, student and staff health and counseling centers, and hearing and speech clinics provide patient care services. Auxiliary enterprises, which typically are expected to be self-supporting, include residence and dining halls, bookstores, student unions, parking and transit operations, and—in some cases—intercollegiate athletics.

Rather than request specific data about this wide range of secondary revenue sources, IPEDS includes a category for miscellaneous activities that are not part of the primary academic mission. The miscellaneous revenue category also may include gains on the sale of surplus property (such as obsolete or unneeded equipment), insurance recoveries resulting from natural disasters or other property damage, or licensing royalties from commercializing research outcomes. Though relatively insignificant on their own, in the aggregate, these secondary revenue sources often represent a substantial sum.

- **Independent institutions:** Revenues from sales and services represented 10.2 percent of total revenues (exclusive of investment gains/losses) at independent four-year institutions and 7.7 percent of revenues at independent two-year institutions.[72] The corresponding amounts for other revenues were 7.6 percent and 3.5 percent, respectively.[73]
- **Public institutions:** Revenues from sales and services represented 8.6 percent of revenues at public four-year institutions and 3.9 percent of revenues at public two-year institutions.[74] The comparable amounts for other revenues were 9.7 percent and 3.2 percent, respectively.[75]

Hospital Sales and Services

The United States has 136 accredited medical schools, served by nearly 400 teaching hospitals and health systems.[76] Although approximately two-thirds of the revenue generated by academically related hospitals benefits public four-year institutions, the percentage of total revenues (exclusive of investment gains/losses) it represents is very close to the percentage of revenues provided to independent four-year institutions. The percentage for public institutions is 12.1 percent, and the corresponding amount for independent institutions is 11.1 percent.[77]

Investment Income

Colleges and universities typically have idle cash balances that they invest to generate additional revenues. In addition to cash management programs, many institutions have sophisticated short-term investment programs. Both cash and short-term investment programs are intended to use all available resources to generate additional revenues for the institution. (For the public institutions not authorized to make independent investments of idle cash or other resources, the state typically manages investment of the funds and retains the investment earnings.)

Many institutions also maintain long-term investment programs. The majority of resources invested in long-term programs are in the form of endowments—gifts provided by donors with a stipulation that the principal be invested in perpetuity. Investment income earned on idle cash balances or through short-term investments usually can be used for any institutional purpose. (At many public institutions, an affiliated foundation holds the endowment investments; the practices discussed here also apply to them.)

Endowment income is subject to special spending rules. A portion of annual endowment income—which might include dividends, interest, rents, and royalties—is made available for the purpose specified by the donor or, if no purpose was specified, for the institution's general purposes. A formula determines the amount available in a given year, referred to as the spending or payout rate. This rate usually is based on the endowment's historical market value and also may factor in the amount made available the previous year.

If investment income generated by the endowment in a given year is not sufficient to meet the spending level authorized under the payout calculation, the income is supplemented from accumulated gains and market appreciation. These amounts accumulate when the combined value of gains, market appreciation, and investment income exceeds the amount determined under the spending rate calculation. When this occurs, the institution reinvests the funds in the endowment as a hedge against economic downturns.

The use of a spending rate based on historical market values has a smoothing effect on payout rates; it removes some of the volatility that can occur with long-term investment returns. A typical approach relies on a 12-quarter rolling average of historical market values. This approach has proven effective over time, although in some periods, continued negative returns eventually caused the budget support from endowment income to flatten or decrease. This was the case in fiscal year 2010, when the major financial losses in fiscal years 2008 and 2009 caused the endowment income available through the spending formula to decrease.

Uniform Prudent Managment of Institutional Funds Act

Nearly all states have passed a version of the Uniform Prudent Management of Institutional Funds Act (UPMIFA), which builds on the foundation established in the early 1970s with the Uniform Management of Institutional Funds Act (UMIFA).

UMIFA provided explicit authorization for endowments to be managed using the "total return concept." The key element of this concept is distributing a portion of accumulated appreciation with cash income (for example, dividends and interest) when the income is not sufficient to meet the spending requirements.

Before enactment of UMIFA, many endowments were managed under trust theory, which requires the segregation of income from principal (original gifts) and appreciation. Under trust principles, only cash income was available to support endowment objectives. This resulted in many endowments being heavily invested in fixed-income securities to maximize the value of current income. The emphasis on current income came at the expense of the long-term increase in value that could be achieved by investing endowments in equity securities (for example, the stock market).

UPMIFA continues the key elements of UMIFA but adds one critical feature that proved fortuitous when financial markets collapsed in 2008—the ability to spend from "underwater" endowments. Many endowments dropped in value below the amount of their original gift because of the market collapse—what's referred to as being under water. Under UMIFA, such underwater endowments may not receive income distributions in amounts greater than the cash income generated. Given the history of distributing earnings using the total return concept—that is, income plus a portion of accumulated appreciation—there now was insufficient income to meet the spending needs of many endowments.

UPMIFA takes into consideration the reality that endowments are intended to last into perpetuity and will weather highs and lows in the markets. As such, UPMIFA allows the prudent use of a portion of principal to meet current spending needs. Many institutions have used the new spending authority to sustain programs supported by endowments that find themselves under water. They're carefully dipping into principal to fund programs while they wait for the endowments' market values to recover.

Endowment size varies dramatically. Harvard University holds the largest higher education endowment; its market value on June 30, 2011, was $31.7 billion.[78] Among public institutions, the University of Texas System has the distinction of having the largest endowment—$17.1 billion as of June 30, 2011.[79]

Although impressive, these endowments are not representative of higher education overall. In fact, the combined value of the 823 endowments participating in the "2011 NACUBO-Commonfund Study of Endowments" amounted to $408 billion.[80] Seventy-three institutions account for 70 percent of the total value reported in the study. These institutions, each with an endowment valued at $1 billion or more, represent $285 billion of the total market value.[81] Of the participating institutions, 433 have an endowment valued at less than $100 million.[82] More than 16 percent of the participants have endowments valued at less than $25 million.[83] Thus, for the vast majority of institutions, endowment income is quite small.

It is not possible to determine the value of investment or endowment income revenue earned by institutions during fiscal year 2009. The reporting models dictating the manner in which financial information is reported to IPEDS do not require separate disclosure of investment income, gains, and losses. All income, gains, and losses are combined and netted to produce a single number labeled investment income. For fiscal year 2009, independent four-year institutions reported net investment losses of $64.1 billion, while independent two-year institutions reported losses of $32 million.[84] Public four-year institutions reported losses of just under $10 billion.[85] The only sector to report positive net investment income was public two-year institutions, which generated positive net returns of $47 million.[86]

Federal Student Aid Programs

It is impossible to consider higher education revenues without also examining the effect of federal student financial aid. During the 2007-08 academic year, 5.2 million full-time undergraduate students, representing 63 percent of all such students, received some form of federal financial aid.[87] The comparable number for part-time undergraduate students was 4.9 million, representing 38.6 percent of all part-time undergraduate students.[88] The various forms of undergraduate federal financial aid are described below.

Pell Grants. Established by the Education Amendments of 1972, the Basic Educational Opportunity Grants Program—now called the Federal Pell Grant program—provides a minimum level of assistance for students to use at any postsecondary institution eligible to participate in the programs authorized under Title IV of the Higher Education Opportunity Act. The funds, collected and managed by the institution, are awarded to eligible students based on their FAFSA need analysis calculations.

The need analysis system is scaled so that the amount awarded decreases as family income increases. Actual award amounts are based on the total costs of attendance at a particular institution minus the Expected Family Contribution–the amount students and their families are expected to contribute toward their higher education expenses. Federal appropriations limit the total amounts available to students. Because of the program's entitlement nature, the maximum allowable award is revised downward by a reduction formula to ensure that the program has sufficient funds. The Department of Education received a $41.7 billion appropriation for Pell during federal fiscal year 2011.[89] The maximum award per student was $5,550.[90]

Campus-based programs. Unlike Pell, an entitlement program administered directly by the federal government, campus-based programs are operated by the institution using funds from the federal government supplemented with required institutional matching funds. Current regulations require institutions to provide a match equal to one-third of the federal funds.

Although students must demonstrate financial need under the same FAFSA process used for all federal financial aid programs, campus-based programs are awarded by the institution's financial aid office. The federal campus-based program funds (though administered separately) are usually pooled with financial aid from other sources, including the institution itself, and awarded in the form of grants, work-study programs, or loans.

There are three types of campus-based aid programs. Federal Supplemental Educational Opportunity Grants (FSEOG), previously known as the Educational Opportunity Grants Program, were established by the Higher Education Act of 1965 to provide federal grants for financially needy undergraduate students as identified by the institution. FSEOG funds, distributed to institutions according to a state formula based on undergraduate enrollments, are supplemented by the institutional match and used to make grants to students. First priority for FSEOG must be given to students who also receive Federal Pell Grants. The Department of Education received a $736 million appropriation for FSEOG during fiscal year 2011.[91]

The Economic Opportunity Act of 1964 established the Federal Work-Study (FWS) Program. Both undergraduate and graduate/professional students who have financial aid are eligible to receive FWS awards. Funds for FWS are distributed to institutions according to a state allocation formula based on the state's proportion of higher education enrollments, high school graduates, and children in poverty-level families. Supplemented by the institutional match, they pay wages to needy students employed by the institution or a local nonprofit organization or private for-profit businesses. The Department of Education received an appropriation of $978.5 million for FWS during fiscal year 2011.[92]

The National Defense Education Act of 1958 established the National Defense Student Loan Program—now called the Federal Perkins Loan Program—to provide low-interest loans to financially needy students. Funds are distributed to institutions according to a state allocation formula based on undergraduate enrollments. The program operates as a revolving fund. Federal funds (called a Federal Capital Contribution) are matched by the institution, then combined with the principal repayments and interest earnings from previous loans, to make new loans.

From fiscal years 2006 through 2009, Congress appropriated no funds for new Federal Capital Contributions for Perkins Loans; amounts available to the program were limited to loan cancellations.[93] Even that minimal support changed for fiscal year 2011, when the cancellations were not made available.[94] This is consistent with the Department of Education's plan to shift loan support from the Perkins program to the William D. Ford Direct Loan program (see below).

Even with no additional funding, the Perkins program remains a revolving fund. Barring a directive otherwise, the repaid principal and interest on past loans will be lent for the foreseeable future. Some loans are cancelled in return for various forms of community service, and others are simply not repaid. The latter typically are removed from the institution's portfolio and transferred to the federal government.

Leveraging Educational Assistance Partnership (LEAP) Programs. The Higher Education Act of 1972 established the Federal-State Student Incentive Grants Program, now called the LEAP. Also established was the Special Leveraging Educational Assistance Partnership (SLEAP). These programs encourage the creation of state scholarship and community service work-study programs for needy students.

The states received total appropriations of $63.9 million for LEAP [95] and $33.9 [96] million for SLEAP during fiscal year 2011. The amount of aid available for award from all LEAP/SLEAP sources was $161.6 million for LEAP [97] and $101.6 million for SLEAP.[98]

Federal Family Education Loan (FFEL) Program. The Higher Education Act of 1965 established the Guaranteed Student Loan Program, now called the FFEL Program. Loans no longer are being made under the program, although substantial amounts of loans remain outstanding.

William D. Ford Federal Direct Loan Program. The newest federal loan program actually is a variant of previous programs. The Student Loan Reform Act of 1993 established the Federal Direct Student Loan Program. Under the program, the federal government is the lender and provides funds directly to student and parent borrowers through higher education institutions. The program offers four types of loans:

- **Direct subsidized Stafford loans** are subsidized low-interest, variable, or fixed-rate loans based on established financial need. The federal government pays the interest while the student is in school and during grace and deferment periods.

- **Unsubsidized Stafford loans** are low-interest variable or fixed-rate loans available to students regardless of financial need. The federal government does not pay interest on unsubsidized Stafford loans.

- **Federal Parent Loans for Undergraduate Students (PLUS)** loans are available to the parents of dependent undergraduate students and to graduate and professional students. The federal government does not pay interest on PLUS loans.

- **Consolidation loans** allow borrowers with existing student loans to combine their obligations and possibly extend their repayment schedules based on the total amount of outstanding student loan debt. The Department of Education received an appropriation of $2.8 billion for the direct loan program during fiscal year 2011.[99]

State Student Aid Programs

Typically, state financial aid programs for needy students match federal money provided under the LEAP and SLEAP programs. The overall amounts provided under these programs far exceed the seed funding provided by the federal government.

Many states have established competitive financial aid programs. In some states, students must achieve a specified level of academic performance in high school (such as a "B" or 3.0 overall grade average) in order to receive scholarships throughout college, provided the students maintain the specified level of academic performance. In other states, awards are provided based on students' financial need without regard to academic performance.

Programs vary widely, but it is not uncommon for state programs to have maximum awards limited to tuition or an established dollar ceiling. Many states also award funds to students who attend out-of-state institutions. A number of states have experienced revenue shortfalls leading to some qualified individuals not being able to access the aid specified for the programs. The total amount expended under state student aid programs during fiscal year 2010 was $8.6 billion.[100]

A Diverse Pool

Clearly, higher education has a diverse pool of resources with which to fund its operations. The key for institutional success is having a diverse mix of revenues, with reduced reliance on any one source.

Figure 4-1 presents each of the revenue types. The characteristics common to public and independent institutions are presented first for each type of revenue. Features peculiar to the sectors are presented separately. The figure does not identify student aid as a source of institutional revenue because it flows into the institution indirectly through students.

It's noteworthy that, for almost all sources of student aid, the institution actually receives and manages the funds. And although the institution may recognize grant, endowment income, or contribution revenue for amounts received for student financial aid, tuition and fee revenues are reduced by these amounts when the financial statements are presented.

Figure 4-1 Institutional Resources by Source and Type

Source	Type of Revenue	Received Through
Students	Tuition and fees	Customer charges
Government		
Federal	Appropriations	Subsidy
	Grants and contracts	
	–Direct costs	Exchange for services
	–Indirect costs	Reimbursement for services
State and local	Appropriations	Subsidy
	Grants and contracts	
	–Direct costs	Exchange for services
	–Indirect costs	Reimbursement for services
	On behalf payments (A)	Subsidy
Private		
Individuals	Contributions	Gifts
	Contributed services (B)	Subsidy
Corporations and	Contributions	Gifts
foundations	Grants and contracts	
	–Direct costs	Exchange for services
	–Indirect costs	Reimbursement for services
	Contributed services (B)	Subsidy
Investments	Endowment income	Investment of long-term pooled funds
	Investment income	Investment of idle cash balances
Sales and services	Educational activities	Customer charges
	Auxiliary enterprises	Customer charges
	Patient care	Customer charges
Licenses	Royalties	Contractual payments

Notes:
A—It's common for some state governments to pay salaries, fringe benefits, and debt service for public colleges and universities. Such payments are recognized as both revenues and expenses.

B—Contributed services meeting specified criteria are recognized as revenues by independent institutions, but not by public institutions. The value of such services is recognized as both a revenue and an expense.

Figure 4-2 identifies the relative amounts of revenue from the several sources available to higher education institutions. The information is segregated by sector and level of institution.

Figure 4-2 Sources of Revenue for Institutions of Higher Education by Sector and Level of Institution, Fiscal Year 2009

Source: National Center for Education Statistics

	Total	Public Institutions Four-Year	Public Institutions Two-Year	Independent Institutions Four-Year	Independent Institutions Two-Year
Government		Amounts in Billions			
Federal	$61.887	$32.538	$8.325	$20.965	$0.059
State	77.426	58.120	17.490	1.796	0.020
Local	20.228	9.648	10.005	0.574	0.001
Capital appropriations	7.039	4.988	2.051		
Subtotal	**$166.580**	**$105.294**	**$37.871**	**$23.335**	**$0.080**
Tuition and fees	105.548	43.478	8.362	53.409	0.299
Auxiliary enterprises	34.917	19.391	1.967	13.522	0.037
Hospitals	42.105	27.302		14.803	
Private gifts, grants, and contracts	17.672			17.626	0.046
Gifts	9.676	9.019	0.657		
Other	33.645	21.906	1.626	10.096	0.017
Net investment (loss)/gain	(73.693)	(9.958)	0.470	(64.173)	(0.032)
Total Revenues Net of Investment Loss/Gain	**$336.450**	**$216.432**	**$50.953**	**$68.618**	**$0.447**

	Total	Public Institutions Four-Year	Public Institutions Two-Year	Independent Institutions Four-Year	Independent Institutions Two-Year
Government		Percentage Distribution			
Federal	18.4%	15.0%	16.3%	30.6%	13.2%
State	23.0%	26.9%	34.3%	2.6%	4.5%
Local	6.0%	4.5%	19.6%	0.8%	0.2%
Capital appropriations	2.1%	2.3%	4.0%		
Subtotal	**49.5%**	**48.7%**	**74.2%**	**34.0%**	**17.9%**
Tuition and fees	31.4%	20.1%	16.4%	77.8%	66.9%
Auxiliary enterprises	10.4%	9.0%	3.9%	19.7%	8.3%
Hospitals	12.5%	12.6%		21.6%	
Private gifts, grants, and contracts	5.3%			25.7%	10.3%
Gifts	2.9%	4.2%	1.3%		
Other	10.0%	10.1%	3.2%	14.7%	3.8%
Net investment (loss)/gain	-21.9%	-4.6%	0.9%	-93.5%	-7.2%
Total Revenues Net of Investment Loss/Gain	**100.0%**	**100.0%**	**100.0%**	**100.0%**	**100.0%**

Figures 4-3 through 4-6 indicate the relative percentage of revenue from each source. These figures exclude net investment losses—except for Figure 4-4 for public two-year institutions, which had net investment gains for the period.

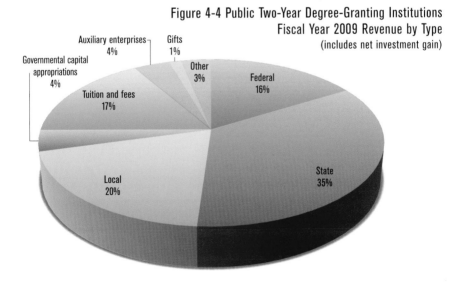

Figure 4-3 Public Four-Year Degree-Granting Institutions
Fiscal Year 2009 Revenue by Type
(excludes net investment loss)

Gifts 4%
Other 10%
Federal 14%
Hospitals 12%
State 26%
Auxiliary enterprises 9%
Tuition and fees 19%
Local 4%
Governmental capital appropriations 2%

Figure 4-4 Public Two-Year Degree-Granting Institutions
Fiscal Year 2009 Revenue by Type
(includes net investment gain)

Auxiliary enterprises 4%
Gifts 1%
Governmental capital appropriations 4%
Other 3%
Federal 16%
Tuition and fees 17%
Local 20%
State 35%

Figure 4-5 Independent Four-Year Degree-Granting Institutions
Fiscal Year 2009 Revenue by Type
(excludes net investment loss)

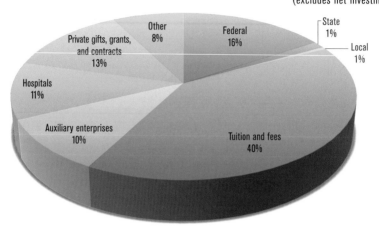

Other
8%

Private gifts, grants,
and contracts
13%

Federal
16%

State
1%

Local
1%

Hospitals
11%

Auxiliary enterprises
10%

Tuition and fees
40%

Figure 4-6 Independent Two-Year Degree-Granting Institutions
Fiscal Year 2009 Revenue by Type
(excludes net investment loss)

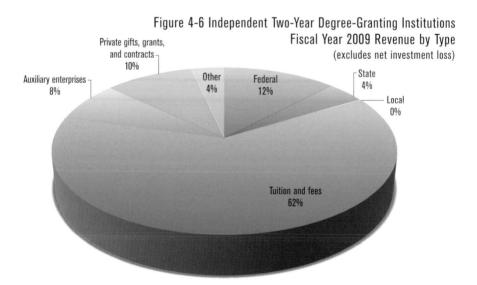

Private gifts, grants,
and contracts
10%

Auxiliary enterprises
8%

Other
4%

Federal
12%

State
4%

Local
0%

Tuition and fees
62%

Key
Points

- Higher education has two major revenue categories: tuition and fees—provided by students and their families—and governmental appropriations from federal, state, and local sources.

- Some institutions receive revenue through sponsored programs, which provide both direct and indirect costs to underwrite research, training, and various other activities. This type of support comes primarily from the federal government, corporations, and foundations.

- Major sources of philanthropic support include individuals, foundations, and businesses. Additional revenue often comes from the sale of nonacademic goods and services via bookstores, residence halls, and dining operations, and from investment income—either generated by endowments or idle cash balances.

- Depending on their financial situation and ability to pay for college, students may receive need-based financial aid to help defray the cost of their education. Need is determined based on the Free Application for Federal Student Aid (FAFSA).

With minor variations, two- and four-year public and independent two- and four-year institutions engage in the same activities, so the types of costs they incur are fairly standard. What varies is the way costs are reported and the relative percentages invested in different categories of expense between the various sectors.

Two different entities establish the accounting and reporting rules applicable to higher education institutions (see Appendix). Public institutions must adhere to one set of rules, while independent institutions must comply with a different set. Public institutions must differentiate between operating and nonoperating expenses when they report financial activity, while independent institutions are not required to segregate expenses.

Additionally, certain cost categories that public institutions can present separately must be allocated by independent institutions to the primary functional categories. For this reason, this chapter presents cost analysis separately by sector and category.

One other note: The following discussion is organized by functional category, such as instruction, academic support, and operation and maintenance (O&M). Functions refer to the purpose for which expenses are incurred. The alternative method for presenting expenses, called natural classification reporting, focuses on the type of expense incurred rather than its purpose. Natural classification includes expenses such as salaries, utilities, and travel.

The data presented below, for fiscal year 2009, are drawn from IPEDS. IPEDS does not collect expenses by natural classification, so it is not possible to provide information about these categories of expense.

Public Institutions

Instruction

All higher education institutions focus on instruction. Although it is not the largest category, instruction is considered the most important and, therefore, appears as the first expense category in the grouping of educational and general (E&G) activities. (E&G activities are an institution's primary academic, administrative, and related activities; they do not include auxiliary enterprises and hospitals.)

This category includes the natural classification expenses (salaries, travel, supplies) incurred by academic units involved in teaching and directly related activities.

Instructional expenses at public four-year institutions amounted to $57.3 billion, representing 25.4 percent of total expenses. The comparable amounts for public two-year institutions were $17.8 billion and 37.4 percent.[101]

Research

Research occurs in institutes and centers as well as in traditional academic departments. Doctoral institutions typically have larger volumes of research activity than other four-year institutions. Research at two-year institutions is relatively insignificant in terms of dollars expended, but some discoveries are just as likely to materialize at these institutions as at their four-year counterparts.

This category includes natural classification expenses related both to internally funded research and sponsored research. Research expenses at public four-year institutions amounted to $26.6 billion, representing 11.8 percent of total expenses. The comparable amounts for public two-year institutions were $22 million, representing less than 1 percent.[102]

Public Service

Public service expenses encompass a multitude of activities that provide benefits to external groups. This category includes conferences, executive training, advisory services, and other activities that deliver value outside the institution. Other examples include public broadcasting services for radio and television, and cooperative extension services that support regional agricultural interests. Their mission dictates that public two-year institutions are much more likely to engage in public service activities than research.

Public service expenses at public four-year institutions amounted to $10.5 billion, representing 4.7 percent of total expenses. The comparable amounts for public two-year institutions were $745 million, representing 1.6 percent.[103]

Academic Support

This category consists of expenses that benefit the primary missions of instruction, research, and public service. The largest category of expenses usually is for libraries, but depending on the institution and its mission, significant expenses might be incurred for audiovisual services, museums, gardens, or academic administration.

Academic support expenses at public four-year institutions amounted to $15.3 billion, representing 6.8 percent of total expenses. The comparable amounts for public two-year institutions were $3.5 billion, representing 7.3 percent.[104]

Student Services

In this category, the common theme is support for students' emotional and physical well-being, along with their intellectual, cultural, and social development outside the classroom.

There are two broad types of student services activities. The first relates to the administration of operating areas that support students, such as financial aid and the registrar's office. (Intercollegiate athletics are reported in this category when not operated as a revenue-generating activity within auxiliary enterprises.) The second type represents opportunities for student participation or interaction, such as student clubs and organizations, cultural events, student newspapers, intramural athletics, career guidance, and counseling.

Student services expenses at public four-year institutions amounted to $8.6 billion, representing 3.8 percent of total expenses. The comparable amounts for public two-year institutions were $4.3 billion and 9.1 percent.[105]

Institutional Support

This category is sometimes referred to as the general and administrative (G&A) expense category because it represents the nonacademically related administration of the institution. Traditional institutional support activities include executive leadership, planning, accounting and related fiscal services, legal services, human resources, logistical services (for example, procurement and printing), insurance (other than property insurance), public relations, and fund-raising.

Many institutions use the institutional support category to report operational expenses related to the chief academic officer and chief student affairs officer. Other institutions report these expenses as academic support and student services, respectively. This category excludes O&M, which has its own category.

Institutional support expenses at public four-year institutions amounted to $16.5 billion, representing 7.3 percent of total expenses. The comparable amounts for public two-year institutions were $6.6 billion and 13.8 percent.[106]

Operation and Maintenance of Plant

With the exception of depreciation, O&M includes expenses related to the built environment—the infrastructure, facilities, and grounds of a college or university. The expenses cover a wide range of activities, including utilities, custodial services, noncapital repair and maintenance, grounds maintenance, fire protection, security, property insurance, and similar items.

Usually, the expenses reported in this category are limited to those related to the institution's E&G activities. When non-E&G activities report their expenses, they typically include an appropriate share of O&M expenses.

O&M expenses at public four-year institutions amounted to $13.8 billion, representing 6.1 percent of total expenses. The comparable amounts for public two-year institutions were $4 billion and 8.5 percent.[107]

Depreciation

This category constitutes the annual charge for physical assets—buildings and equipment—with a limited life extending beyond one year. Rather than charge operations with the full cost of a building or large piece of equipment, the item is recorded as an asset, and its cost is recognized as an expense ratably over the estimated useful life of the asset.

Given the capital-intensive nature of higher education, depreciation represents a significant expense for most institutions. The exception would be institutions relying primarily on rented space. In that case, the institution's depreciation expense would be relatively low, but its O&M expenses would be significant.

Depreciation expenses at public four-year institutions amounted to $11.7 billion, representing 5.2 percent of total expenses. The comparable amounts for public two-year institutions were $2 billion and 4.2 percent.[108]

Scholarships and Fellowships

Scholarship and fellowship expenses relate to student financial aid. Scholarships typically are awarded to undergraduate students, while graduate and postdoctoral students receive fellowships.

To avoid double counting revenues and expenses, the vast majority of aid awarded to students is recognized as an offset to tuition and fee revenue. Although a variety of governmental, private, and institutional sources award significant amounts of financial aid to students, the expenses are relatively small compared to the total value of student aid. Only the portion disbursed directly to the student (versus applied to the student's account in the college business office) is recorded as an expense.

Student aid expenses at public four-year institutions amounted to $7.2 billion, representing 3.2 percent of total expenses. The comparable amounts for public two-year institutions were $3.9 billion and 8.3 percent.[109]

Other Operating Expenses

This catchall category includes expenses related to ongoing activities that do not align with standard programmatic categories. It is the final category in the E&G grouping of expenses.

Some institutions engage in unique activities that, while related to their mission, are not common enough to be reported in a standard programmatic category. Rather than distort data that may be used for various types of analysis, these amounts are reported as other operating expenses. One example might be the operation of historical venues that are not deemed museums or galleries (which would be reported with academic support).

Another example would be a major federal research laboratory operated on a contract basis and designated as an independent operation.

Other operating expenses for public four-year institutions amounted to $4.3 billion, representing 1.9 percent of total expenses. The public two-year institutions expended $1.5 billion for other operating expenses, representing 3.1 percent.[110]

Auxiliary Enterprises

One of two major activities that fall outside the scope of E&G, auxiliary enterprises is the collective term used to describe activities that provide fee-based services and goods to students, faculty, staff, and—occasionally—the general public. They generally operate on a self-supporting basis and frequently must cover both their operating and capital costs from user fees and charges. Public institutions often expect auxiliary enterprise units to reimburse the E&G units for services provided to the auxiliaries.

The most common auxiliaries found on a campus are bookstores and dining operations. Other activities frequently operated as auxiliary enterprises include parking, transportation, student health, and various retail outlets (especially for computers and other end-user technology). In some cases, institutions outsource their auxiliary activities to commercial entities; these arrangements vary from campus to campus, but it's common for the service provider to share revenues with the institution.

Depending on the magnitude of operations and the revenue generated, intercollegiate athletics is another candidate for treatment as an auxiliary enterprise. Large-scale NCAA Division I athletics almost always are treated as an auxiliary enterprise. When not classified as auxiliary enterprises, athletics operations are reported as student services.

Auxiliary enterprises expenses at public four-year institutions amounted to $18.3 billion, representing 8.1 percent of total expenses. The comparable amounts for public two-year institutions were $2.3 billion and 4.8 percent.[111]

Hospitals

Teaching hospitals represent a significant non-E&G activity for some universities. A number of institutions operate multiple hospitals with different specialties, as well as various clinics serving different constituencies.

In addition to reimbursing E&G units for services received, hospitals typically provide financial support to the institution's medical school. At a minimum, the physicians providing care in the hospitals and clinics usually have a faculty appointment in the medical school. In these cases, the hospital and the medical school share responsibility for compensating the physicians.

Although many public two-year institutions have relationships with hospitals as part of their educational efforts to train students for health-care careers, no two-year institutions reported expenses related to hospitals. Hospital expenses at public four-year institutions amounted to $25.9 billion, representing 11.5 percent of total expenses.[112]

Interest and Other Nonoperating Expenses

The final expense categories for public institutions include interest, usually related to capital construction or purchases, and nonoperating expenses that do not fit neatly in one of the designated programmatic categories for higher education. Interest expense is significant in public higher education because most of the capital construction is financed using long-term debt.

The source data do not explain the nature of the expenses reported in the other nonoperating category. They likely include noninvestment losses from the sale of capital assets, typically equipment, losses on refinancing long-term debt, or costs incurred as a result of natural disasters. To the extent that the losses are not fully covered by insurance, the write-off would be treated as an other nonoperating expense. (Investmenst losses are netted against investment gains and investment income. The net amount—whether positive or negative—usually is reported among revenues.)

Interest expense at public four-year institutions amounted to $2.4 billion, representing 1 percent of total expenses, while other nonoperating expenses represented $7 billion and 3.1 percent. The comparable amounts for interest for public two-year institutions were $618 million, representing 1.3 percent, and other nonoperating expenses were $307 million, amounting to 0.6 percent.[113]

Figure 5-1 identifies the relative amounts of expenses by functional category, segregated by sector and level of institution.

Figure 5-1 Functional Expenses of Higher Education
Institutions, Fiscal Year 2008–2009

		Public Institutions	
Purpose of Expense	Total	Four-Year	Two-Year
Operating Expenses		Amounts in Billions	
Instruction	$75.079	$57.266	$17.813
Research	26.651	26.629	0.022
Public service	11.244	10.499	0.745
Academic support	18.805	15.300	3.505
Student services	12.940	8.613	4.327
Institutional support	23.079	16.506	6.573
Operation and maintenance of plant	17.839	13.805	4.034
Depreciation	13.720	11.720	2.000
Scholarships and fellowships (student aid)	11.104	7.156	3.948
Auxiliary enterprises	20.588	18.293	2.295
Hospitals	25.945	25.945	
Other operating expenses	5.777	4.297	1.480
Subtotal	$262.771	$216.029	$46.742
Nonoperating Expenses			
Interest	2.973	2.355	0.618
Other nonoperating expenses	7.286	6.979	0.307
Subtotal	$10.259	$9.334	$0.925
Total	$273.030	$225.363	$47.667

		Independent Institutions	
Purpose of Expense	Total	Four-Year	Two-Year
		Amounts in Billions	
Instruction	$46.453	$46.287	$0.166
Research	15.262	15.262	
Public service	2.299	2.295	0.004
Academic support	12.580	12.538	0.042
Student services	11.012	10.944	0.068
Institutional support	19.401	19.259	0.142
Scholarships and fellowships (student aid)	0.758	0.751	0.007
Auxiliary enterprises	13.708	13.671	0.037
Hospitals	11.931	11.931	
Other expenses	7.945	7.915	0.030
Total	$141.349	$140.853	$0.496

Figures 5-2 through 5-5 indicate the relative percentage of expense for each category. The differences in presentation reflect the differences described in the text.

Figure 5-2 Public Four-Year Degree-Granting Institutions Fiscal Year 2009 Operating Expenses by Function

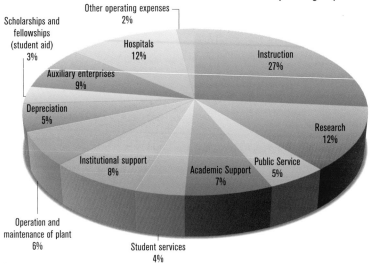

Scholarships and fellowships (student aid) 3%

Other operating expenses 2%

Hospitals 12%

Auxiliary enterprises 9%

Instruction 27%

Depreciation 5%

Research 12%

Institutional support 8%

Academic Support 7%

Public Service 5%

Operation and maintenance of plant 6%

Student services 4%

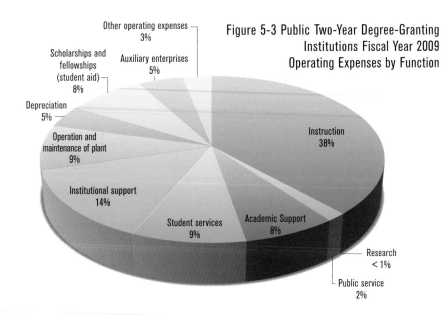

Other operating expenses 3%

Figure 5-3 Public Two-Year Degree-Granting Institutions Fiscal Year 2009 Operating Expenses by Function

Scholarships and fellowships (student aid) 8%

Auxiliary enterprises 5%

Depreciation 5%

Operation and maintenance of plant 9%

Instruction 38%

Institutional support 14%

Student services 9%

Academic Support 8%

Research < 1%

Public service 2%

Figure 5-4 Independent Four-Year Degree-Granting Institutions
Fiscal Year 2009 Total Expenses by Function

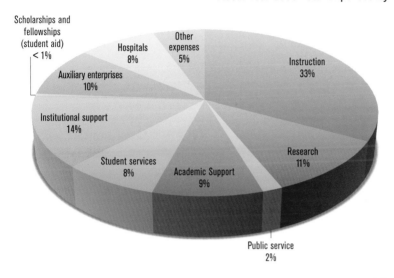

Figure 5-5 Independent Two-Year Degree-Granting Institutions
Fiscal Year 2009 Total Expenses by Function

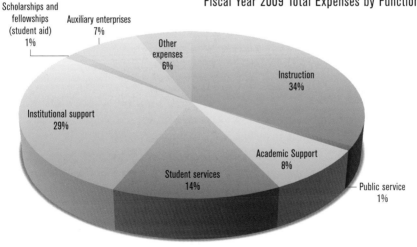

Independent Institutions

In their financial reporting, independent institutions use most of the same expense categories as public institutions, with three exceptions: interest expense, depreciation expense, and expenses for facilities-related costs (referred to as O&M of plant). Expenses in the three omitted categories must be allocated to the other categories.

Because the IPEDS database doesn't include details about the allocation methodology, it is not possible to disaggregate the data to present comparable amounts for independent institutions. Despite the fact that the same terminology is used, the measurement differences make comparisons between public and independent institutions meaningless.

- In the category of **instruction**, independent four-year institutions expended $46.3 billion, amounting to 32.9 percent of their total expenses. The comparable amounts for independent two-year institutions are $166 million and 33.5 percent.[114]

- **Research** expenses for independent four-year institutions represent $15.3 billion and 10.3 percent of their total expenses.[115] No research expenses were reported by independent two-year institutions.

- Not surprisingly, given the private nature of their funding, independent institutions do not invest as many resources in **public service** as their public institution counterparts. Independent four-year institutions expended $2.3 billion for public service, amounting to 1.6 percent of their total expenses. The comparable numbers for independent two-year institutions are $4 million and 0.8 percent.[116]

- **Academic support** at independent four-year institutions consumed $12.5 billion, representing 8.9 percent of total expenses. Independent two-year institutions invested $42 million in academic support, amounting to 8.5 percent of their total expenses.[117]

- Independent institutions make large investments in **student services** expenses. The amount in this category for independent four-year institutions was $10.9 billion, representing 7.8 percent of total expenses. Independent two-year institutions invested $68 million, or 13.7 percent.[118]

- **Institutional support** appears significantly larger at independent institutions compared to their public institution peers, but major required allocations inflate these numbers. For instance, interest expense frequently is allocated entirely to institutional support. Independent four-year institutions invested $19.3 billion for general and administrative purposes, amounting to 13.7 percent of total expenses. The comparable numbers for independent two-year institutions were $142 million and 28.6 percent.[119]

- The amount of **scholarships and fellowships** reported as expenses is modest because most financial aid is treated as an offset to tuition revenue. Independent four-year institutions expended $751 million for financial aid, amounting to 0.5 percent of total expenses. Their two-year counterparts invested $7 million in aid, representing 1.4 percent of their total expenses.[120]

- In the category of **auxiliary enterprises,** independent four-year institutions consumed $13.7 billion, representing 9.7 percent of total expenses. The comparable numbers for independent two-year institutions were $37 million and 7.5 percent.[121]

- As with public institutions, only independent four-year institutions report **hospital expenses.** Independent institutions expended $11.9 billion for hospitals, amounting to 8.5 percent of total expenses.[122]

- Because independent institutions are not required to differentiate between operating and nonoperating activities, the **other expenses** category would contain both types of expenses, representing the same activities as described for public institutions. Other expenses at independent four-year institutions consumed $7.9 billion or 5.6 percent of total expenses. The comparable numbers for their two-year counterparts were $30 million and 6 percent.[123]

As these statistics demonstrate, higher education incurs significant expenses. Both public and independent institutions make major investments in delivering instruction and related services to their most important constituency: students. But it doesn't stop there. With the exception of independent two-year institutions, the sectors conduct significant amounts of research on behalf of the federal government, foundations, and corporations. And this is beyond what is being funded from institutional resources.

Public institutions, in particular, expend large sums on public service, with the objective of enhancing the well-being of their local communities or regions. Beyond these expenses classified as primary objectives, institutions spend large percentages of their budgets on supporting and ancillary services. Although it doesn't have the bottom-line profit motive that exists in the for-profit commercial sector, higher education has a huge impact on the nation's economy.

Key
Points

- The expenses incurred by colleges and universities fall into two broad categories: functional or natural classification. Functional categories, referred to as E&G expenses, represent the core academic and related activities: instruction, research, public service, academic support, student services, institutional support, O&M of plant, and student financial aid.

- E&G expenses do not include these two functional expense categories: auxiliary enterprises and hospitals. The former are the "businesses" operated by the institution to serve the needs of faculty, staff, students, and the general public, such as bookstores, residence halls, and dining facilities.

- While functional expenses describe the nature of the activity being supported, natural classification expenses refer to the type of expenses incurred. For instance, within the functional expense category of instruction, natural classification expenses would be incurred for salaries, benefits, travel, and utilities.

Who should participate at each stage of the budgeting process? Is the budget merely a continuation of what was done last year? Should tuition and fees increase next year—and, if so, by how much? Which departments should receive increased resources next year, and which ones should experience reductions? What are the implications for fringe benefits if salaries increase by 2.5 percent?

Such questions commonly arise during the budget process. Over time, participants in the process become more skilled at raising the right questions at the right time to ensure they influence resource allocations. They learn the best opportunities to influence the budget occur during the planning stage.

Because plans guide effective budgets, planning should precede and link to the budget process. To wield meaningful influence, a participant should contribute to both the planning process and the budget process. The major decisions behind resource allocations are both process related and content related. For instance, the institutional representatives who participate in the process affect resource allocations just as much as the amount of resources available for allocation.

Participants generally expect that they can affect resource distribution if they analyze the institution's programs and activities in a logical, orderly manner. The issues raised in this chapter provide a framework for analytical thinking—an essential element of planning. Still, the effect of politics on budget decisions cannot be overlooked or underestimated.

The political environment and the spheres of influence of people within an institution's community vary from one campus to another. Through friendships with trustees or legislators, for example, a department chair may have political connections that provide influence far beyond that normally indicated by such a position. An administrator or faculty member, who has long participated in the planning and budget processes, may gain enough institutional knowledge and political clout to become a powerful figure during budget negotiations. And some participants are simply more articulate than others and, therefore, enjoy greater success at garnering resources.

In general, the more complex the budget process and the greater the individual interconnections, the more complex the political environment becomes. The framework outlined below enables institutions to strike a balance between rational planning and the inevitable political maneuvering. In fact, an effective planning process—one that involves key stakeholders and is built on transparency—can reduce the impact of politics on resource allocation decisions.

The wide range of planning activities undertaken by higher education fall into three main categories:

- **Strategic planning** takes the long-term perspective; it sets the agenda for major investments and guides the institution's development for a five-year period. A strategic plan identifies and focuses on only a handful of priority areas.

- **Infrastructural planning** fills in the gaps between the handful of strategic priorities and the core functional and essential support areas that represent the institution's ongoing activities.

- **Operational planning**, which focuses on one year of activities, drives the resource allocation decisions that determine an institution's operating budget. It must be linked to and driven by the strategic and infrastructural plans.

Ideally, an institution integrates these various plans with one another, with the resource allocation process, and with ongoing assessment activities.

A Question
of Trust

Whether discussing planning or resource allocation, the institutional representatives engaged in the budget process cannot communicate too much. Stakeholders need to know not only the strategic priorities but also how to garner additional resources. Widespread sharing of information must occur at every step of the process.

An institution's desired level of openness and transparency will influence the way it communicates. Having open and transparent processes—and disseminating information about the processes and their outcomes—will create a more stable environment on campus. On the other hand, failure to disseminate information will likely create a void that stakeholders will fill with rumors—and rumors rarely are positive. Others on campus will devote significant amounts of time to speculating about the budget decisions being made and their implications.

What's more, a lack of available information also produces a lack of trust among stakeholders. If the administration or the board take actions in secret, any existing trust in the institution will erode. Trust within an organization is fragile—and very difficult to restore. To avoid this problem, communicate openly and honestly: Share both the good news and the bad.

Strategic Planning

Strategic planning sits at the highest level of institutional planning. It is holistic—in other words, it focuses on the entire institution. Although many campus operating units will refer to their strategic plan, strategic planning does not happen at the unit level. Units can engage in strategic thinking—but their plans must be driven by the institution's strategic plan and supportive of its established goals.

Effective strategic planning is inclusive and provides opportunities for broad participation and input. Within practical limits, the more perspectives influencing the strategic plan, the better the end result.

The process should be conducted by a task force representative of the institution's diversity and championed by a senior institutional leader—typically the president, chief academic officer, or chief financial officer. Some larger institutions have a chief planning officer serving on the president's cabinet, who could serve as the strategic planning champion. The champion does not necessarily serve on the planning task force; instead, he or she ensures that the task force has the resources, cooperation, and support to do its work, including access to the president and the cabinet as needed.

By its nature, strategic planning covers a multiyear period—typically five years. Some institutions develop 10-year plans, which can be problematic because dramatic changes can occur that make pursuit of the plan impractical or misguided—especially in the out years. A five-year plan, reviewed annually and adjusted for new realities, provides appropriate guidance while still responding to changing circumstances.

The best strategic plans focus on a limited number of strategic themes or priority areas—five or six at the most. Too often, especially when written to make all constituents feel good, plans ignore the practical realities that institutions simply can't afford to spread their resources across more than a handful of major areas. Many important activities occur on college and university campuses, but they cannot all be strategic priorities at the same time.

Strategic planning produces a written document that articulates the institution's vision five years into the future. It identifies strategic themes, which represent the handful of priority areas that support the vision and will serve as the institution's focus during the period. Finally, the plan identifies the major goals within each strategic theme, along with their time frames and success measures.

Just as the strategic planning process requires an overall champion, each strategic theme needs an identified champion. A similar requirement applies to each of the goals supporting the various strategic themes. One senior-level official must own the goal and take responsibility for ensuring its achievement.

Infrastructural and Operational Planning

Once developed, the strategic plan should guide other aspects of campus planning. Infrastructural plans, which cover core programmatic and essential support areas, address the many ongoing operational activities that fall outside the five or six strategic themes.

Occasionally, a strategic theme will align perfectly with a core programmatic or essential support area. More likely, however, the strategic themes will address a portion of a programmatic area or touch on multiple areas. For example, a strategic theme focused on the need to alter the teaching/learning environment by dramatically increasing technology use clearly falls within the academic plan but also has significant implications for the IT plan.

In the core programmatic areas, separate plans will relate to academics, student engagement, learning resources, athletics, and the auxiliary enterprises plan. In the area of essential support activities, plans typically address enrollment management, institutional advancement, facilities, IT, and administrative support functions not addressed in the other support plans.

The financial plan, represented by the operating and capital budgets, pulls together the various infrastructural plans. While infrastructural plans typically focus on a two- to four-year period, operational plans guide what happens on a day-to-day basis for one to two years. Institutions historically have not intentionally planned at the unit level. Instead, they allow the budget to guide what happens, usually based on what happened the previous year. True operational planning focuses primarily on one or two fiscal years, although some initiatives can extend beyond this period. The objective is to establish plans guided by the strategic and infrastructural plans that, in turn, guide the deployment of resources.

Given this planning hierarchy, influencing how resources are allocated starts with the planning process. Anyone who wants to make a difference on how resources will be utilized should seek to participate at the earliest possible point.

Ancillary Planning Issues

One issue related to planning doesn't fit neatly into strategic, infrastructural, or operational planning: the need to benchmark progress through peer comparisons. In fact, higher education institutions are noted for their efforts to monitor what happens at other institutions and use it as a yardstick for comparison with their own efforts.

Benchmarking has two critical elements:

1. **Identifying the comparison group.** The objective is a group appropriate

for comparison across the institution. Realistically, however, perfect matches won't exist. More likely, the selected institutions will match up well on some elements, such as enrollment size, operating budget, and endowment, but not well on other elements, such as the number of academic programs or specific majors offered.

Political issues often creep into the identification of comparison institutions. Some constituents, for instance, will not feel comfortable with true peers and instead seek to identify institutions that clearly are better performers. Both groups will provide valuable information but generally not within the same comparison set. A better approach is to agree on a set of institutions that match up well currently—true peers—and a different set of institutions that can serve as an aspirational comparison group.

Many states assign their public institutions a set of peer institutions for comparison purposes. This works well if the institution participates in the process of identifying the peer institutions but may prove challenging if the peers are unilaterally assigned.

Independent institutions select their own peers. A good approach is to examine both the formal and informal affinity groups in which the institution participates, such as consortia, athletic conferences, or other membership organizations. Of course, not all members of a particular group will represent a good fit. For instance, an athletic conference like the Big Ten provides good peers for all institutions other than Northwestern, the conference's only independent institution. The remaining institutions all are large public research universities, albeit with some mission differentiation. As a starting point, this makes a good comparison group.

2. **Determining the comparison factors.** Institutions have an endless list of topics for comparison. To illustrate the alternative approaches available, the examples below use two topics: benchmarking instructional costs and measuring institutional health through financial ratio analysis.

Because salaries represent one of their largest costs, institutions have great interest in determining whether their costs of instruction are reasonable for faculty engaged in teaching (versus research or other activities). One way to assess this is by participating in the National Study of Instructional Costs and Productivity (The Delaware Study). Nearly 600 four-year institutions have participated in the study, which originated at the University of Delaware in 1992.[124] It relies on self-reported data on various aspects of costs and faculty teaching load. Study participants can access information by academic discipline and course level, sorted by type of institution. This allows them to compare their cost structure against national norms as well as customized peer sets.

As for financial ratios, one of the most valuable is the Composite Financial Index (CFI) developed by KPMG and Prager, Sealy & Co. LLC.[*] The CFI consists of four weighted ratios that measure an institution's financial health:

- Primary reserve ratio—Does the institution have sufficient resources to carry out its mission?

- Viability ratio—Does the institution practice strategic debt management in carrying out its mission?

- Return on net assets ratio—How well do the institution's physical and financial assets perform financially in supporting the mission?

- Net operating revenues ratio—Is the institution able to carry out its mission without spending reserves?

The final three ratios are supported by secondary ratios that dig deeper into the CFI's underlying factors. Secondary ratios include, among others, the age of facilities ratio—indicating whether an institution invests sufficient resources to maintain its physical plant's suitability—and the debt burden ratio—measuring the portion of total expenditures devoted to annual debt service.

The developers of the CFI indicate that it is not intended for institutional comparisons because too many different factors affect institutional character. Instead, they recommend comparing on the basis of the four primary ratios, which rely on information generally available in institutions' audited financial statements. For the most part, if one can obtain the statements, one can calculate the ratios.

In terms of planning, ratios can be used to drive institutional performance. If the institution's financial health is unsatisfactory, the ratios can be used to direct actions that result in improvement.

Financial equilibrium offers another way to assess financial health. Generally speaking, the term refers to the minimum performance to which all institutions should aspire. Financial equilibrium has four components:[**]

- **Maintaining a balanced budget.** This element ties directly to one of the four primary ratios in the CFI—the net operating revenues ratio. A balanced budget actually means a budget with at least a modest surplus; even nonprofit organizations must generate a surplus to survive.

- **Investing in human capital.** The faculty and staff who conduct the various operational activities are essential to an institution's success. As such, the institution must compensate them well, provide for their

---

[*] For an in-depth discussion of the CFI and additional general information about ratio analysis, see Phil Tahey, Ron Salluzzo, Fred Prager, Lou Mezzina, and Chris Cowen. *Strategic Financial Analysis for Higher Education.* 7th ed. (San Francisco: Prager, Sealy & Co., LLC., KPMG LLP, and Attain LLC, 2010).

[**] The discussion of financial equilibrium draws on the work of William S. Reed, *Financial Responsibilities of Governing Boards* (Washington, DC: Association of Governing Boards of Universities and Colleges and NACUBO, 2001).

well-being following employment, and invest in their ongoing professional development. Unfortunately, too few institutions invest adequately in this area, especially during times of economic difficulties.

- **Preserving physical assets.** Too many institutions abandon scheduled maintenance during difficult economic times, thereby threatening their long-term financial health. Delaying essential maintenance typically occurs because so many aspects of maintenance are invisible to the average person. Unless a leaking roof or temperamental boiler affects people directly, they rarely recognize the problem. (See Chapter Nine for a deeper discussion of deferred maintenance.)

- **Maintaining the endowment's purchasing power.** Endowments are perpetual resources intended to last forever, so management of them should ensure long-term viability. "Intergenerational equity" refers to the concept that an endowment should be managed so current beneficiaries are treated equitably—as well as, but not better than—when compared with future generations.

Unless an institution is appropriately addressing these four elements, it will find itself in financial disequilibrium. Financial disequilibrium eventually will threaten the institution's long-term viability.

Strategic Planning

From *Collaborative Strategic Planning in Higher Education* by Patrick Sanaghan

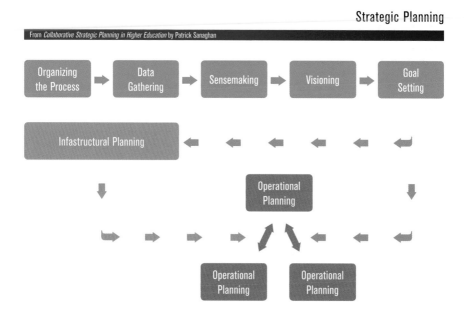

Integrating Planning, Resource Allocation, and Assessment

After planning establishes the institution's priorities, resource allocation decisions must ensure the priorities can be carried out. It may not be possible to direct all resources to established priorities; at the very least, institutional procedures should confirm that resources are not used in a manner counter to established priorities.

Ongoing assessment represents the final element of integration. Its results should influence plans and drive resource allocation decisions. What is learned through assessment should result in an intentional decision to stay the course, alter the course, or abandon the trip entirely. Assessment that isn't intended to have an impact, unless externally mandated, should not be undertaken.

As part of the planning and budgeting processes, an institution should establish success measures long before the assessment effort gets underway. Knowing in advance what you're trying to achieve—and formally articulating it—dramatically enhances your likelihood of accomplishment.

Effective integration of planning, budgeting, and assessment relies on common sets of data and information. This requires the institution to not only generate and disseminate information widely on the campus but also encourage extensive dialogue and interaction. Yet many institutions approach integration activities the same way they approach routine activities in their day-to-day operations—via silos. They establish one structure for planning, another for budgeting, and still a third for assessment (if this has a structure at all).

The following sections suggest ways to facilitate integration and the roles various constituents can play.

Participation and Involvement

Budget development can involve budget staff and administrators or expand to include faculty, students, and other constituents. Constituent groups may take part in the process through mechanisms such as advisory committees and budget hearings. The effectiveness of the budget process will depend on the quality of the participants; their level of institutional knowledge; the support participants receive from budget staff; and the budget office's willingness and ability to provide meaningful, usable data.

Role of the board. How intimately involved should the governing board be in the development of the budget? Should they influence tuition rates or the salary increase pool? Should they directly influence the amounts allocated to department A versus departments B and C? Or the distribution of resources between ongoing operations and strategic initiatives? What about

Opening Up

In large part, an institution's culture will determine the degree of openness in the budget process. Colleges with small faculties and staffs and a strong sense of shared governance typically have relatively open deliberations, followed by an all-faculty meeting to discuss the proposed budget. Larger institutions, because of the sheer number of people involved, rarely have the same depth of participation.

Institutions without a highly participative governance structure will more likely have a relatively closed budget process without much transparency or input from constituents. Even when the process is transparent and involves extensive participation by various constituents, the numbers participating will represent only a small fraction of the college's or university's community. In these situations, communication becomes paramount.

Generally speaking, the more open the process, the better. Closed processes tend to simply perpetuate past practices—including their flawed elements. A more open budgeting process has the benefit of including new and differing perspectives. It may, however, take longer as participants raise difficult but necessary questions related to making resource allocation decisions and negotiating levels of support. The criteria for distributing resources may be more widely debated—but also more widely understood.

participating in budget hearings?

The answers to these questions will vary from campus to campus. It's not possible to articulate all the possible variations or the specific factors that favor one approach over another. The goal here is to describe an effective approach that would serve the majority of institutions; it will be necessary to adapt the approach to particular campus environments and cultures.

Governing boards in higher education must distinguish between their governance responsibilities and the administration's responsibility to manage and operate the institution. Boards' governance responsibility clearly translates into establishing major institutional policies. Management is responsible for adhering to the policies as they carry out the mission of the institution.

Simply put, the governing board should focus on planning and leave resource allocation to management. Boards fulfill their responsibility to govern the institution by influencing and approving plans. In so doing, they leave to management the details—how to achieve the results specified in the plans.

That's why board members normally should not participate in budget hearings. Their mere presence will alter the nature of the conversation and potentially prevent the discussion of critical issues. Nor would it be appropriate for the board to delve into issues such as the amount of resources allotted to particular departments or cost centers. On the other hand, it is totally appropriate for the board to influence the allocation of resources between strategic and operational objectives. This is a natural outgrowth of their responsibility to oversee planning and ensure that plans can be accomplished.

The board influences and ultimately approves the assumptions on which management builds the budget. That role includes approving tuition rates and salary increase pools, plus providing the broad guidance that shapes the budget's development. They also must approve the budget developed by management. And they must engage in assessment by periodically examining the administration's success in fulfilling plans and living within the budget. The board also would be expected to review and approve any budget revisions that would affect the bottom line.

Still, the board's most critical role comes during the planning stage when key decisions are made. Part of the planning process is confirming the appropriateness of the institution's mission. The board must validate the mission and confirm its continued appropriateness. Then, by participating in the planning process—particularly the strategic planning process—the board ensures that the plans support the mission.

Role of operating departments. Should these departments have a role in developing the budget, or should central budget office personnel have sole responsibility? In part, the answer depends on the kinds of expectations the institution wishes to encourage among departments. For example, if the institution will have insufficient revenues to satisfy requests for additional resources, involving departments may raise expectations that cannot be met.

On the other hand, if the institution has a culture of openness and inclusiveness, involving departments ensures that the best information about resource needs is available. With this approach, requests and justifications are based on information that might not otherwise become available to participants at later stages of the budget process. As departmental staff and faculty become aware of the constraints, their expectations may become more realistic; this creates an opportunity to build support for the chosen direction.

Role of faculty and students. The level of involvement for faculty and students, in particular, significantly influences their satisfaction with the decisions that shape the resource allocations. Faculty appropriately believe that they offer unique perspectives with respect to academic program development (including new instructional endeavors), research initiatives, and service programs.

Students are not necessarily as active on campus as faculty—especially compared with earlier generations—but they still seek to influence budget decisions. As the cost of an education has risen and the federal government has increased the use of loans in lieu of grants, students have started paying closer attention to decisions that affect their costs. Even when students don't have a formal voice in budget matters, they make their views apparent through their enrollment decisions. If students elect not to enroll in certain programs, for instance, the institution eventually will have to reduce resources allocated to those programs.

When faculty or students participate, there generally is a formal campus procedure for selecting representatives. Specify in advance the nature of the participation (advisory or decision making), the elements of the budget subject to review, and the timing of the review. How each of these factors is addressed influences the outcome of the budget process. For instance, selecting constituent representatives by voting may yield the most active participants, but they may not be the ones best able to judge programs and activities. This is especially true if they specifically sought the role. In these situations, it's common for these individuals to have a narrow agenda to pursue; they focus exclusively on the agenda and not the greater good of the institution.

Taking a careful approach to participation calls for having effective ground rules and guiding principles in place. These especially help if some-

Structured Participation

Different governance structures require different levels of involvement at varying stages. A shared governance model may require a high level of faculty, staff, and student participation. These groups typically become involved at the planning stage, as budget assumptions are developed and approved, and may remain involved throughout the budget process as well. Representatives of various constituencies can have significant involvement and see their views reflected in the final budget submitted to the board for approval.

Interestingly, when a process encourages meaningful involvement, constituents frequently adopt a wider, institutional perspective. Rather than merely advocate for the results most advantageous for their own constituency, they recognize the institution's global needs and support what's best for its long-term success.

A less participatory model still provides opportunities for faculty and student involvement through an ad hoc budget advisory committee. This model establishes a small, representative committee when the budget process begins and seeks the committee's input at various steps along the way. Unlike the shared governance model, ad hoc advisory committees frequently discover they do not have much impact. Sometimes the institution seeks the committee's contributions on relatively few issues or issues that are not particularly significant. Then, individual members often become advocates for their constituencies, making it difficult for the committee to agree on positions or recommendations to decision makers.

Some colleges and universities structure formal participation in the budget process through separate faculty, student, and administrative budget committees. The most practical role for faculty and students is to help establish program and activity priorities and recommend general support levels. Faculty participation is appropriate and especially useful in evaluating proposals from deans or program heads for the allocation of faculty positions.

one is obsessed with a particular aspect of the budget.

Factors affecting participation. Reviews that focus solely on academic budgets may not properly address the administrative and support activities essential to the academic units' success. The timing of participation and the amount of time allotted for review will influence the effectiveness of the participation. Participants must have sufficient time to review the materials and consider alternative allocation decisions. The resulting recommendations will be more useful to policy makers at higher levels if available well before the time to finalize decisions.

The benefits of an inclusive process must be weighed against the risk of negative outcomes. Not having input from students or faculty, for example, may result in suboptimal decisions. On the other hand, involving students and faculty but not accepting their input likely will be worse. It may not be possible to accept all the advice provided; if the advice was solicited but not followed, however, the institution has an obligation to explain why.

If an inclusive process is the goal, recognize that meaningful participation will necessarily take more time. In addition, a successful process includes careful explanations to manage the participants' expectations. If the process is not well understood and produces unrealistic or impossible-to-implement recommendations, the effort is likely to produce more negative results than if no involvement had been allowed.

If budgeters are willing to sacrifice the privacy of their deliberations for the sake of broader knowledge of review criteria, they generally have assurance that the information will be communicated accurately to members of the academic community. Still, budget participants in large institutions often find that communication channels are unreliable and transmit distorted or incomplete information. Similarly, the give-and-take of budget review may sometimes generate mixed signals, especially if negotiations occur over an extended period. What was true at one stage of the process may no longer be true as the process approaches its end.

Risks of not allowing adequate participation. If not provided meaningful roles with genuine influence, departmental personnel likely will default to one of two roles: spender or cutter. The spender, or advocacy role, focuses on obtaining the maximum allocation of resources for the spender's unit or activity. The cutter, or restraining role, focuses on conserving resources, either for new initiatives or to increase reserves.

A department chairperson is a typical spender. He or she has the responsibility of protecting the resources in the current budget. If this doesn't happen, the chairperson will have failed in one of the primary responsibilities of the position—being an advocate for the unit. Remember that no unit believes it has sufficient resources to do everything it feels it could—or to achieve the quality levels to which it aspires.

Therefore, if the chairperson can't at least protect the level of resources currently being received, the faculty has a negative response. On the other hand, a chairperson who garners increased resources—especially as compared with peer departments—can fall short in other areas and still be well regarded by the department's faculty. The added resources may be used for new programs, improved staffing, exceptional salary increases, and other purposes. In some ways, it doesn't really matter how the resources are allocated—just that they have been obtained.

The role of the cutter appears at various levels of the institution. For instance, the dean may seek ways to cut resources from one unit to provide resources needed by another unit—or to undertake a new college-level initiative. Although the dean clearly is an advocate for the unit, from the perspective of the department facing a reduction in resources, the dean functions as a cutter.

On most campuses, the budget office is unfairly perceived as the ultimate cutter. This really is not the case, even though the budget office is charged with development of the institution's budget. To produce a budget that reflects the institution's priorities, is fiscally responsible, and has sufficient flexibility to respond to unanticipated circumstances, the budget office likely will be forced to reject requests for additional funds from some academic and administrative units while providing increased funds to others. For example, funds may be allocated to facilities to cover uncontrollable utilities cost increases or to a dean to fund new faculty for a recently authorized graduate program. At the same time, IT must wait for approval to hire a staff position to maintain the network.

Despite the common perception, the budget office staff rarely has the authority to make budget-cutting decisions. Most often, the budget office merely applies the guidance developed either through the planning process or as part of the budget assumptions approved by the board. Nevertheless, they likely will be viewed as omnipotent cutters by many on campus unless the institution makes a concerted effort to have a transparent budget process and clearly communicates various roles. This can be achieved through a broadly participative process.

In an optimal environment, individuals throughout the campus participate in the planning and budget processes in numerous ways. They serve on committees that develop the plans for the institution, analyze the information used to establish the assumptions that guide budget development, and develop the rationales to support the continued investment of resources in the mission-critical activities.

Ideally, institutions have planning and budget processes best described as both top down and bottom up. The top-down aspect recognizes that institutional management is responsible for developing plans and allocating resources to support those plans. The bottom-up element reflects the reality that senior management, despite their best efforts, simply cannot be aware of the various situations in every operating unit. For this reason, the planning and budget processes, though guided through top-down oversight, must be informed by bottom-up realities. This can be accomplished by having a broadly representative operational committee that influences planning, resource allocation, and assessment.

Unfortunately, few institutions have such an inclusive process. All too often, a select group of staff working closely with the senior leaders—but not well connected to the broader institutional community—carefully control the process. Even when institutions have advisory bodies to influence plans and resource allocation, those groups remain separate in carrying out their responsibilities, with little to no interaction. As a result, most individuals on campus do not feel connected to the plans or the budgets intended to implement them. Moreover, they don't really understand the processes and, therefore, distrust them.

Managing expectations. As planning and budget processes evolve over time, involvement by various constituencies will change. People, who seek to influence the amount of resources allocated to a particular activity, usually find involvement at the budget stage less effective than involvement in planning decisions. When an institution plans effectively, budgetary decisions naturally evolve from the planning process. By the time the budget process is under way, the critical decisions already have been made. Nevertheless, because many institutions have yet to develop effective mechanisms for linking planning with budgeting, interested parties always should seek to participate at the budget stage.

Individuals must recognize, however, that even when their involvement is solicited, the institution doesn't weigh all ideas or opinions equally. Some requests are simply pleas for more resources, with little or no evidence demonstrating the benefits to be realized from the additional allocation. Even when a valid, strong case is made for increased resources, the required allocations may not be made if the anticipated outcomes do not line up with the priorities established through the planning process.

Developing a budget is an arduous, time-consuming process. Participants in the process must be prepared to invest the time and effort to become familiar with the issues and the competing priorities for resources. For that reason, excessive turnover within constituent groups seeking to influence budget decisions will be counterproductive. People given the opportunity to participate must commit a significant effort for several years to learn enough to offer meaningful input. Unfortunately, the budget process will take participants away from teaching or research, in the case of faculty, or from studying, in the case of students. Faculty, of course, will be credited with service, but the benefit to students is less tangible.

Three Processes, One Committee

When the goal is integration of planning, resource allocation, and assessment, the best approach is to establish a broadly representative standing committee charged with monitoring and making recommendations to senior management. It is senior management's responsibility to make final decisions related to resource allocation but they do not have the time to devote to extensive analysis and dialogue on the full range of planning and budgeting activities.

Therefore, the committee's contributions are invaluable to senior management because they gain an in-depth understanding of the issues.

The committee reports to an executive champion—typically either the president, provost, or chief financial officer. The champion ensures that the committee's efforts are visible, that they have enough resources to carry out their duties, and that the senior leadership team is fully apprised of key issues.

Ideally, a credible, iconic faculty member and a senior administrator will co-chair this committee. If the co-chairs already do not attend cabinet meetings, they should attend whenever planning, resource allocation, or assessment is on the agenda. Normally, the champion serves as a liaison between the committee and the cabinet, but at times, direct participation may be warranted.

The staffing for the committee should include the "chiefs" of various functional areas: accounting, budget, institutional effectiveness, institutional research, and planning. These chief officers are essential participants because they know more about these subjects than anyone else on campus. Moreover, they have day-to-day responsibility for these areas. In some cases, they may be responsible for more than one area. For instance, the chief institutional effectiveness officer also may oversee institutional research, or budgeting may be overseen by the chief accounting or chief planning officer. However the institution is organized and staffed, the individuals with responsibility for these areas must participate in the committee and contribute their expertise either as full or ex officio members.

Beyond the staff roles described above, the committee must reflect the institution—so it needs to be large enough to ensure representation from all constituencies and many organizational units. Representatives of faculty senate, staff council, and student government automatically have seats on the committee. A large institution with multiple schools and colleges would probably appoint one or two deans to the committee, plus several academic department heads and selected administrative/support managers from units, such as auxiliary enterprises, athletics, facilities, and student affairs. To provide an institution-wide perspective, committee membership also would include faculty and staff from other units. Members should have staggered appointments lasting two to three years, so the collective body always has the benefit of new thinking and perspectives.

Ideally, committee members do not serve as representatives of their specific units but rather as institutional representatives. Their perspectives should be informed by their experience, but their greatest contribution comes when they focus on what's best for the institution overall—even when that may not always be in the best interests of their unit.

Having one committee responsible for planning, budgeting, and assessment makes sense on many levels. First, if the three processes operate independently of one another, with no connection, the institution probably won't achieve its full potential. The people making the budgeting decisions need to understand the plans being pursued with those resources. Similarly, a strong connection should exist between plans and the measures that will determine the success of the plans' implementation. It's not enough for the leaders of separate operational planning, budget, and assessment committees to periodically communicate with one another. Even when the committee chairs do communicate frequently and well—and that doesn't always happen—the message could still become muddled when translated for the relevant committee. Having all the committee members present for all the discussions reduces the likelihood of a communication breakdown.

As mentioned earlier, strategic planning should be conducted in a broadly participative way. In satisfying this objective, the institution can ensure appropriate linkages between strategic planning and the budget by carefully selecting participants for the strategic planning process. Ideally, there would be cross-representation between the strategic planning task force and the standing committee responsible for addressing operational planning, resource allocation, and assessment. If this happens, there would be no excuse for the operational plans, and the resulting resource allocation decisions, not to align with the strategic plan.

Involvement in Budget Implementation and Monitoring

Although planning and budget development can be a highly participatory process involving all segments of a campus, budget implementation and monitoring responsibilities usually are carried out by two specific units: the central accounting office (sometimes referred to as the controller's office) and the budget office.

The *central accounting office* monitors and reports on the progress of the institution toward generating its projected revenues and expending the resources allocated to the various units. Although those with primary responsibility for administering specific pools of resources carry out the day-to-day activities that produce revenues or expend resources, they see only a small part of the overall financial picture. The central accounting office assembles all of the parts to create the high-level picture, indicating whether the institution is on track to meet its budget targets while pursuing its many activities.

The *budget office* engages in at least two specific activities: reviewing requests for changes to the current approved budget and preparing for the next budget cycle. Personnel activities—unexpected retirements, resignations, extended illnesses—necessitate changes in the way salaries and benefits are deployed. When a key faculty member is seriously ill, for example, the department may request supplemental funding to pay overload to others in the department or to engage adjunct faculty to cover the faculty member's class sections. Or a principal investigator may learn of a new grant opportunity that he or she is assured of receiving if the institution can commit matching funds. There is no end to the budget issues that arise each day on a campus. The budget office staff must react to these issues and make recommendations in accordance with the established structure for addressing them.

When addressing individual budget issues on a day-to-day basis, the budget staff also consider future implications. Sometimes the situations are temporary and will resolve themselves by the end of the fiscal year. In other cases, however, budget staff must address the ongoing implications. For instance, if a faculty member receives a multiyear research grant, the demand for matching funds will continue beyond the current period; that ongoing commitment must be factored into future-year budgets.

Similarly, the tenure process, changes in the endowment payout authorized for the future, program expansions or contractions, and new construction would affect future-year budgets. While others make the decisions on such matters, the budget office staff determines the decisions' impact on future budgets and communicates this information to the senior leadership team.

Influence of Infrastructural Planning

In addition to the strategic plan, infrastructural plans—for both core programmatic and essential support areas—guide a college or university. Each infrastructural plan drives operational activities and, therefore, significantly affects the budget.

Core programmatic infrastructural plans address these five areas:

Academics. The academic plan sets the tone for the entire institution by addressing the three primary functional areas: instruction, research, and public service. The plan could cover topics that range from designing a new degree program to setting the average class size within specific schools or colleges, or to establishing new research institutes or centers. The priorities established for the academic plan exert significant influence over the budget process and influence other infrastructural plans, including student engagement, learning resources, enrollment management, and facilities.

Student engagement. This plan addresses issues as diverse as the student organizations that will be authorized, which intramural sports will receive support, key issues related to Greek life, and how various co-curricular efforts will be undertaken. As with most other infrastructural plans, it has close connections to other core programmatic plans—especially academic, athletics, and auxiliary enterprises—and essential support plans, such as enrollment management, facilities, and administration.

Learning resources. This plan covers the fast-changing world of academic libraries and technology. It may deal with digital media replacing traditional books and journals, critical questions about the configuration of library space to facilitate technology-enabled group study, or the implications of mobile technology. The learning resources plan links most strongly to the academic and IT plans.

Athletics. Clearly, major Division I institutions will have an athletics plan; institutions that do not engage in intercollegiate athletics have no need for an athletics plan. Even limited participation in athletics may not warrant a separate plan. In that case, the institution might address athletics as part of the student engagement plan—either because the revenues are not particularly significant or because the institution focuses on intramural rather than intercollegiate athletics. If athletics warrant a separate plan, it likely will have close ties to infrastructural plans for enrollment management, student engagement, institutional advancement, facilities, administration, and possibly auxiliary enterprises.

Auxiliary enterprises. Typically, the auxiliary enterprises plan drives how residence life and the bookstore engage with academics. For example, an institution deliberately attempting to incorporate academic activities in residential facilities or coordinate them with the bookstore will likely address auxiliary enterprises in a separate plan that connects closely to the academic plan. If not closely connected to academics, auxiliary enterprises will be considered an essential support activity. This plan usually has significant interactions with plans for enrollment management, student engagement, facilities, and administration.

Depending on its character, the institution may incorporate the last two categories into other infrastructural plans or not address them at all. For instance, many community colleges do not need an athletics plan and might include auxiliary enterprises in its administration plan. Conversely, a doctoral institution might treat research as a separate core programmatic area.

Infrastructural plans related to essential support address these five areas:

Enrollment management. This plan addresses institutional decisions regarding tuition pricing, tuition discounting, and financial aid management, all of which have significant implications for a budget. It closely relates to infrastructural plans for academics, student engagement, athletics, auxiliary enterprises, and administration.

Institutional advancement. Activities addressed in this plan include fundraising, public relations, community relations, governmental relations, and alumni affairs. Because advancement encompasses annual giving, planned giving, and major gifts, it has the potential to interact with every other infrastructural planning area. The connections to academics could include private support for research, endowed chairs, or a lecture series. As for enrollment management, the scholarship support provided by gifts and endowment income often proves essential to student recruitment. Depending on the priorities for student engagement and athletics, institutional advancement may assist student organizations with fund-raising efforts, provided those efforts don't conflict with larger institutional fund-raising priorities and plans.

The interactions with facilities take many forms, whether assisting with community relations related to proposed construction plans or raising funds to underwrite the cost of a new facility. The same holds true for IT and auxiliary enterprises; either area could have priority needs for private support. Finally, institutional advancement affects administration because accepting gifts carries both compliance and potential liability issues.

Facilities. The facilities plan includes the master plan, which addresses the long-term development of the campus as well as management of deferred maintenance. And because every campus operation is housed in facilities and guided by one or more infrastructural plans, the potential exists for interaction between facilities and all of the other plans.

Information technology. In addition to addressing the deferred maintenance equivalent within IT, this plan typically outlines a reasonable life cycle for upgrading and replacing personal computing, ERPs, and administrative systems to reflect the pace at which technology advances. Like facilities, IT interacts with all other organizational units and, therefore, has implications for those other infrastructural plans.

Administration. This plan provides something of a catchall for activities not addressed in other support plans, including institutional support. It would address plans relevant to units like human resources, general counsel, risk management, internal audit, and compliance among many others. Given the nature of central administration's wide-ranging responsibilities, this plan likely will interact with the plans for all other infrastructural areas.

Key
Points

- Planning helps colleges and universities focus their efforts and deploy resources effectively.

- The way in which information is communicated, along with transparency and openness, can enhance the level of trust throughout the institution.

- Strategic planning provides the long-term direction for the institution, including the vision of its future. A strategic plan focuses on only a few major priority areas. An infrastructural plan addresses a core programmatic area or an essential support activity undertaken as the institution moves toward its vision.

- Strategic planning typically covers a five-year period, infrastructural planning focuses on two to four years, and operational planning covers a one- or two-year period.

- For institutions that fail to undertake operational planning, the operating budget functions as the operational plan. The big disadvantage to this approach is its tendency to perpetuate activities in previous budgets, even if they no longer contribute to institutional success.

Four comprehensive approaches typically characterize budgeting within higher education. The approaches are not mutually exclusive; characteristics of each approach appear in the others. Despite this occasional overlap of some elements, each approach has a distinctive focus and emphasis on the types of information used to determine allocations.

Because of the overlap, many institutions create their own hybrid approach to budgeting that combines elements of one or more of the models described below.

Whatever its elements or its name, the budget needs to be driven by planning and needs to work for the particular institution.

Formula Budgeting

Used primarily in public institutions, formula budgeting is a procedure for estimating resource requirements based on the relationships between program demand and program cost. These relationships, frequently expressed as mathematical formulations, can be as simple as a single student-faculty ratio or as complicated as an array of costs per student credit hour by discipline for multiple levels of instruction (for example, lower division, upper division, master's, and doctoral). Historical data, projected trends, or parameters negotiated to provide desired levels of funding can provide the bases for budget formulas, which combine technical judgment, negotiation, and political agreements.

Budget formulas come in all shapes and sizes. Most, in some way, relate to enrollment or student-credit-hour productivity data. Within the same overall framework, different formulas usually address the distinct functional areas of an institution's operations. Thus, instructional resources may be allocated on the basis of average faculty teaching loads or credit-hour costs (by student level or course level) applied against historical or projected enrollment levels. Library support may be determined on the basis of enrollments and service relationships. Amounts needed for the support and maintenance of the physical plant may not be enrollment based, because the physical plant is a fixed expense relatively immune to enrollment shifts. More likely, the formulas used for the physical plant depend upon the square footage and type of facilities, their age, and/or their replacement cost.

Rather than using distinct formulas for different functional areas, some budget formula frameworks focus on a base function's (usually instruction) resource needs, considering enrollments and instructional costs or workloads. It then computes amounts for other functional areas (such as libraries, academic support, and the O&M of physical plant) as a percentage of the base.

In another approach—focused primarily on staffing—the formula computes only salary expenses for the institution. Nonsalary budget requirements can be determined by various other methods—either as a function of salary expenses or based on other analysis targeted to the particular nonsalary categories.

It is rare to see formula budgeting applied within a college or university. More typically, it is used at a system-wide or statewide level to give public institutions a foundation for developing budget requests and to assist the appropriate control authority with resource allocation. By their very nature, budget formulas are simplified models of how typical institutions operate. This modeling role of budget formulas sometimes puzzles state officials, who assume that funds appropriated to institutions should be spent exactly as they were distributed through the formula. This concept is not practical because all formulas represent the application of an average; only through pure coincidence would an individual institution's needs match perfectly with the results of the formula. For this reason, most institutions abandon the formula when they make internal resource allocation decisions.

The needs justified by the application of a formula routinely exceed available resources. Often, the formula then is modified to yield an allocation approach more consistent with available resources. Or the state may retain the formula but simply fund it at less than 100 percent.

Either approach may be acceptable, provided the formula does not produce results that differ dramatically from the resources available for allocation. If a significant gap exists between the resource needs identified under the formula and the amounts available for funding, the formula itself comes into question. The formula's utility and effectiveness diminish as the gap between needs and available resources grows. If the gap grows too large, the formula may prove counterproductive—simply because it cannot support the objectives that influenced its development.

Advantages: The quantitative nature of most budget formulas gives them the appearance, if not always the reality, of an unbiased distribution. In some cases, formula budgeting has increased institutional autonomy by reducing political influence in budgeting. An even more significant advantage—at least in stable economic climates—is the capacity to reduce uncertainty by providing a mechanism for predicting future resource needs and potential appropriation amounts. The overall process is simplified because budget formulas tend to remain stable over long periods due to the difficulty in developing them.

Disadvantages: Because it tends to rely on historical data, formula budgeting can discourage new programs or revisions to existing programs. Further, given its focus on quantification, it can suffer from many of the faults identified below for incremental budgeting. For instance, a pure formula-budgeting environment tends to avoid in-depth analyses of programs and activities. Perhaps most significant, formula budgeting creates an incentive to retain programs or activities that contribute funding—even if they no longer contribute to the achievement of institutional mission, goals, and objectives.

Formulas also can have an unequal—or even negative—impact on participating institutions. For instance, because most formulas are developed using averages, institutions experiencing increased enrollment will fare better because marginal costs for additional students tend to be lower than average costs. Conversely, the same formula will have a more negative impact if enrollments are falling. To reduce these impacts, some states have developed formulas that differentiate between fixed and variable costs.

Incremental Budgeting

Under incremental budgeting, each program's or activity's budget increases by a specified percentage. (Increasingly common is the flip side of this approach—decremental budgeting, which reduces budgets by a specified percentage.)

Incremental budgeting measures the expected change in allocable resources from one period to the next, then distributes the same percentage uniformly to each program or activity (or broad category). This approach relies on the fact that basic aspects of programs and activities do not change significantly from year to year. And, in most situations, the change in available resources in any given year represents a small percentage of the base budget. Because individuals and organizations spend their resources with little variation, marginal resource additions can accommodate any needed changes.

Unlike many industries, including some equally labor-intensive ones, higher education does not experience significant workforce fluctuations over short periods. Although they contribute to this characteristic, tenured faculty represent a relatively small percentage of the total workforce at most institutions. Rather, the workforce does not change dramatically from one period to another because the number of service recipients—students and, in some cases, patients—does not change significantly from year to year. With salaries and benefits representing the largest component of any institutional budget, yet remaining constant from year to year, the overall budget will remain fairly stable under normal circumstances.

Of course, significant fluctuations in the amounts of resources available—or in the demands placed on those resources—do occur from one year to the next. For example, the recession that began in 2008 resulted in significantly reduced budgets during fiscal year 2009. Although some recovery occurred in 2010 and 2011, the operating budgets at many institutions still remained significantly lower than before the recession began.

The practice of incremental budgeting varies dramatically among campuses. Some institutions use differential factors for various organizational segments. For instance, the first claim on resources usually is for the salary increase pool and other unavoidable cost increases, such as utilities and fringe benefits. Once it has addressed these, the institution may specify a percentage increase for academic units and a different, typically smaller, percentage increase for nonacademic units. Alternatively, it may specify an across-the-board increase for all components. Or the institution may combine across-the-board increases for some categories with differential increases for others—and no increase at all for still others.

Regardless of the approach used, allocating the entire pool of resources through incremental budgeting produces suboptimal results. Because it operates only at the margins, incremental budgeting does not involve serious examination of what the base budget will accomplish. It also avoids the question of whether the institution can find better uses for some of the resources. Budgeters bypass difficult policy choices because questions usually focus on minor changes rather than on an overall approach to the mission.

In essence, incremental budgeting maintains the status quo and generally does not integrate with planning. In fact, planning is relatively unimportant when incremental budgeting is applied to the entire resource pool. By design, planning is intended to alter the established priorities to improve results. Allocating all resources through an across-the-board approach obviates the need to identify priorities.

Advantages: By far, incremental budgeting is the most efficient approach. Institutions find it relatively simple to implement, easy to apply, more controllable, more adaptable, and more flexible than almost any other approach because of the general lack of emphasis on analysis. In addition, it minimizes conflict because—for the most part—it treats all institutional components equally.

Disadvantages: Incremental budgeting carries two faulty assumptions. First, it assumes that the current distribution of resources across activities and programs is optimal—which is highly unlikely. Some units typically have more resources than they can productively use, while others are significantly under-resourced given their potential for success.

Second, incremental budgeting assumes that a standard percentage increase (or decrease) will enhance (or impair) each program or activity optimally relative to the whole. Again, this is highly unlikely. Neither increased nor decreased resources will greatly affect the units with more resources than they need. Conversely, the units with insufficient resources may not receive enough new resources to allow them to succeed—or the cuts may curtail their efforts to the point of hurting the institution.

Over time, this approach will drive the institutional activities toward mediocrity. Poorly performing units will continue to consume resources that provide little return in terms of enhanced institutional success. At the same time, high-performing and high-potential units do not garner enough resources to leverage their efforts for better results.

Despite its shortcomings, incremental budgeting endures. Without question, this is attributable to the model's straightforward and easy application. It is practiced by the largest number of institutions throughout higher education—at least for a portion of their resource pool. Unfortunately, some institutions sacrifice effectiveness for efficiency by distributing their entire resource pool through incremental budgeting.

A Quick Guide

Here are the main distinctions among budgeting models commonly used in higher education:

- **Formula budgeting** relies on quantitative measures to distribute resources.

- **Incremental budgeting** focuses primarily on increases or decreases to the base rather than on analysis of the activities being supported. The implicit assumption is that the base—in whole or in part—has been rationalized in previous budget cycles.

- **Responsibility center budgeting (RCB)** classifies individual programs and units as either revenue or cost centers. Revenue centers control the revenues they generate and are responsible for financing both their direct and indirect costs. Cost centers are funded from central revenues and taxes assessed on revenue centers.

- **Zero-based budgeting** examines some or all programs and activities during each budget cycle to ensure each contributes to organizational success and consumes an appropriate level of resources in doing so.

These four comprehensive models allocate all of an organization's resources. The next two models focus on only a subset of those resources, so they must be employed along with one of the comprehensive approaches:

- **Initiative-based budgeting (IBB)** focuses on the identification and funding of activities that support established priorities; resources are distributed through some type of competitive process.

- **Performance-based budgeting (PBB)** involves allocating resources based on a program's success on achievement of specific established targets.

Responsibility Center Budgeting

Also known as cost center budgeting, profit center budgeting, and revenue responsibility budgeting, responsibility center budgeting (RCB) emphasizes program performance rather than central budgetary control. The essential characteristic of RCB—that units manage and control the revenues they generate—contributes to this approach being referred to informally as "every tub on its bottom."

Under RCB, schools, colleges, and other organizational units become revenue centers, cost centers, or a combination of the two. All revenues generated by the units remain under their control. This includes tuition and fees, overhead recovered on research grants and contracts, gifts, endowment income, and proceeds from sales and services of educational activities.

For instance, a college of engineering is credited with the tuition revenue generated by classes taught by its faculty. Additionally, the college receives credit for students majoring in engineering. Similarly, all overhead recovered from the sponsored programs awarded to faculty of the college count as revenue. If the college's instructional activities lead to commercially viable products or services, the college retains any revenues generated. Essentially, any revenues that can be connected directly to the efforts of the college of engineering come under that dean's ultimate control.

In exchange for controlling the resources it generates, the college of engineering also assumes responsibility for funding all of its direct and indirect costs. This includes faculty salaries and benefits as well as space-related costs for labs and classrooms. In addition, the college must share in the funding of the various cost centers that serve it—such as the library, human resources, and the budget office—because these academic and institutional support units do not generate revenues from external sources.

Some cost centers—especially those providing easily monitored and measured services, such as the physical plant—rely on charge-back mechanisms; they charge the cost center's internal customers for the services received, based on established rates. The rates, which are designed to recover fully all costs and balance out over time, usually are subject to an approval process that ensures that service recipients are not being overcharged. Typically, the same rates apply to sponsored programs that receive services from support units. When this occurs, federal guidelines outline the method for calculating rates.

In addition, campuses impose a tax on the unrestricted revenues that revenue centers generate. The tax proceeds, combined with other central revenues—such as investment income, unrestricted gifts, and unrestricted endowment income—create a subvention pool that funds cost centers as well as revenue centers that don't generate enough revenues to be self-sufficient.

Central administration collects and redistributes the taxes, playing a key role in the institution's resource allocation decisions.

Responsibility center budgeting forces institutions to ask questions about how to share revenues and how much to fund central services. Because all support services are fully costed and all academic units receive credit for their share of total institutional revenue, RCB forces a much broader understanding of institutional finances.

Advantages: RCB provides incentives for units to enhance revenues and manage costs. It puts them in a position to better recognize the importance of revenue sources, such as tuition and overhead recoveries from sponsored programs. Also, RCB can help instill an awareness of the actual costs of relatively scarce campus resources, such as space and IT.

Without RCB, many overhead costs are borne centrally and consume institutional resources before allocations for other purposes are made. When costs are treated in this manner, faculty and staff tend to lack an appreciation of the true cost of the services provided on campus. On the other hand, having access to cost information changes faculty and staff demand for services and resources. When people understand their department will have to pay, they become more likely to pursue optimal space utilization rather than request additional space. For instance, faculty will be assigned class times during nonpeak periods to take better advantage of existing space.

Responsibility for managing resources results in surpluses being carried forward from one fiscal year to the next, while deficits become liabilities that must be satisfied using resources from future-year budgets. RCB encourages the removal of central controls and gives more attention to performance or outcome measures. The budgeting system also drives home the reality that academic decisions have financial consequences.

With RCB, recipients of campus services become better and more demanding customers. In turn, because campus providers charge for their services, they become more responsive—especially when forced to compete with the private sector. If outside vendors can provide comparable or better services at competitive prices, the campus will turn to them. Using outside vendors may not be possible for services, such as payroll, accounting, or purchasing, but internal customers will still let providers know if service does not meet acceptable levels.

Disadvantages: Detractors complain that RCB focuses unduly on the bottom line and does not respond adequately to issues of academic quality or other priorities. Another common complaint is that decisions made by individual units—though advantageous for the units themselves—may have negative consequences for the institution as a whole. For instance, units often establish their own internal service provider operations instead of using central services. Or individual colleges or schools add courses in disciplines already housed in other academic units simply to retain the revenue from those courses. And, as units gain greater budget autonomy, a lack of coherence between planning and budgeting may evolve.

Despite these concerns, RCB remains popular. Historically practiced at a small number of independent institutions, RCB has made inroads among public institutions. By 2011, nearly half of all independent doctoral universities and more than 20 percent of public doctoral universities employed some form of RCB.[125] This represents a 15 percent increase among publics and an 8 percent increase among independents as compared with 2008.

Zero-Based Budgeting

In many ways, zero-based budgeting (ZBB) and incremental budgeting are at opposite ends of the spectrum for allocating resources. While incremental budgeting emanates from centralized management and employs across-the-board distributions, ZBB focuses on the individual program or activity. It assumes no budgets from prior years; instead, each year's budget begins at a base of zero. Each budget unit evaluates its goals and objectives and justifies its activities based on each activity's benefits and the consequences of not performing it.

This evaluation takes the form of a decision package, which includes a description of the activity, a definition of alternative levels of activity (including minimum and maximum levels), performance measures, costs, and benefits. After being ranked by priority, decision packages at one level of the organization are forwarded to the next level for review. Successively higher administrative levels rank the decision packages and then make allocation decisions for each unit.

Advantages: Proponents of ZBB contend they gain a much better understanding of their organization through the preparation and review of the decision packages. And, by its very nature, ZBB eliminates a protected budget base for each activity. With no funding guarantee, each activity must prove its own worth; this can help eliminate programs that no longer contribute to the institution's success.

Disadvantages: Preparing the decision packages can consume significant amounts of time and generate a large volume of paperwork. Another criticism: Agreeing on priorities often proves difficult. Some contend that the centralized pre-audit of lower-level decisions reduces decision-making autonomy and responsibility. Others suggest that simply conducting periodic program reviews, which incorporate a financial component, will obtain ZBB's same benefits with less effort.

The disadvantage cited most often is that ZBB assumes no budget history. Thus, it does not recognize continuing commitments–such as tenured faculty and contracts with key administrators–and cannot be easily altered in the short run. Like most labor-intensive organizations, colleges and universities cannot initiate and terminate activities quickly.

When attempting ZBB, managers often assume a fixed complement of activities and a corresponding base of support. For instance, they might begin with the assumption that 80 percent of the previous year's budget will continue as a base, then apply ZBB techniques to the balance of the budget. This strategy, however, compromises ZBB's ability to eliminate a protected budget base.

ZBB often is considered an "all or nothing" proposition, but this does not have to be the case. An institution can apply ZBB techniques selectively, rather than to the entire organization, or implement them cyclically. For instance, administrative and support units might use ZBB exclusively. Or each unit might participate in the ZBB process on a periodic schedule–say, once every five years. Under this approach, 20 percent of the campus would employ ZBB each year, while the remainder of the units would use a different budgeting approach.

Initiative-Based Budgeting

Unlike the four comprehensive budget models described above, initiative-based budgeting (IBB) represents a structured approach to distributing resources for new initiatives that support established priorities. To finance the initiatives, institutions typically take one of three common approaches:

- **Capture centrally a percentage of the expected increase in resources for the period.** This typically modest amount of revenues (for example, 2 percent) is isolated in a pool that then supports priorities established through the planning process.

- **Establish reallocation targets for each unit.** After examining their operations and identifying activities to discontinue or curtail, units free up resources to meet the reallocation target. This approach provides the side benefit of ensuring that units review the productivity of their existing activities.

- **Rely on the contingency funding included in the expense budget.** If the institution does not need the contingency to cover cost overruns or revenue shortfalls, it can devote some or all of the funds to IBB.

Reallocating to Fund New Initiatives

With the reallocation approach to initiative-based budgeting (IBB), the resource pool is created from resources returned to central administration. In theory, the units provide the resources by discontinuing lower-priority or unproductive activities. The funds then are redistributed in support of the priorities agreed upon during the institution's planning process.

Here's how it works. Assume that a campus imposes a 2 percent reallocation target on all campus units. Each unit identifies activities or programs it can eliminate or modify, thus reducing its base budget by the specified target. Notice that this approach focuses on base budget rather than the unit's entire budget. The base budget usually excludes nonrecurring projects, such as sponsored programs or other one-time activities that are not part of the unit's continuing operations.

To meet the reallocation target, an administrative unit—such as environmental health and safety—may propose changing its approach to staff training. Rather than incurring the cost of sending campus personnel off-site for required safety training, a current staff member will become certified to conduct the training on-site. Although some overtime pay may be necessary because of the trainer's shifting workload, the unit will be able to achieve the 2 percent target.

To meet its target, a school within the university might propose consolidating two of its academic departments in response to shifting demands that coincide with the retirement of one of the department chairs. The salary and benefits savings from the elimination of the chair's position, coupled with consolidation of the two departments' support staffs, will allow the unit to contribute more than the required 2 percent savings. This situation gives the dean some flexibility to take other actions to meet the school's 2 percent target.

The savings from environmental health and safety, the school, and all other units are consolidated into an initiatives pool and then redistributed based on criteria established during the planning process. Typically, redistribution entails a proposal process. All units seeking to obtain funds from the pool submit a proposal identifying the planned activities, the institutional priorities that the activities support, the benefits to be generated, and the amount requested.

There may be slight variations in IBB based on whether the proposed initiative requires one-time or continuing funding. Continuing funding usually is more difficult to obtain because it reduces the funds available for future initiatives. Another possible variation centers on whether both administrative and academic units compete for funds. Funds reallocated from administrative units, for example, may not necessarily be reserved for administrative initiatives; if the institution's priorities focus exclusively on academic initiatives, the administrative reallocation may be used to fund academic initiatives.

Reallocation strategies prove particularly valuable because they enable departments to achieve the target in various ways each year. A department may meet its target one year through program reduction in response to reduced demand. The next year, it may find a less expensive provider for needed services.

Accomplishing IBB through reallocation, however, cannot continue indefinitely—especially as it relates to core academic and administrative activities. At some point, a payroll office that continually gives up 2 percent of its budget without successfully obtaining replacement funds will erode its ability to meet the institution's needs for payroll services. Similarly, a core academic unit attempting to meet increased enrollment demands may find it impossible to achieve a 2 percent savings. Any reallocation program must provide a mechanism for waivers and for reallocation back to core activities.

Performance-Based Budgeting

During the early development of public administration budgeting and planning, the budget was viewed as an instrument of expenditure control. Performance-based budgeting (PBB), which emerged in the late 1940s, signaled a shift to a management orientation by focusing on programs and activities that became ends in themselves. Specifically, PBB focuses on outputs and outcomes. The number of graduates, for example, is an output, while the number of graduates finding employment in a relevant industry or gaining acceptance to graduate school is an outcome.

This technique has enjoyed a recent rebirth of interest, particularly at the state level. The modern form of PBB:

- Relates resources (inputs) to activities (structure) and results (outcomes)

- Defines specific outcome measures in either quantitative or qualitative terms

- Has accounting structures that attempt to relate resources to results

- Defines explicit indicators of input-output relationships or indexes relating resources to outcomes

- Specifies goals in terms of performance measures (that is, desired input-outcome ratios)

Applying the newer forms of PBB in the public arena often proves challenging. The development of performance measures typically flows from the state to the institution and frequently doesn't reflect an understanding of the factors that influence the measures. Outcome indicators sometimes are viewed as relatively meaningless because they are linked with program budgets only at the highest level of aggregation. This may disconnect the indicators from the activities that actually drive the results. Quantitative measures are more widely employed than qualitative measures, which may be more meaningful indicators of success. Finally, performance measures at high levels of program aggregation are not easily linked with organizational divisions and departments—the structure used for resource allocation on most campuses.

As currently practiced, PBB usually applies only to a small percentage of available resources, such as 2 or 3 percent. It typically starts with the identification of a series of metrics for measuring performance—such as specific target scores, a specific required percentage improvement in performance, or an institution's relative ranking among peers. If the institution achieves the target scores or rankings, it receives supplemental resources; if it misses the target, it does not receive the supplemental allocation. Rarely do states assess penalties if the institution does not achieve the desired results, although this practice would not be inconsistent with PBB principles.

A few states have considered expanding the use of PBB, even to the point of linking the majority of an institution's state appropriation to specific performance objectives.

Key Points

- Higher education commonly uses two operating budget models: Comprehensive budget models address the entire range of an institution's operational resources and investments, and special-purpose budget models address only a portion of the budget.

- Comprehensive budget models include formula budgeting, incremental budgeting, RCB, ZBB, and a hybrid (which relies on elements of other comprehensive budget models and also may incorporate features from the special-purpose budget models).

- Special-purpose budget models fall into two categories. The first, IBB, focuses on directing resources toward the priorities established during the planning process. This model usually deals with a small portion of the operating budget, typically just a few percentage points or less. The second approach, PBB, also addresses only a small portion of the budget—typically no more than 1 or 2 percent.

In the aftermath of the 2008 recession, numerous public institutions in the United States experienced dramatic budget cuts triggered by state revenue shortfalls, and both public and independent institutions felt the effects of distressed financial markets on their endowment and fund-raising revenues. Such significant changes led institutions to readjust their resource allocation patterns.

Tuition-dependent institutions, for example, increased amounts for attracting students—both in the form of marketing and tuition discounting. To avoid or minimize operating deficits, many institutions dipped into reserves, reduced employee benefits (or increased the portion of premiums paid by employees), instituted travel bans, froze salaries, or mandated employee furloughs. Others took more dramatic actions, such as eliminating programs and laying off tenured faculty and programmatic staff.

Individual characteristics dictate differences in how an institution approaches and implements the budgeting process. The larger the institution, for example, the more likely its budget process will include many participants and be decentralized. Smaller institutions may rely exclusively on a centralized approach using top-down directives.

Summarized below are the factors that exert the most influence on the budget process; understanding these factors leads to an understanding of how to influence the process.

Institutional Character

Each of the nearly 4,500 public and independent degree-granting higher education institutions in the United States has a unique personality, shaped by its size, mission, type of funding, culture, operating climate, administrative structure, and history. When considered together, these various elements describe an institution's unique character.

Not all independent institutions are created or operated equally. The same statement applies to public institutions. Public land-grant universities, for instance, often enjoy a "flagship" status that translates into strong political support in the state legislature—an asset that doesn't appear on the institution's balance sheet. In contrast, small regional public colleges with lower profiles may have more financial constraints, especially if they are "open admission" institutions with low student-retention rates.

The type of student the institution attracts will shape institutional character as well. For instance, students at an inner-city community college are more likely to have remedial needs compared to a campus in a suburban setting. Similarly, the presence (or absence) of vocational partnerships with local industry will draw different types of students, as will the level of co-ordination with local K–12 educational systems.

One might argue that the relationship between the budget and institutional character is a "chicken-and-egg" proposition, in that they influence one another. Institutional character frequently drives resource allocation decisions. Similarly, that character is, in many ways, a function of past resource allocation decisions.

Shifts in institutional character do occur, although they aren't always obvious. Identifying the shifts requires paying close attention to tangible factors that can be easily monitored and tracked over time, such as articulated plans, administrative priorities, revenue fluctuations, and assessment results.

A Change in Character

Large organizations typically resist change. That tendency, coupled with higher education's deep sense of tradition, often leaves institutional character mired in inertia. In other words, participants in the planning and budget processes should not expect an institution's character to change within a single budget cycle. Nevertheless, they can use the budget to effect desired change as guided and shaped by the planning process.

An institution can change its character, albeit slowly, by changing the way in which it allocates its resources. Such decisions will, in and of themselves, bring about major change, although some will provide a stronger push than others. For instance, an institution not noted for its research proficiency may make great strides in a relatively short period simply by establishing and staffing a small office of sponsored programs. Moreover, if it couples this step with providing seed money to faculty interested in pursuing sponsored support, the institution can move from having little or no external support for research to measurable results within a few years.

A number of colleges and universities have attempted to change their character through intercollegiate athletics. Several have changed divisions within the NCAA classifications, with most moving to a higher, more expensive division. On the flip side, a few institutions have dropped a major sport or moved to a classification requiring less investment. Either action creates an opportunity for the institution to change its character—sometimes dramatically.

Dramatic changes in institutional character also may stem from:

- **Shifts in enrollment patterns or increased demand for certain programs.** For instance, current social and political events may influence students to pursue some disciplines in numbers far exceeding typical patterns. If the shifts prove more than a short-term phenomenon, the institution should realign resources to meet the demand.

- **Changes in employment demographics.** The United States will experience a dramatic increase in employee turnover as the baby boom generation reaches traditional retirement age. This affects higher education as well, with many senior-level positions remaining vacant (or held by interims) for extended periods of time as qualified individuals pursue other opportunities. In response, institutions have increased their nontraditional hires, such as chief financial officers hired from the private sector, government, or health care. Similarly, colleges and universities increasingly turn to the business and nonprofit sectors to fill the president's position; at state institutions, legislators or executives from various branches of state and local government often fill the presidencies. This influx of employees from outside higher education, coupled with looming retirements, will undoubtedly reshape institutional character.

Whether thrust upon the institution by external forces or nurtured from within the institution, the impetus for change can be addressed through the planning and budget processes to achieve specific objectives.

An institution's character contributes to the way in which participants in the budgetary process interact. Simpler logistics typically permit smaller colleges and universities to allow more individual participation by faculty and students. Smaller institutions can involve a comparatively smaller number of participants in the budget process and still have representation from all institutional segments. This breadth of participation becomes more difficult for a large institution, which might involve the same number of participants but not achieve the same level of representation.

Some community colleges and smaller four-year institutions adopt a highly centralized approach to budgeting, simply to reduce the demands placed on their smaller workforces. In situations involving fewer discretionary resources and streamlined management structures, involving a relatively small number of people in planning and budgeting can work if a high level of trust exists on the campus.

At well supported public and elite independent institutions, budget participants will ask different questions about resource allocation than their counterparts at struggling institutions. Because they rely on some public funding, public institutions are accountable to a broader constituency than independent institutions. They must be responsive to legislators, state agencies, and the public in ways that independent institutions are not. Even states that grant a high level of autonomy to higher education will require institutions to provide information to state agencies. These demands may shape the formats for budget requests, accounting structures, and other aspects of regulatory oversight. Both public and independent institutions are subject to extensive accountability requirements for resources provided by the federal government—whether directly to the institution in the form of research grants or to students, through the institution, in the form of financial aid.

One unique characteristics of higher education is how much institutions share best practices with one another. Although they compete for sponsored program funding, the most qualified students, financial support, and athletic titles, colleges and universities willingly share their ideas and successes. Entire conferences are devoted to the sharing of success stories, best practices, and innovative approaches to a variety of management issues.

Budgeting is no exception in this regard, and the character of the institution will influence how readily a new strategy can be implemented. Typically though, change is introduced incrementally. Few institutions have a culture that can tolerate a completely new approach to something as crucial as budgeting. As a result, institutions commonly retain the basic elements of existing budget strategies while introducing new approaches through pilot programs or for only a portion of the overall budget.

Decision-Making Authority

A continual source of tension among decision makers in any organizational setting—but especially when dealing with resource allocation—is determining the level of authority at which to make decisions. Most budget participants will express a desire for greater autonomy: Department chairpersons feel constrained by deans, deans feel constrained by the provost, and—in public institutions—everyone complains about approvals required by the legislative or executive branch.

At what level should financial decisions be made? Most experts say the best decisions are made closest to the action. In fact, the real issue is where the organization falls on the continuum between control and accountability. A system of accountability allows greater latitude with respect to decision making compared to one that relies on controls to prevent problems from occurring.

An accountability system can include controls, but they need not be the dominant factor. It might be appropriate to allow a system of accountability to operate for most transactions and decisions, with control being exercised only for selected issues that represent significant dollar or political risk. For instance, a higher authority typically is required to approve transactions above a certain dollar level or to sign off when the institution makes an official salary offer to a prospective employee. This level of control ensures that proper procedures have been followed and that the financial commitment fits within the institution's overall structure.

Some hiring decisions carry political risk. For example, a public institution's hiring of a former state official might be viewed as politically motivated rather than driven by the individual's qualifications. Academic units typically enjoy a significant amount of autonomy in the hiring process—except in situations involving positions that come with the granting of tenure. Yet it still would be appropriate to require departments to seek approval before extending an offer to current or former governmental officials.

To maintain an appropriate balance between the level of control and the amount of latitude provided to operational managers, some institutions use sophisticated systems and processes to ensure expenses are incurred in accordance with the budget. These automated systems support line-item budgeting, where funds allocated for supplies must be spent for supplies, funds budgeted for travel can be used only for travel, and so on. Institutions that use a line-item budget system for control will not process transactions that would produce deficits in the individual budget categories.

An example of a higher level of control is an aggregate nonsalary expense pool. In this environment, supplies or travel expenses may not fall within specific budgets. Instead, such expenses are charged against the nonsalary pool. Assuming that transactions are appropriately chargeable to the nonsalary pool, they are processed as long as funds remain available.

Enhanced accountability mechanisms offer an alternative to this type of control environment. Rather than relying on preventing problems, an accountability environment shifts the decision-making authority to the unit responsible for managing a given budget. It also charges unit managers with addressing problems that may arise. Returning to the example above, a control system would simply prevent a department from overspending its budget for travel. In a system relying on accountability, the transaction would be processed, and the department would be responsible for alleviating any resulting budget deficit. The responsible managers might need to request additional resources from the next unit up the organizational chain, or they might transfer resources into the travel category from another category within the departmental budget. In either case, the accountability system relies on them to make the decisions that are most appropriate while still following overall institutional guidelines.

Transparency

The degree to which the budget process is open to review by those not actively involved in the deliberations dictates the amount of flexibility decision makers have in their negotiations over resource allocations. At the same time, the institution's character and structure for involvement will determine the openness of the process. In general, the greater the number of participants in the budget process, the more open it will be.

Some institutions carefully control openness to prevent unintended consequences. For instance, if the budget provides for changes that will result from outsourcing some physical plant operations, the institution will want to take great care in communicating these potential changes. Outsourcing analysis usually includes a plan for existing employees. Nevertheless, when staff learn about the outsourcing possibility through the budget process, the news will likely alarm them—and may result in significant service disruptions until the matter can be addressed.

As a rule, budgets should not contain surprises for the campus community. Address important issues before they affect the budget—ideally, through an engaged and inclusive planning process. If difficult issues arise at the budget development stage, separate them from their budgetary implications. Communicate first with the affected parties and then inform the broader community before addressing the decision's budgetary implications. This approach doesn't necessarily prevent acrimony or concerns, but it will help forestall challenges to the budget as a whole. If the budget contains major surprises—especially ones that could have been addressed in a more open manner—the entire process becomes suspect.

Thanks to "open meetings" legislation and regulations, public institutions have opened their policy-making and decision-making arenas to a wider audience. On the positive side, this development enhances the accountability of people in public positions. It can have negative consequences, though. By its nature, budget development is a process of negotiation and trade-off. So even when conducted in an above-board and appropriate manner, it can be viewed in a negative light. The negotiation process likely will result in identifying some institutional activities to sacrifice in favor of others that will provide substantial long-term benefits. Voicing this fact publicly can raise the hackles of some constituents—especially those who will be affected by the loss of the activity.

Recognizing the need for a balance between openness and privacy, some institutions have designed the budget process to allow relevant groups to be represented while sensitive discussions about competing priorities take place. Accordingly, they structure communications to the broader community to minimize the negative impact that budget decisions may have on individuals, programs, and activities. In these circumstances, the need for openness in the budget process is balanced against the need for privacy during delicate negotiations and deliberations.

Public institutions will be more transparent with certain budgetary information. Independent institutions, for instance, rarely disclose individual salaries; for public institutions, compensation information usually is available in the library, if not the local newspaper.

Levels of Trust

The more administration, faculty, and other stakeholder groups trust one another, the more likely the campus will employ a budgeting process that features significant information sharing. In turn, an open and transparent process helps build a climate of trust because participants don't feel as if they are being left out of important discussions or barred from seeing critical data.

In organizations that lack trust, the budget process usually involves a small group of people and produces a final product that few outside the group understand well. This type of closed process ultimately will erode whatever trust might exist. In fact, when a campus has a problem with trust, the budget process frequently contributes to the situation.

Communication

Academic, administrative, and other support units often submit their budget requests at the beginning of the process and receive only limited information before seeing the final budget approved by the governing board. Along the way, the departments have no idea whether they succeeded in making a case for additional resources or how their requests were perceived relative to others in the institution.

To avert this situation, distribute information about the status of the budget throughout the process—especially to lower-level units that may not have direct access to decision makers. Given the ease of Internet communication, there is no excuse for failing to disseminate information regularly.

Periodically sharing information throughout the budget process will help allay concerns and allow the process to proceed smoothly. Keeping the community apprised of the progress on developing the budget will help avoid rumors and the resulting distrust that accompanies them. It also can discourage people from taking actions that may prove counterproductive in the long run. As for the amount of information to share, more is always better.

Key
Points

- An institution's size, mission, type of funding, culture, operating climate, administrative structure, and history all contribute to its unique character. In turn, institutional character will influence how a college or university approaches the budgeting process.

- Both external forces and internal decisions—identified through the planning process and addressed through the budgeting process—can significantly reshape institutional character.

- The greater the number of participants involved in the budget process, the more open it will be. And the more transparent the process, the more faculty, administrators, and other constituents will trust one another to keep the institution's best interests in mind.

- Issuing regular reports on how the budget process is progressing will help allay concerns within the community and minimize rumors. The more information shared, the better.

Public and independent institutions tend to follow the same general budget process: People in the same positions take the same steps, in the same sequence, in roughly the same time frame. The key variant, applicable to some public institutions, is the impact the state (or local) government's budget process has on the timing of specific aspects of the institution's process.

The timetable for various activities within the budget process is referred to as the budget cycle. Budget cycles typically overlap, with multiple budgets being used, developed, or analyzed retrospectively at the same time. For example, in late summer/early fall of a fiscal year, the prior year's financial results are being finalized in preparation for the financial statement audit. At the same time, the current year's budget cycle is guiding expenditures and influencing hiring decisions. Finally, it's possible that the budget cycle for the next fiscal year has already begun.

Depending on the institution, the overall budget cycle can last up to 24 months. For public institutions, the cycle can go even longer—especially those located in states with a biennial budget cycle.

At any given time, a campus will be in the midst of both an operating budget cycle and a capital budget cycle. Both processes are complex and require a concerted effort to build on the planning work that should precede them. Each step in the process contributes to the development of the budgets and, if executed properly, will help contribute to the likelihood of successful execution of the activities addressed in the respective budgets.

Operating Budget Cycle

Operating budgets address revenues and reserves, both of which may be sources for projects addressed in the capital budget. Similarly, the facilities projects covered by a capital budget will affect the operating budget once they are completed and placed in service. The expenses for maintaining the facilities become part of operating expenses and, if the facilities are debt-financed, the interest on the long-term debt will be a claim on resources. That's why operating and capital budgets cannot be developed in isolation.

Budgeting is an iterative process at both public and independent institutions. The approach may appear straightforward and sequential, but many steps may be revisited and repeated along the way. Even with this "back-and-forth" method, here are the 16 steps in a typical budget process, listed in the sequence in which they usually occur:

1. Develop plans to guide the resource allocation process.

The budget development process begins with a review of the results that emerged from planning efforts, along with information about past actual results measured against the budget. The combination of these factors will shape the budget being developed.

Areas of need should be evident from an analysis of past results, while priority areas should flow from the planning process. Similarly, the plans should disclose areas that will be de-emphasized in the upcoming period. The budget process requires extensive negotiation, so having well-defined plans will make the process run smoother. Not every decision will flow easily from the plans—but the absence of plans will make each decision a struggle.

Although listed here as the starting point, planning is not a discrete activity that occurs once per budgeting cycle. Planning is an ongoing process that never stops. As the budget process gets underway, participants review the cumulative results of all planning efforts, assess how they may impact the operating budget, and use the results to shape the overall process.

Effective planning processes involve participation by all campus constituencies, including the board (see Chapter Six). The board influences the overall organizational direction through their involvement in the planning process, and management uses the budget as the primary tool for carrying out the plans. Several steps in the budget process, however, require board involvement. The board, for example, reviews and approves the assumptions on which the budget is built. This is a natural outgrowth of the planning that has occurred up to the point when the operating budget cycle begins.

A Typical Budget Process in 16 Steps

1. Develop plans to guide the resource allocation process.
2. Close out the prior fiscal year.
3. Analyze year-to-date results for the current year and final results for the prior year.
4. Project enrollment.
5. Establish budget assumptions for the board's approval.
6. Project central revenues.
7. Project expenses.
8. Develop and distribute guidelines for preparing budget proposals.
9. Develop and submit budget proposals.
10. Participate in budget hearings.
11. Analyze submissions.
12. Consolidate the budget.
13. Obtain board approval of the budget.
14. Begin budget implementation.
15. Monitor performance against the budget.
16. Prepare audited financial statements.

The board also reviews and approves the final budget to ensure it aligns with previously approved plans.

After approving the final budget, the board monitors the status of planned efforts and the resulting budgetary implications. If circumstances change and the overall budget requires revision, the board should review and approve the changes. Finally, well after the end of the fiscal year covered by the budget, the board formally accepts the audited financial statements prepared by management and reviewed by external auditors. In preparation for the board's final budget review, management should reconcile the financial statements to the budget.

2. Close out the prior fiscal year.

Prior-year closeout entails finalizing all revenue and expense activity in preparation for the annual audit of the institution's financial statements. The process begins well before the fiscal year ends to ensure sufficient time to conduct and conclude financial activity. Public institutions, for instance, need time to ensure they wisely spend funds that otherwise may revert to the state legislature. Similarly, departments within an independent institution that recaptures unexpended funds centrally at year-end will do their best to expend as much of their budget as possible.

Because last-minute spending may result in the acquisition of unneeded goods, institutions usually have a supplemental process for reviewing transactions above a certain dollar amount that are initiated close to year-end. Similarly, campuses commonly specify that some types of purchases—particularly equipment—cannot be initiated after a certain date. These procedures stem not only from concerns about workload for procurement staff but also from questions about the motivation behind the purchase. Yet even when an institution imposes such constraints, it typically makes exceptions for legitimate purchases, such as new equipment needed for a sponsored project that begins late in the fiscal year.

3. Analyze year-to-date results for the current year and final results for the prior year.

The most recently completed budget will provide valuable information about the actual receipt of revenues and expenditures throughout the period. It will highlight shortfalls and indicate programs that may be in their downward cycle. It also will identify opportunity targets for increased investment—for example, units experiencing increased demand that shows no signs of tapering off. Examining the budget for the current period will give early warning signs of potential problems and other issues that may require attention in the upcoming budget.

The budget analysis typically looks at past experience with diverse types of revenue—such as investment income, gifts, sponsored program, and other revenues monitored centrally—and with expenses. To the extent possible, analyze expenses to determine whether they can be projected more accurately. For instance, if one can establish a strong relationship between a particular category of expenses and a generally available cost index, monitoring the cost index will provide an early indicator of changes in expense levels. (This technique is common with health-care costs, which are monitored using a cost trend rate to provide early warning of significant increases in premiums.)

4. Project enrollment.

A few, enviable institutions cap their enrollment and enjoy excess demand, enabling them to develop a budget using the same enrollment numbers as in the past. The vast majority of institutions, however, must predict enrollment accurately for the upcoming year.

For tuition-dependent institutions in particular, the gain or loss of just a few students can significantly impact their bottom line. Even for those less dependent on tuition as a source of revenue, the number of projected students has a ripple effect on the entire budget. Enrollment numbers affect financial aid, the number of faculty, inventory costs for the bookstore, and staffing in dining halls, to name just a few areas. For this reason, the planning process should focus in large part on enrollment and related issues.

Many institutions—especially public institutions—face expanding enrollments each year. Although the number of graduating high school seniors is trending downward, more nontraditional students now enroll in college—primarily because they can't find employment. Unfortunately, this tremendous demand for education comes at a time when many states can't provide enough resources to cover educational expenses. This situation usually leads to extensive negotiation of enrollment levels, corresponding appropriations, and tuition levels for both in-state and out-of-state students.

Beyond the potential pool of applicants, pricing decisions affect enrollment. Tuition discounting refers to the practice of offering institutionally funded aid to students beyond their demonstrated need. Essentially, the institution uses some of its resources to attract students who might otherwise not enroll. By offering even a partial scholarship, an institution can attract students with particular skills or qualities to fill a void in the expected incoming class.

In some cases, tuition discounting focuses less on student qualities than on economics. If an institution has excess classroom and housing capacity, attracting a student by offering a partial scholarship results in increased net revenues. For instance, an institution charging $20,000 for tuition and $9,000 for room and board can realize approximately $19,000 of additional revenue if it attracts a student with a $10,000 scholarship. Some costs may increase by serving that additional student, but they will be insignificant compared to the additional revenue.

5. *Establish budget assumptions for the board's approval.*

Every budget builds upon a series of general assumptions. Plans describe what the campus intends to accomplish; assumptions create the framework for the plans.

Usually, the budget office develops assumptions with input from other offices, including planning, admissions and financial aid (or enrollment management), institutional research, human resources, housing, and the treasurer's office. The assumptions address issues, such as:

- The likely increase or decrease in enrollment by level

- The expected inflation rate for various expense categories

- Planned salary increases for various employee categories (faculty, administrators, staff)

Commercially available applications—including Future Perfect, Alight Planning, Oracle Hyperion, and BPC from SAP—can facilitate the financial analysis that helps develop assumptions. They are especially valuable for conducting "what-if" analysis.

The governing board should review and approve the budget office's assumptions. Doing this simplifies the later step of obtaining the board's approval of the finalized budget.

6. *Project central revenues.*

Departments have substantial influence over some revenue streams, especially at the graduate level. When considering other revenues—such as undergraduate tuition and fees, gifts, investment and endowment income, and even sponsored program overhead recoveries—central offices are better positioned to project revenues for the upcoming budget. The same is true for aid, which typically is addressed concurrently with tuition and fees. As a general rule, the central office establishes the number of undergraduate students for the entire institution, recognizing that they are distributed among various colleges and departments.

Typically, the treasurer or controller projects income from endowments and investments. Endowment income tends to be a firmer number, because most institutions employ a spending formula based on historical market values. On the other hand, several factors—including the budget itself—affect investment income.

Investment income for operating purposes usually comes from investing idle cash balances in short-term investments. Cash balances fluctuate depending on factors both within the institution's control, such as success in collecting receivables or managing the timing of expenditures, and outside its control (for example, national economic conditions).

Decisions made during the budget process also influence the availability of cash. For this reason, the treasurer typically provides both an expected earnings rate and a range of revenue likely to be earned. A budget that anticipates significant increases in reserves–institutional savings–likely will provide more investment income. On the other hand, a budget that anticipates spending from reserves usually will reflect reduced investment income. Cash flow analyses–predictions regarding the timing of the receipt and disbursement of cash–take on particular significance when projecting investment income.

With fund-raising, as a general rule, the past serves as a reliable indicator of the future. Absent major economic changes or special initiatives, such as a capital campaign, development officers can use an analysis of the most

Projecting State Appropriations

Depending on the type of public institution (for example, research, doctoral, or liberal arts) and the state's funding approach, state appropriations may contribute as little as 9 percent or as much as 60 percent of all revenues. In states that allow institutions to set tuition rates, the operating appropriation usually is the biggest factor affecting those rates. Even in states that have not granted tuition-setting authority, the state's support greatly affects various expense categories–especially salaries and benefits.

The process of projecting state operating appropriations will depend, in part, on the state's process for establishing its own budget. In some states–especially those relying on well-defined formulas–the campus can project revenues based on factors, such as enrollment, employment levels, and usable space. Applying formulas to the projected data will yield results to incorporate into the assumptions, with the budgets developed accordingly. Other states use a more fluid process that forces institutions to incorporate more contingencies in their budget as protection against shortfalls in anticipated support.

In the aftermath of the 2008 financial crisis, some state institutions began the fiscal year without knowing how much financial support the state would provide. In a few cases, the state did not determine the final appropriation until well into the fiscal year. That meant institutions either had to build a conservative preliminary budget or start the year assuming no changes to the previous year's base budget.

The difficulties deepened in those states that approve tuition levels as part of their appropriation process. Not only were administrators challenged to develop a budget without knowing the levels of appropriations and tuition, students and their families had limited time to arrange financing for the upcoming fall semester due to uncertainty about tuition levels.

recently completed fiscal year, supplemented with current-year experience, to make reasonably accurate projections about giving levels, especially in the area of unrestricted support.

The vast majority of overhead recoveries for a given year will be a function of awards already received. Therefore, the starting point is the analysis of existing and pending awards. Indirect cost recoveries, however, are relatively small compared with the rest of the budget. Therefore, projecting these revenues conservatively avoids the risk of overlooking a source while still protecting the institution against shortfalls. Over time, the experience gained through analysis will pay dividends as projections become more accurate.

7. Project expenses.

Except in institutions relying on RCB (see Chapter Seven), central administration projects virtually all expense categories. Compensation, encompassing the categories of salaries and fringe benefits, represents the largest expense for higher education institutions. Although institutions have significant investments in facilities, infrastructure, equipment, and technology, the annual depreciation and amortization charges related to these assets is modest compared with the expenses incurred for human resources.

The expenses for selected benefits can be tied directly to salaries and wages. To determine any expense assessed as a percentage of salaries—for example, the Federal Insurance Contributions Act (FICA), unemployment insurance, and workers' compensation—simply apply the applicable rate to projected salaries (while considering any ceilings that may apply). Other benefits, however, don't link so easily to salaries. For instance, rates for health insurance—usually the most expensive fringe benefit for higher education—are negotiated annually, and extraordinary increases are not uncommon.

Central administration also determines the inflation factor to apply to various expense categories. In the largest categories, projections reflect specified percentage increases influenced primarily by institutional decisions. Other items are subject to external influences beyond the institution's control yet still must be adjusted for inflation.

The failure to address inflationary factors affecting significant portions of an operating budget essentially imposes a budget cut on units incurring costs in those areas. If the budget process doesn't provide adjustments for this type of increased expense, the unit will have to cover the increased cost by reducing costs in other areas.

8. Develop and distribute guidelines for preparing budget proposals.

To help departments develop their budgets—and to minimize the likelihood of unrealistic submissions—the budget office should provide instructions and electronic forms to everyone responsible for the accounts and activities that will appear in the final budget. The guidelines cover a wide range of issues, such as enrollment trends and their implications for staffing, the distribution of tenured and nontenured faculty appointments, the distribution of part-time faculty, anticipated tenure and promotion decisions, anticipated sabbaticals, and the distribution of instructional workload for departments.

Nearly all institutions rely almost exclusively on electronic submissions transmitted either via e-mail or an intranet. The forms used for electronic submission typically incorporate various edits and diagnostics to prevent submissions that are not consistent with the instructions.

The budget process at most institutions requires approval at intermediate levels of management. As the submission moves through the applicable organizational layers, decentralized management can address unit-specific guidelines. For instance, a dean may require all departments in the college to allocate a specific percentage for curriculum development. Or a major administrative unit may require its departments to identify a portion of their budgets for reallocation to fund special initiatives. At the department level, these types of guidelines may have greater influence on the budget than those imposed by central administration.

In addition to providing budget guidelines, larger institutions often conduct online tutorials or live workshops to convey the important aspects of developing a budget submission. Interestingly, campus personnel—including faculty and academic administrators—almost always find time to attend budget-related training, unlike training on many other administrative topics. Most individuals with budget development responsibility recognize there is much to lose if they are not fully aware of the budget guidelines and procedures.

9. Develop and submit budget proposals.

Ultimately, the unit head is responsible for the budget submission. Depending on the size and complexity of the unit—and both unit and institutional policy—this individual may involve numerous others in the process or simply rely on the unit financial administrator.

The larger the unit, the more likely faculty and additional departmental administrators are to participate in developing the budget submission. For very large departments with significant amounts of gift support and sponsored programs activity, several departmental administrative personnel will probably perform most of the work required to complete a budget submission. Conversely, in small units, the unit head may handle the entire process with clerical support from a departmental secretary. The latter approach also is typical in situations relying primarily on an incremental budget process.

Budget submissions are prepared at the lowest unit level and submitted for review and approval by successive levels of management. At each step, the responsible individual (for example, division head, dean, or vice president) reviews the submissions to ensure they collectively represent the best possible proposal for the unit. Once each level is satisfied that the combined budgets are consistent with the established plans, address all identified priorities, and comply with relevant guidelines, the budgets are submitted to the next management level and, finally, to the budget office.

10. Participate in budget hearings.

Not all institutions have budget hearings, which can occur at the institution or unit level. At the institution level, the hearings usually involve the institutional leadership group that will make the final resource allocation decisions. Hearings at the unit level typically entail a small committee led by a senior unit leader, such as the vice president for administrative units or dean for academic units.

During the meetings, individual unit heads amplify their budget submission to explain the importance of the efforts to be undertaken with the resources requested. They elaborate on the significance of these efforts, establishing the connection to the institution's plans and priorities.

The appropriate body—either institution-level group or unit committee—will weigh the information obtained through the hearings and modify the budget submission accordingly. If the process operates effectively, the group will steer resources toward the activities that align with priorities established through the planning process.

11. Analyze submissions.

The budget office reviews the various submissions from the units to ensure they comply with the established guidelines and to assess how well they align with planning priorities. To the extent anomalies emerge, the units are required to submit revised budgets. Some submissions may be returned because they outline unrealistic proposals.

The overall budget process cannot continue until all unit submissions comply with the guidelines and priorities.

12. Consolidate the budget.

After accumulating all unit and central account budget proposals, the budget office develops the consolidated institutional budget, usually using budget software. Automating the process enables the budget office to produce a consolidated budget as submissions are received. They then can assess how things are coming together and spot any problems that materialize.

While ERPs, such as Banner or PeopleSoft, are excellent transactional systems, they provide only limited analytical capability. The embedded reporting applications are unsophisticated and lack flexibility. This leads to the need to extract data from the ERP for use in a report-writer or spreadsheets.

Modifying the Erps to meet analytical needs becomes expensive because the modification must be repeated each time the vendor releases a new version of the software.

Complex organizations sometimes use dedicated budget applications referred to as business performance management (BPM) systems. These systems provide:

- Standardized templates, methods, and processes for developing operating budgets

- A single source for all financial and budget data that can provide both real-time and end-of-period data as well as multiyear budget-to-actual comparisons

- Standard report and query templates with access to data based on user authorization

BPM systems enable decentralized users to access, view, revise, and report budget data—often via an intranet. Available systems include SAS Financial Management, Oracle Hyperion, XLerant, Host Analytics, Adaptive Planning, and Prophix. Though not designed specifically for higher education they still facilitate managing the budget process by making high-level adjustments, forecasting, and providing analytical tools useful to senior management.

Although highly automated and frequently utilizing an intranet, these tools more likely are *interfaced to* other administrative software, such as the accounting system, rather than *integrated with* it. For this reason, stand-alone software may not incorporate much historical information unless it is intentionally uploaded to the application.

Institutions without the capacity to employ commercial solutions must manually load budget details into whatever tool (for example, Excel) is used to produce the consolidated budget—a time-consuming and labor-intensive process. These institutions are less likely to produce preliminary consolidated budgets. Instead, they focus on entering all source information and produce the budget once everything has been received and processed. A manual process is more likely to yield mistakes that require correction before production of an accurate budget. As such, significantly more time is required for manual processes—both for input and error correction.

Once the consolidated institutional budget has been produced, it must be analyzed. The objective is to ensure that the final budget is consistent with the institutional plan, addresses all priorities, and contains numbers that meet the target established in the assumptions phase.

13. Obtain board approval of the budget.

Next, management submits the budget to the board for review and approval. Assuming the board was consulted during the development of the institution's plans—and approved the budget assumptions—and the budget is consistent with those plans and assumptions—board approval should not be a problem.

The board usually seeks assurance about specific issues identified during the planning process or asks about special risks embodied in the budget. Two issues routinely arise when boards review budgets: the tuition increase and the level of contingency built into the budget. Management should anticipate these questions and provide supplementary narrative information. After hearing answers to their questions and discussing the budget's implications, the board generally gives its stamp of approval.

If, however, the board determines that the budget deviates from the approved plans or assumptions in some way, they may withhold approval. In that case, management typically directs the budget office to make the changes necessary to address the issues raised by the board. This may entail asking selected units to submit revised budgets. Everything comes to a halt if the board remains unwilling to approve the budget. If the budget is consistent with the plans overseen by the board and with the budget assumptions they approved, this suggests a serious problem. The board and management need to invest the effort required to resolve the issues that stand in the way of finalizing the budget.

14. Begin budget implementation.

Once the board has approved the budget—ideally, well before the beginning of the new fiscal year—the accounting system must be updated to reflect the new resource allocation decisions. This step is necessary because various administrative processes must occur to be ready for the fiscal year. Depending on how soon the academic year will start, for example, it may be necessary to process new hires into the payroll system, issue purchase orders, or execute leases for rental space.

Some administrative systems allow activity for a future year to begin in the current fiscal year. In fact, some systems will allow multiple fiscal years to operate simultaneously. This feature is beneficial in one sense but also problematic: Care must be taken to ensure transactions are processed in the appropriate fiscal year. The earlier the budget can be finalized and implemented, the better prepared the campus will be for the next academic year.

15. Monitor performance against the budget.

To ensure it carries out the plans embedded in the budget, the institution must track the progress of revenue generation along with the expenses being incurred.

Unlike some other enterprises, higher education revenues are not earned ratably throughout the fiscal year. Some categories are more stable, such as investment income and selected auxiliary enterprises, but tuition and fees arrive in large chunks. Most institutions have two major revenue spikes: the start of the fall and spring semesters, which each bring in significant amounts of tuition and fee revenue within a short time. A third potential revenue spike comes with summer school tuition.

Many expenses—particularly faculty salaries—are committed before the academic year starts, although the actual expenses tend to be incurred evenly throughout the year. A large expense, like faculty salaries, will drop off during the summer at most institutions, but this can be mitigated at some large research institutions. In either case, monitor expenses periodically throughout the year to ensure things remain on track.

Revenues that do not materialize as planned, or expenses that run higher than expected, may call for action. If the deviations can be accommodated through the contingency incorporated in the expense budget, management can make the adjustments without board involvement (although notification is advisable). If the bottom line is materially affected, however, the board will likely need to review and approve the budget revisions.

16. Prepare audited financial statements.

Well after the fiscal year has ended and the institution has turned its attention to the new budget, the budget office needs to close the door on the previous year. The audited financial statements—the last step in the budget cycle—facilitate this process.

At this stage, final revenue and expense numbers are available. Some analytical effort will be required to reconcile the budgetary and financial statement reporting. Once this has occurred, the board can compare the budget as approved by them—both initially and as revised throughout the fiscal year—with the audited financial statements.

Figures 9-1 and 9-2 illustrate the operating budget cycles for a large public institution and a large independent institution. Because a public institution must integrate its approach with the state's budget process, it must take additional steps linked to state submissions. The nature of the state budgeting cycle requires campuses and other state agencies to meet various deadlines and, in most cases, to submit information on a somewhat piecemeal basis.

In contrast, the independent university's process appears to flow in a more natural sequence. Despite the differences, the basic tasks must occur on both campuses. Although smaller, less complex institutions may rely on a more streamlined budget process, the general flow presented in Figures 9-1 and 9-2 could be adapted to any public or independent institution.

Figure 9-1 Sample Public University Operating Budget Development Cycle

(For a state utilizing a biennial budget cycle)

Jun 30   The prior fiscal year ends.

Sept   *In odd-number years, submit base operating budget and activity-based budget for the upcoming biennium to the state.*

ept–Oct   Present operating and capital budget requests (odd-number years) or amendments (even-number years) to the governing board for approval.

Oct   *Submit the biennial budget request. In even-number years, the request represents an amendment to the existing biennial budget; in odd-number years, the request is for the upcoming biennium.*

Dec   *The governor submits the proposed budget to the legislature.*

     Distribute upcoming fiscal year budget development instructions and templates to vice presidents for distribution to reporting units (after applying any unit-specific revisions).

     Process all modifications that will affect target budgets for the upcoming fiscal year.

     Tuition, housing, and board fee increase requests for the upcoming fiscal year are due for designated programs.

Jan   *Submit budget amendments to the legislature for items not addressed by the governor's proposed budget.*

     Distribute internal budget targets to the vice presidents for distribution to reporting units (after applying any unit-specific adjustments).

     Application, activity, and other fee increase requests for the upcoming fiscal year are due.

     Begin development of the tuition proposal and financial aid allocations.

Feb   *State budget bills cross over from house and senate.*

     Mandatory fee increase requests for the upcoming fiscal year are due.

     Full budget submissions are due from the auxiliary enterprise, selected other self-supporting units, and various academic units.

     Present upcoming fiscal year housing rates and budget development assumptions to the governing board for approval.

Mar   *Joint conference committee forwards the legislature's budget bill to governor.*

Apr   All remaining budget submissions, including addenda requests, for the upcoming fiscal year are due.

     Present dining, tuition, and mandatory fee proposal to the governing board for approval.

     The appropriation act is approved by the legislature and governor.

May   Carryforward requests for the current fiscal year budget are due.

     Present the budget to the governing board for approval.

     Distribute the approved budget and addenda to vice presidents.

     Update the financial system with the new fiscal year budget.

Jul 1   The new fiscal year begins.

Items in italics represent submissions to the state or activities that occur at the state level.

Figure 9-2 Sample Independent University Operating Budget Development Cycle

Jun 30	The prior fiscal year ends.
Oct	The board of trustees budget committee meets to review final budget performance results for the prior fiscal year and the planning schedule for the upcoming fiscal year's budget development process.
Oct–Nov	The planning and budget advisory committee meets to:

- Review and discuss budget planning strategies/procedures

- Review and discuss program priorities

- Review and discuss preliminary revenue planning assumptions

- Set planning parameters for the upcoming fiscal year

Dec–Feb	Central administration staff (including the planning office, budget office, finance office, and provost's office) meet with deans and other unit heads to review and update strategic plans (preplanning meetings).
	University administration meets with deans and other unit heads to discuss strategic plans (planning and budget meetings).
Feb	Preliminary allocation materials are distributed.
	The board of trustees budget committee reviews the preliminary budget performance report for the current fiscal year and receives a status report on the upcoming fiscal year's budget planning.
	Trustees review and approve tuition and room and board rates for the upcoming fiscal year.
Mar	Faculty salary planning guidelines are distributed to schools.
Apr	Upcoming fiscal year budget allocations are finalized.
	The budget office prepares and distributes final budget allocation materials and detailed budget preparation materials for the upcoming fiscal year.
	Faculty salary plans are due to the provost's office.
	Detailed upcoming fiscal year appropriated budgets are due to the budget office.
	Faculty hiring plans for all schools are due to the provost's office.
May–Jun	The budget office reviews upcoming fiscal year appropriated budget details and reconciles with the final budget summary.
	The budget office prepares a budget summary for the upcoming fiscal year for review by the president and trustees.
	Exempt and nonexempt staff salary plans are due to human resources.
	The board of trustees budget committee reviews and endorses the final upcoming fiscal year operating budget and receives a status report on the current fiscal year's budget performance.
	Upcoming fiscal year budget details are entered into the financial system.
	Upcoming fiscal year budgets are distributed to the units.
Jul 1	The new fiscal year begins.

Operating Budget Calendar

The budget calendar must have sufficient flexibility to allow for the routine reexamination of individual components. Some units may need to revise their budget proposals to adhere to guidelines or targets, and the board may request revisions as well. Consequently, the entire budget process can take anywhere from six to 12 months at midsize independent institutions and appreciably longer at large independent and public institutions—particularly because of the influence of state agencies.

The end point usually is keyed to the board's meeting schedule, so it's good practice to include a month or more of cushion within the budget calendar. Otherwise, the board may have to convene in a special meeting for the sole purpose of reviewing and approving the budget. When this occurs, the board may want to examine the budget in greater detail than would have been the case under the normal schedule.

Every institution should aim to have the budget approved well before the fiscal year starts. Ideally, approval for nonfaculty positions should happen sufficiently early to begin the recruitment process for these positions. Faculty recruiting requires even more lead time, especially if new faculty will be teaching sections in the fall semester or if any other approved positions are expected to generate revenues during the year. Unless the revenue projections contemplate hiring delays, revenue shortfalls are likely if the new positions are not filled early in the fiscal year.

Since the 2008 recession, state legislatures and governors often have struggled to agree on a state budget, making it difficult, if not impossible, for some public institutions to finalize their own budgets much in advance of the new fiscal year. Like the federal government, several states have operated with continuing resolutions, executive orders, or similar administrative stopgap measures to enable state government, including public higher education, to operate without the benefit of an approved statewide budget. Although temporary authorization allows public institutions to conduct most routine operations, it impairs effectiveness, stifles innovation, and creates anxiety about the possibility that cutbacks may be needed later in the fiscal year. Also, it frequently interrupts progress on construction projects, especially when the capital appropriation is provided on a fiscal year basis rather than a project basis. When this occurs, project completion costs typically rise because of inflation in the construction industry.

Some states use biennial budgets, which forces institutions to project far into the future—sometimes more than two years from the latest completed period. The discipline that accompanies a multiyear model can be beneficial when a public institution chooses to use it internally to manage operations more effectively. When imposed by the state, however, it can become a hardship.

When projecting two or more years into the future, budgeters typically reduce the uncertainty by using current experience as a base. Adjustments are made at the margin to reflect anticipated changes in revenues and expenses, which in turn are determined by such variables as program mix, enrollments, market factors affecting the availability of job candidates, inflationary influences, and investment yields.

Scheduled changes, such as the introduction of a new degree program or tighter admissions standards, can be planned. But it is difficult to predict more extreme events, such as new environmental regulations, dramatically changing interest rates, changes in federal student assistance programs, or the impact of an international crisis. As a result, public institutions in states with biennial budgeting are forced to default to incremental budgeting and to include significant contingencies as a protective measure.

Capital Budget Cycle

The typical capital budget cycle includes fewer steps than the operating budget cycle but lasts appreciably longer. Although individual programs may continue for years (for example, a multiyear sponsored research project) and activities—such as instruction—will occur as long as the institution exists, an operating budget covers only the activities occurring within a single fiscal year.

In contrast, the capital budget extends over several years. It covers physical assets, such as buildings, and the dollar magnitude of individual projects usually dwarfs items in the operating budget. Even a very large sponsored project usually will not represent as large a financial commitment as the typical project addressed in a capital budget, which may range from the acquisition of a single major item of equipment, to the renovation of a laboratory, to the acquisition or construction of a campus building. Similarly, it's not uncommon for an individual capital project's budget to exceed the combined annual operating budgets for a number of academic departments.

Depending on institutional policies and procedures—and the volume of capital activity ongoing at any time—the capital planning and budgeting processes at large institutions can be as complex as those for the operating cycle. At institutions with few resources available for capital activities, the processes may be relatively informal and include minimal formal planning. Instead, the institution might maintain a "wish list" of projects to undertake as resources become available or in response to operational problems.

Regardless of the type of institution, the most desirable way to address both new projects and ongoing maintenance involves a formal process for identifying and addressing capital needs. Outlined below is a recommended six-step process.

1. Establish the Need for Space.

The need for new space—or significant renovations to existing space—is first identified at the department or school level. The unit develops the rationale for additional space, citing the specific activities that will occur there. The request might focus on increased sponsored programs activity, the introduction of a new academic program, improved faculty-student interaction because of technological upgrades, or enhanced campus-corporate training partnerships.

The request usually includes an analysis of existing space resources and an explanation of why they are not sufficient to accommodate the new activities.

2. Search for Existing Space.

Once the need has been identified and shown to be consistent with the institution's plans and priorities, the search begins for other space on campus that could be reassigned without adversely affecting other institutional activities. If no existing space is available, efforts begin to acquire or construct space.

Depending on the activity's importance and urgency, an interim arrangement to rent space might accommodate the identified need temporarily.

3. Review Campus Master Plan.

After the addition of new space has been approved in concept, review the campus master plan to determine the appropriate location for the space. Master plans address long-term facilities and infrastructure needs, and identify how the physical space will be developed over time.

An effective master plan typically covers a 10- to 20-year period. Its purpose is to guide a campus as it develops its physical resources to maximize their programmatic benefit and aesthetic value, and also ensure that financial resources invested in facilities and related areas provide the maximum benefit. Plans typically are reviewed and revised regularly and rewritten approximately every five years.

Campus master plans identify specific areas reserved for academic expansion, along with the designated location for any new residential facilities, administrative space, athletics and recreation venues, and other buildings. Within the constraints of the institution's political climate, a master plan also indicates potential boundary expansion for the campus.

This sensitive issue typically is not addressed in the master plans of independent institutions. Public institutions, however, usually must disclose expansion plans even though doing so may complicate relationships with the local community. Unlike most independent institutions, public institutions are subject to open meeting and open records laws and regulations, which require that official actions taken by the board or management be open to the public.

This burden is somewhat offset by the fact that a public institution may be able to invoke eminent domain to acquire land in support of its mission. Under eminent domain, the public institution directly, or through the local government, forces the transfer of privately owned land to the institution (with appropriate compensation to the owner). This is a last resort; it is much more typical for public institutions to acquire land through normal competitive purchase.

4. Assess Feasibility.

Rarely will a campus undertake space acquisition or new construction to address a single need for space. More typically, several identified needs will be combined to determine the best overall solution. It may be desirable to acquire an available commercial facility, or it may make more sense to construct a new on-campus facility.

The decision to buy, lease, or build considers such factors as:

- The suitability of available commercial space
- The overall cost comparison between building/leasing new space and acquiring/renovating commercial space
- The availability of space to rent until a permanent solution can be implemented
- The time needed to construct the needed space

5. Obtain Approvals

As a general rule, approval of land or other significant capital acquisitions—such as those above a certain dollar threshold—by independent institutions occurs only at the board level. Rarely does anyone outside the institution need to authorize the institution's acquisition of capital assets. (Sometimes, an independent institution seeking to acquire land locally must obtain approval from the local municipality. The approval usually is linked to concerns regarding the property tax implications that arise when a tax-exempt organization acquires property and removes it from the tax rolls.)

Public institutions have a more substantial approval process that requires significant lead-time. Most states, for example, have statutory requirements related to the acquisition of land and buildings. Various state agencies will be required to approve the acquisition or construction of new facilities. In some states, this occurs only if state funds will be used to finance the acquisition or construction; other states require approval of all transactions at the state level.

Along with concerns related to demonstrated need, states may raise environmental concerns (such as asbestos or ground contamination), building and related construction code regulations, and other issues related to public policy. If the transaction requires debt financing, additional approvals will be required from various state financial offices.

6. Acquire or Construct.

Once all approvals have been obtained, the purchase is consummated or the actual construction begins. Depending on the nature of the project, this step may take several years. During this period, the capital budget will be reviewed regularly to ensure the overall capital portfolio is being managed effectively.

Cost overruns are common with construction projects, and it is not unusual for an individual project budget to have a sizable contingency factor. Although the amount will vary by project, a 5 percent contingency is customary and a 10 percent contingency is not uncommon.

Capital Budget Calendar

Due to the types of projects included in a capital budget, its cycle will be much longer. Several years may elapse from the time a project is conceptualized until it has been completed, placed in service, and removed from the budget. The capital budget extends through the end point for the longest-term project that has been formally approved within the institution. Because multiple projects may be in different phases at any point, capital budgets tend to stretch out for years—especially at public institutions.

Because of the lengthy capital project approval process in some states, and the fact that many states employ a biennial budget cycle, a single project could have a six- or eight-year life. For instance, the institution could internally approve a project in year one and then embark on a two- or three-year process to obtain approval for the project from the relevant state departments and agencies. Once approved by the state, the project will wait until resources become available. Depending on debt markets and competing priorities, this process easily could take one or two years.

Once funding has been secured, the process begins to program the project specifics and issue invitations to bid for the various project components. This will lead to the awarding of contracts followed by actual construction. It's not uncommon for major projects to require two or more years for construction.

Deferred Maintenance

Deferred maintenance refers to the scheduled routine repair and maintenance of facilities that is postponed, thereby creating a backlog. Every campus has some amount of deferred maintenance resulting from various operational considerations. Say a particular classroom facility is due for interior painting, but because of increased demand for the program housed in the facility, the decision is made to postpone the painting until spring break during the following academic year. Or a roof scheduled for replacement

Figure 9-3 Sample Public University Capital Budget Development Cycle for Fiscal Years 4-9

(For a state with a June 30 year-end utilizing a six-year capital planning cycle)

May FY 1	Distribute the call to vice presidents for FYs 4–9 six-year capital plan.
Jul FY 2	Project initiation forms are due for each new project.
	Prepare a six-year capital plan.
Aug FY 2	Present the six-year capital plan to the executive review committee for review and approval. Emphasis is on 1) biennial plans, 2) project justifications, and 3) funding (state general fund, bond, and gift-funding proposals for each biennium, and the impact on student fees).
Oct FY 2	The university architect's office completes project formulation documents for proposed projects.
Nov FY 2	The vice president for finance completes business plans and the debt assessment impact for proposed capital projects.
Dec FY 2	Present the six-year capital plan, business plans, and debt assessments to executive committee for review and approval.
Feb FY 2	*The state planning and budget department notifies agencies of the submittal schedule for FYs 4–9 six-year capital plan and unfunded projects from FYs 1–5 six-year capital plan eligible for the preparation of detailed submissions.*
Mar FY 2	The six-year capital plan is presented to the special governing board committee for final review and approval.
Apr FY 2	*The six-year capital plan is submitted to the state planning and budget department.*
Jun FY 2	*Detailed documents for projects approved by the state in February are submitted to the state planning and budget department.*
	Notification by the state planning and budget department of six-year plan projects are approved for detailed submittal.
	Notification by the state planning and budget department of maintenance reserve subprojects that meet required criteria occurs.
Aug FY 3	*Detailed documents for projects approved by the state in June are submitted to the state planning and budget department.*
	Annual maintenance reserve plan documents are submitted to the state planning and budget department.
Sept FY 3	Complete financial feasibility studies for revenue bond projects.
Nov FY 3	*The governor submits the six-year capital improvement plan to the legislature.*
Dec FY 3	*The governor submits the FYs 4–5 biennial budget to legislature.*
May FY 3	*The FYs 4–5 appropriation act is approved by the legislature and governor.*
Jul 1 FY 4	Approved FYs 4–5 project authorizations take effect.

Items in italics represent interactions with the state or activities that occur at the state level.

must continue in service because the specialized materials it requires are temporarily unavailable. Such situations are not problematic when they are short term.

On the other hand, many institutions have large backlogs of deferred maintenance that developed because of financial stress. In other words, revenue shortfalls or expense overruns in prior years prevented the institutions from making the repairs or conducting the maintenance in accordance with the established schedule. A modest deferred maintenance backlog may be manageable, but once it grows too large to address within normal operating cycles, facilities begin to deteriorate rapidly. Even relatively new facilities will not operate optimally if not properly maintained.

For these reasons, institutions seek to quantify the deferred maintenance backlog so they can address it through the operating budget, the capital budget, or both. Normal repairs and maintenance are considered operating expenses. As such, they typically are managed by including an amount in the operating budget to address at least a portion of the backlog. And if the institution ends the year with unanticipated surpluses, it may allocate a portion of the surplus to addressing the backlog.

When the operating budget (or surpluses it generates) cannot accommodate the backlog, the institution usually turns to its capital budget, which includes a special category to address critical aspects of deferred maintenance. The major concern for such projects is the funding source. It is unlikely that bonds can be sold to finance deferred maintenance projects, so other sources must be found. Many public institutions receive special appropriations for this purpose. Independent institutions, however, must generate the funds themselves through operating surpluses or fund-raising.

Trade-offs are necessary between demands for new or enhanced space and the need to maintain and repair existing space. Some institutions rely on outside firms to assist with the analysis required to determine the appropriate mix between routine scheduled maintenance, facilities renewal/upgrades, and new construction.

Unlike many other indicators of financial stress—such as reduced enrollment resulting in declining revenues, increased bad debts from students not paying their bills, or increases in accounts payable due to liquidity problems—deferred maintenance backlogs do not appear in the audited financial statements. Some effects of deferred maintenance may be visibly apparent, but nothing in generally accepted accounting principles (GAAP) requires disclosure of the amount of the backlog. Stakeholders must ask the right questions to ensure that the backlog does not become unmanageable.

Attending to existing backlogs poses a financial challenge—one that can become worse as institutions add new facilities. The campus building boom of the late 1990s and early 2000s has resulted in significantly increased deferred maintenance burdens. One strategy being employed by a number of institutions is to place a moratorium on new facilities projects unless they come with a dedicated renewal and replacement reserve for the facility. In other words, the source of ongoing maintenance funds must be identified at the start of any new capital project to ensure the new facilities do not contribute to the deferred maintenance backlog.

Obviously, this approach addresses only part of the problem because it does not generate funds to address the existing backlog. Still, it represents a step in the right direction.

Key
Points

- An operating budget covers activities occurring within a single fiscal year, while a capital budget covers physical assets—such as buildings—and extends over several years.
- The operating budget cycle consists of 16 steps, while the capital budget cycle has six steps.
- Public institutions must perform the same budgeting steps as independent institutions, plus whatever processes are needed to satisfy the expectations of various state agencies.
- The calendars for the operating and budget cycles typically are not linked because of the differing objectives for the two budgets. The operating budget calendar usually begins before the start of the fiscal year it pertains to and ends when the board approves the audited financial statements. The capital budget calendar has a much longer time line: It begins with the internal approval of a capital project and continues as long as any approved project remains unfinished.

Inevitably, things will not always play out as projected. There is no guarantee that revenues projected in the budget will actually materialize. Enrollment targets, for example, might fall short because students offered admission chose to enroll elsewhere, or previous students did not return for another year. Financial markets may not deliver the investment income anticipated when the budget was developed.

Conversely, some expenses might prove larger than expected. Major winter storms could drive snow removal costs beyond anything considered possible. The contracted Internet service provider may go bankrupt, forcing the institution to rely on a backup provider with rates originally set only for short-term consumption.

Any of these situations could wreak havoc on resource allocation plans. Building flexibility into the budget enables institutions to better respond to such changing circumstances and conditions—and the financial implications that accompany them. In fact, one mark of a well-managed institution is its ability to take advantage of unforeseen opportunities and respond to unanticipated problems.

Ultimately, flexibility comes from having adequate revenues to conduct activities and programs. One way to provide flexibility is through **contingency funding** to cover revenue shortfalls or expense overruns. Unrestricted revenues—such as tuition and fees, unrestricted gifts and endowment income, some state appropriations, and surpluses in auxiliary enterprises or other self-supporting activities—can provide the resources that cushion an institution against unforeseen events. The challenge comes in identifying the cushion and preserving it despite the demands of daily operations.

Apart from contingency funding, **maneuverability** is a key element supporting flexibility. For example, funds with the fewest restrictions on their use can be held back and not allocated at the outset, making them available to address unanticipated needs. All institutions must deal with the reality that some donated funds carry donor-imposed restrictions. In these situations, the donor explicitly states what the funds may be used for—either specific programmatic objectives (for example, research or student financial aid) or specific types of expenses (for example, salaries, or library materials).

Not all unrestricted funds are equal. When a donor makes an unrestricted gift, the only constraint on using those funds is that they be used for lawful purposes consistent with the institution's mission. Although state operating appropriations (general funds) are considered unrestricted, regulatory requirements cause them to be managed as if they carried restrictions. For instance, the state may have established rules about special approvals to obtain when state general funds are used to pay for a personal services contract. Or it may be necessary to utilize an established procurement contract when acquiring certain commodities. In other words, the state doesn't identify the particular program that must be supported with the funds it provides, but it may dictate how to support whichever program is chosen.

Public institutions can enhance flexibility by allocating state general funds to qualifying activities while preserving completely unrestricted resources for other uses. Resources, such as gifts and endowment income–when not restricted–and any other resources with no strings attached, usually are preserved to support activities that are not eligible for state funding.

Risk tolerance also relates to flexibility. The greater the institution's aversion to risk, the more important the need to develop a budget that provides maximum flexibility through contingency funding and maneuverability. Not allocating all anticipated revenues to committed expenses or investments helps avoid the risk that resources will be insufficient to meet all commitments. A budget that allocates all anticipated revenues runs the risk that some planned expense or other investment will have to be deferred due to revenue shortfalls or cost overruns.

Five Change Factors

One of five factors typically causes significant changes in an institution's revenues or expenses. All are major reasons for building cushion into the budget.

1. Enrollment fluctuations. If enrollments fall below expected levels, institutions will lose tuition revenues and, in the case of public institutions, may lose state appropriations as well. Unless the expense budget contains a cushion, the institution will face a deficit for that year.

Similarly, excess enrollment can create budget problems. Additional class sections may be required to accommodate the unanticipated increase in enrollment, but the revenue generated from the additional students may not cover all additional costs. Unanticipated enrollment increases also may affect auxiliary units. Dining operations can probably accommodate more students with ease, but bookstores may not have adequate textbook inventories to meet demand. Or the campus may not have enough residence halls to accommodate the additional students who need housing.

Sometimes, enrollment patterns do not follow historical trends. For instance, enrollment may shift dramatically among majors, making it impossible to reallocate resources. The institution may need to engage adjunct faculty or identify additional graduate students to serve as teaching assistants to meet the increased demand, even though no savings can be realized in the programs experiencing the enrollment declines.

2. Revenue fluctuations. Revenue shortfalls occur in sources other than tuition and fees. Investment income may not meet targets due to unanticipated market conditions, or adverse publicity may result in declining donations. Similarly, economic problems might affect state revenues, thereby causing the state to reduce appropriations to public institutions. If the problem develops late in the fiscal year, the state may even require the institution to return funds already received.

3. Expense fluctuations. An unanticipated utility hike, increased insurance costs due to a spate of natural disasters, or price increases for required repair materials are examples of expense increases that collectively could create the potential for an operating deficit. Campuses are like small- or medium-sized cities. Price increases in almost any commodity will affect them. If the increase relates to a widely used commodity, the impact can be significant.

4. Financial emergencies. Although most campuses have several types of insurance, a natural disaster can strike at any time and lead to significant unplanned expenses to meet policy deductibles or cover costs not protected by insurance. Other emergencies might range from paying dramatic increases in health-care premiums to complying with a federal audit of sponsored programs. In the latter case, institutions often deem it more practical to negotiate a financial settlement than aggressively challenge the federal government, even if they have followed all the rules governing the sponsored research.

5. Unforeseen opportunities. Say a faculty member needs a substantial commitment of institutional-matching funds to secure a major research project that will raise the institution's profile. Or perhaps another college or corporation suggests collaborating on a new initiative that dovetails with a priority area identified through the institutional planning process. Rather than pass up such opportunities, an institution with a discretionary or contingency fund could take advantage of them.

A Three-Tiered Approach

One institution's approach to contingencies relies on multiple funds. The first level is a contingency fund for use in an emergency. If none arise, the contingency amount will be added to reserves at year-end.

The second level, a tuition reserve fund, solely addresses revenue shortfalls caused by unexpected drops in enrollment. The final category, known as the president's discretionary fund, provides resources to deploy if unique opportunities arise.

Creating the Cushion

At each level of the budget process, participants have the opportunity to allocate every potential resource to its fullest or maintain a cushion for responding to expense overruns or revenue shortfalls. Although modest, a cushion created at the department level will allow the unit to respond to issues that might arise.

More cushion is needed at the highest levels because of the greater magnitude of issues to deal with. A cost increase for a special laboratory supply may affect only one or two units and probably can be accommodated with a modest amount of cushion. On the other hand, a major spike in health-care premiums can absorb an institution's entire contingency reserve.

Some people view financial flexibility as a sign of inefficiency and poor administration, even referring to contingency funding in an institutional budget as "fat." One extension of this philosophy is the notion that a leaner budget translates into greater accountability or improved efficiency. In fact, the most effective organizations can readily marshal their resources to respond to challenges or take advantage of opportunities.

Recognizing the importance of flexibility, most budgeters will protect the budget contingencies from those above and below in the hierarchy. They must take care, however, not to go to extremes and forget that contingency funds exist for use when needed. The funds should not be spent unwisely, but neither should the institutions miss opportunities because of a misguided desire to build reserves at all costs.

Managers typically seek to shift uncertainty to others. Department heads routinely turn to deans or central office personnel for resources needed to respond to emergencies or opportunities. For instance, a department that encounters unanticipated price increases for needed supplies or higher-than-expected salary demands by an adjunct filling in for a temporarily disabled faculty member may expect the provost to provide funding to address the situation.

Conversely, deans and central administrators may take on the burden of monitoring departmental spending closely to anticipate problems, or they may use their contingency funds to address problems within departments rather than use them for opportunities at the college level. At the state level, officials often shift uncertainty to public higher education systems or individual campuses by establishing regulations that prohibit operating deficits.

Flexibility changes from one budget cycle to another as circumstances change. New resources must be found to adapt to different conditions, and new strategies must be utilized to create contingency funding in the budget. Although budgeters at all levels seek to include cushion in their portions of the budget, they are reluctant to label it as such for fear that others may seek to claim the amounts—with good reason. It's not uncommon for presidents and provosts to try to spend the cushion, occasionally even attempting to spend the same dollar multiple times.

Ideally, to avoid deficits, the institution should establish an institutional-level contingency fund to address significant revenue shortfalls and expense overruns. The chief financial officer must ensure the president and provost understand the nature of the cushion and what it is intended to cover. The optimal level of cushion is 3 percent of the operating expense budget. This is large enough to address most situations that might arise but small enough to realistically incorporate into the budget.

On rare occasions, an institution will receive an unanticipated windfall—such as a large bequest with no restrictions—and it should know immediately how to deploy such funds. In fact, plans at the institutional level should include a list of priorities to address if resources become available, either through unanticipated savings or a windfall. Truly effective institutions take it a step further. They develop a complementary list of areas that will experience resource reductions if expenses must be curtailed. This approach protects high-priority areas when revenue shortfalls or expense overruns occur.

Hidden Costs That Limit Flexibility

No one—especially someone with budget responsibility—likes surprises. To limit the impact of surprises, budgets should include contingency funding that can be reallocated to meet unanticipated expenses, provide funds to take advantage of new opportunities, or allow the institution to withstand revenue shortfalls.

Even with contingency funding, however, some policy decisions carry hidden costs. Here are some common examples:

New facilities. Institutions rarely fail to acknowledge the costs of constructing or acquiring a new facility. Occasionally, however, they ignore the ongoing O&M costs incurred when the new facility enters service, erroneously assuming that existing budgets will absorb these costs.

In addition to ongoing operating costs, a new facility needs funding for equipment and furnishings. Again, so much attention usually is focused on the building or space itself that its related costs are ignored or underestimated.

New academic programs. Typically, the obvious costs—salaries and benefits for new faculty and staff, space needs, workstations, supplies, and so on—are anticipated and factored into the budget. But the less obvious items—the ancillary cost and revenue impacts of the new programs—may not be addressed.

If, for instance, the new program attracts more students, complementary programs will probably experience increased demand for their courses and need to hire additional instructors. Or rather than significantly increasing enrollments in existing departments, the new program may prompt students to transfer in from existing departments. The net result may be that courses in existing departments become under-subscribed, causing those departments to be overstaffed.

The question becomes: Who should provide the resources to meet the increased or shifted demand for instruction? More than one department must bear the burden of curricular changes that affect several programs. Although the question has no single correct answer, the obvious implication is to consider all additional costs—and lost revenues—before making programmatic changes.

Making the Case

Whenever a new program, activity, or facility is being considered, borrow a standard practice from the corporate sector and develop a written "business case" to support the decision-making process. The documentation for each initiative should include:

- **The rationale.** Describe what the effort will accomplish and how it will contribute to institutional success. Also identify any anticipated ancillary impacts—both positive and negative—that might occur if the initiative is pursued.

- **Estimated financial impact.** Project expenses, other costs, and revenues for at least three years (and, when possible, for five years). With a capital project, the business case must identify the total project cost, even if it extends beyond five years.

- **Project details.** If the initiative relates to an academic program, estimate the projected numbers of students, faculty, and support staff. Explain any anticipated involvement or participation by other organizations and any dependencies—other things that must occur for the initiative to succeed.

In short, a business case presents all relevant factors in one place. This puts decision makers in the best possible position to make the most appropriate choice for the institution, based on what is known and can be reasonably expected.

Elimination of activities or programs. Hidden costs have the potential to erase some or all of the anticipated savings. For example, continuing academic programs that require courses or services from the program being eliminated will have to find substitutes or provide the services themselves.

If program curtailment results in the release of personnel, reduction-in-force policies may require that the personnel displace other less senior staff or receive significant severance payments.

Space usually is at a premium on campuses, so vacated space will be in high demand. Nevertheless, a unique single-purpose space may be abandoned when a program ends. Even if the vacant space no longer incurs ongoing maintenance costs, at some point the institution will have to convert the space for an alternate use.

Human resources. Positions protected by tenure policies or job security established through individual contracts or collective bargaining agreements can greatly affect budget flexibility. In some institutions, for example, job permanence makes it difficult to reallocate positions from one activity to another or to reduce the number of positions assigned to an activity. As for tenured positions, an assistant professor may receive tenure at age 30 and continue working until age 70. If the professor earns an average salary of $75,000 plus benefits throughout his or her career, the decision to grant tenure represents a financial commitment approaching $4 million.

Seed funding. Grants or other temporary sources can help launch a new program or activity. Once operational, however, the program or activity may require support from other resources—unless it generates resources on its own through gifts, service fees, or tuition.

Higher education is not noted for its ability to terminate programs or activities, so an established program is likely to continue even if anticipated revenues do not materialize. Prepare for the possibility of a new program not generating sufficient funds to sustain itself by recognizing and accommodating these potential costs at the outset.

Strategies to Increase Flexibility

Flexibility is structured according to the portion of the budget to which it pertains. Compensation costs can represent as much as 70 percent of college or university budgets, with fixed expenses, such as utilities and physical plant maintenance, absorbing another 10 to 15 percent. The balance usually is spent for operating expenses, such as service contracts, technology, supplies, communications, noncapital equipment, and travel.

Constraints on the use of funds differ from one expense category to another. For example, it is possible that amounts budgeted for compensation may not be spent for other operating expenses. Instead, unspent amounts could be captured centrally for reallocation or, in some public institutions, reverted to the state. Strategies for creating flexibility tend to be tailored to the activity, the expense constraints affecting the institution, and the level of operation within the institution.

Outlined below are specific strategies an institution might employ to increase financial flexibility. Not all will work in every situation, but they offer the potential to achieve enhanced results from the budget process.

(*Note:* For public institutions, success with these strategies might backfire. Accumulating unrestricted balances as a cushion against economic difficulties can create a juicy target for state officials looking for more resources. In some instances, states have recaptured what they perceive as excessive fund balances or simply reduced appropriations and directed institutions to spend down their existing balances. Public institution officers and appropriate state officials should talk about what actions can be taken to protect the reserves developed through prudent management.)

Change the framework. The potential for operating and budgetary flexibility may simply disappear through atrophy. In other words, budget practices will become stale if not examined and modified regularly. The same things will happen year after year, with the participants comfortably replicating what had been done the year before—which also had been done the year before that, and the year before that, and so on. Absent a comprehensive approach to examining the process, participants tend to allocate resources as in years past, usually with only marginal change. This is especially true in institutions that do not employ a rigorous planning process to drive budgetary decisions.

Ample evidence suggests that budget practices remain static. For instance, the historical growth driven by program expansion rarely has a corresponding contraction resulting from program elimination. Focusing on new programs or activities that might enhance the operating environment or make the institution more appealing to its applicant pool comes easily. It proves much harder to identify programs and activities that no longer contribute to success.

An institution may be able to capture excess resources by analyzing the current distribution of resources. Taking a holistic approach that focuses on the entire operating budget—addressing both academic programs and nonacademic programs—affords the opportunity for an in-depth review. An alternative approach focuses on activity clusters—it simultaneously examines a particular academic program and all of its related activities, both administrative support and student support.

ZBB (see Chapter Seven) and its variants entail an in-depth assessment of program and activity costs compared to program accomplishments to determine whether the investments are reasonable. By examining the costs of all program elements and linking them to specific levels of service or quality, the institution may be able to select the appropriate level of investment in light of competing demands for resources.

Alternatively, closely related academic or support programs might be analyzed in terms of the degrees and services they provide. Another analytical strategy would involve investigating similar activities across common dimensions, such as clerical or support staffing, specific operating expense categories (such as travel and equipment repair contracts), use of graduate assistants in academic departments, or faculty and staff productivity.

Examine cost structures. In general, academic programs have many fixed costs—costs incurred no matter how many students are served. As an example, every institution, no matter its enrollment, has some form of chief academic officer. Every institution also has a registrar for managing student records and determining when a student has met the requirements for a degree. For a third example, consider the faculty member who teaches biology courses. Whether that faculty member is tenured or adjunct is irrelevant; as long as the institution intends to offer a biology program, it will have fixed costs related to faculty for those courses.

The alternative to fixed costs is variable costs—costs that rise or fall based on levels of service. When a community college offers multiple sections of algebra, the number of faculty becomes a variable cost. There may be some fixed costs for algebra because a minimum number of faculty is needed each term. Overall, however, this represents a variable cost once that fixed number has been exceeded. If eight sections of algebra are offered with a standard class load of four, two faculty members will be needed. If student demand dictates that the college offer 16 sections, two additional faculty will be needed.

A further refinement of variable costs is known as step-variable costs. These costs do not vary proportionally as volumes increase or decrease. Instead, they remain steady until a specific threshold is reached. In the example involving sections of algebra, it's likely that a step threshold is established. If the objective is to limit each algebra section to 25 students, the step threshold is 25. A new class section will be offered for every 25 additional students seeking to take a class in algebra. Another step variable threshold would be established for the number of faculty teaching algebra. If the established teaching workload results in a faculty member teaching four sections of algebra, one additional faculty member will be added for each four additional sections.

In reality, of course, the numbers don't necessarily work out. What happens if 12 additional students instead of 25 want to take algebra? Do you add a section for the 12 students or distribute them among existing sections, thereby increasing the student count beyond the standard of 25? Similarly, what happens if 18 sections are needed? Presumably, four faculty will teach the first 16 sections. Will the additional two sections represent overload for two faculty, or will they hire one or two adjuncts to meet the additional demand? Such situations arise routinely on campus, so the institution needs to have policies and practices in place as a decision-making guide.

Fixed or Variable?

It's not unusual for participants in the budgeting process to make erroneous assumptions about a cost's true nature. Too often, costs are assumed to be fixed when, in fact, they are variable. Just because a cost has been incurred every year, for as long as anyone can remember, does not mean it can't be eliminated.

Resource allocation decisions must be informed by cost analysis to determine whether they truly can be eliminated without adversely affecting the program or activity. The lower the fixed costs incurred by a program or activity, the greater the flexibility an institution has over its operating budget. And when program and activity planning are linked to the budget process, costs become much more variable.

Conduct an in-depth revenue analysis. Revenue analysis focuses on the individual activities (such as programs, courses, and projects) that actually generate revenue. It will reveal, for example, which academic programs generate the most revenues and which have the highest costs.

Some individual courses produce significant amounts of net revenue because they rely on a single faculty member lecturing to large groups of students without the need for significant capital investment (psychology, business, and English are three examples). Unless variable tuition pricing applies, these revenue-generating courses subsidize more labor- or capital-intensive programs, such as nursing, music, or engineering. Linking the analysis to productivity indicators, such as numbers of students served, student credit hours generated, and number of course sections offered, provides even greater value.

The point of the analysis is not necessarily to encourage the institution to invest more in courses that provide greater returns (although that may be appropriate in some situations). Instead, the goal is to develop an understanding of cost and revenue structures so that informed decisions can be made. If results show that a particular program produces significant net revenues but is under-enrolled, it would make sense to align recruitment efforts in this direction. Conversely, it may make sense to establish enrollment caps for other, high-cost programs to avoid incurring marginal costs to accommodate anything less than a full (or nearly full) cohort of students.

The analysis will help identify which programs might be attractive targets for competitors from the for-profit education sector. For the most part, these organizations are not interested in competing to offer instruction in the hard sciences or engineering; those programs require substantial investments in facilities and equipment. Instead, they want to capture the high-volume, high-return programs and courses to generate profits for their investors.

Gaining an in-depth understanding of cost and revenue structures also is crucial for campus business operations, such as auxiliary enterprises and charge-back units (for example, central stores, the physical plant, and copy centers). Based on the results of an analysis, units will know whether they are pricing goods and services appropriately to recover all costs.

Build reserves. Perhaps the simplest strategy for creating a central reserve of resources at the institution, college, or department level is to withhold a small percentage of the funds that otherwise would be available for distribution within that level of the organization. For instance, the president may withhold 2 percent of the anticipated overall increase in revenues to create a discretionary fund. The fund might finance new initiatives, respond to emergencies and opportunities, or cover expense overruns in central budgets. Similarly, a dean may divert a small percentage of the school's unrestricted resources to provide funds for crosscutting initiatives that will benefit the school as a whole.

All operating budgets should include at least a modest level of contingency funds. The central reserve goes beyond such contingencies. It provides a pool of resources—at whatever level it is created—to enhance the operational flexibility enjoyed at that level. Reserves might fund the creation of a research laboratory, for instance. Working with his or her senior cabinet, the president may decide the research laboratory represents the best use of the funds that otherwise would have been dispersed throughout the institution.

By drawing on the reserve, the institution can pursue initiatives that individual units probably can't afford. Reserves, however, represent a one-time, special use of resources. Initiatives should not consume central reserves on an ongoing basis.

Fewer Restrictions on Endowment Spending

Nearly all states have enacted versions of the Uniform Prudent Management of Institutional Funds Act (UPMIFA), which loosened prohibitions on spending from underwater endowments—those whose current market value had fallen below the original amount establishing the endowment. The previous restrictions were deemed impractical given that true endowments have a perpetual life.

Two major features of the act benefit colleges and universities. The most significant is the provision for prudent spending from underwater endowments; this provides institutions with the flexibility to spend a portion of principal to support the endowment's objectives.

The other provision establishes a streamlined process for addressing small endowments whose restricted purpose no longer is relevant. Following procedures established in their state, institutions can consolidate such endowments and use them for a purpose consistent with the donors' original intent.

Capture savings from position vacancies. Rather than impose specific targets for salary savings on operating units, an institution may require all (or a portion of) position vacancy savings to be captured centrally. Under this "lapsed salary" approach, whenever a position becomes vacant and the salaries and benefits are not expended as originally planned, the funds revert to a central account for distribution within the institution (or for addition to reserves).

It is not always possible to capture any savings, either because a replacement is hired immediately at a comparable salary or the savings must cover the payout of accumulated vacation and sick leave. When this is not the case, however, the savings generated by midyear departures or the delay in recruiting a replacement can enhance institutional flexibility.

Reduce the grade or rank of vacant positions. A college or university can centrally capture some surplus resources simply by downgrading positions that become vacant. In essence, this forces the hiring of replacements at lower salary levels, with the savings used for other purposes.

This strategy won't work in all situations. For instance, if a senior-level administrative position becomes vacant because a long-serving incumbent departed, the marketplace has likely changed; the replacement may demand an even higher salary. Similarly, if a senior researcher retires, creating a position vacancy, the overall research mission may dictate the recruitment of an equally accomplished researcher as a replacement.

Employ part-time or temporary faculty. Temporary faculty hired on a course-by-course basis are significantly less expensive than tenured faculty. Some department chairpersons routinely hold certain faculty lines vacant so that the unspent funds can be used to employ temporary faculty, thereby increasing the department's budget flexibility. This practice also is customary when faculty are on sabbatical or leave without pay. The salary savings generated can be used to meet other departmental needs, such as travel or small equipment.

While appealing from a flexibility standpoint, this strategy has drawbacks. Temporary faculty often become academic nomads, moving from one temporary position to another each semester or each year because they are unable to find permanent positions. And although these faculty may be well qualified in the classroom, they may not be as accessible to students and colleagues as permanent faculty. Their presence also can have a negative impact on the morale of the permanent faculty, who see positions being filled by people who may not be as committed to the institution or the discipline.

Withhold some salary-adjustment funds. Public institutions commonly receive funding for a specified percentage of total budgeted salaries to cover salary adjustments. This is true even when some positions remain vacant. Therefore, it is possible to gain increased flexibility at central or school/college levels by withholding the salary adjustment for any position not currently filled. The resources captured in this way then can be applied to other campus or unit priorities.

Carry over balances. State systems or independent institutions that permit the carryover of year-end balances from one fiscal year to the next have a natural source of budget flexibility. This liberal use of year-end balances reduces the pressure on units to spend all of their resources before year-end and encourages the saving of resources for major purchases or projects. It imposes additional burdens on central administration to ensure that the overall amount carried forward is reasonable.

In states that do not allow balance carryover, the institution must monitor the level of resources that units seek to carry forward, along with the amounts by which other units are prepared to overspend their budgets through accelerated purchases. This process would begin in the latter part of the fiscal year and continue through year-end. By matching up these situations, the institution can avoid either a surplus or a deficit for a portion of the budget while still achieving unit objectives.

In the subsequent year, the situation will be reversed, with the prior year's overspending units reducing their budgets by amounts equal to their prior year's overspending. This enables the previously underspent units to spend more in the current year. While this process provides flexibility, it also creates a significant administrative burden on the central offices that manage the effort.

Pursue sponsored research and training activities. Grant and contract awards include many direct costs (such as salaries, graduate student support, travel, and supplies) that enhance the financial position of the institution. External support also provides financial relief for committed research activities.

Recover overhead costs. Facilities and administrative costs charged to sponsored projects are based on actual expenses incurred to support all projects. When collected from the sponsor, however, there is no requirement to use the funds for purposes related to the specific sponsored projects generating the recoveries. With some modest limitations established by federal policy, the institution can use the funds for any purpose it deems appropriate.

In most independent institutions, overhead recoveries represent another revenue source similar to tuition or investment income. For some public institutions, however, state guidelines may require returning the funds to the state treasury—the source of funds for the original investments in support costs. Or states may impose specific rules about how the institution can utilize these funds.

A number of states allow institutions to retain and use overhead recoveries to support research. For instance, the funds might be used to make internal grants to young investigators to help them start their research. Alternatively, they may be allocated to cover the cost of travel to professional meetings at which faculty present their research findings.

Enhance fund-raising efforts. The financial support received from alumni, foundations, corporate allies, and friends is invaluable in helping meet institutional or constituent needs. Yet while all gifts provide value to institutions (or they should not be accepted), unrestricted gifts bring the added benefit of flexibility. With that in mind, work with donors so they understand the importance of gifts that carry no restrictions.

Engage in technology transfer. Technology transfer refers to the practice of leveraging an institution's intellectual property for commercial gain. Essentially, it involves licensing the use of inventions or discoveries to share knowledge and generate revenues.

At research institutions in particular, faculty and graduate students are continually engaged in the pursuit of knowledge; many undergraduate students engage in research activities as well. Sometimes their research results in a commercial application for which companies will pay substantial sums. Many institutions rely on a third party to commercialize discoveries, although others have established related foundations or internal units for this purpose. In these situations, revenues come from either a one-time sale or ongoing royalties from use of the discovery.

Some campuses elect to commercialize the discovery directly, and the resulting revenues represent a return on investment. Various models can apply to leveraging the discoveries, including a distribution of net revenues to the institution, the home department, and the researcher(s)—whether faculty, technicians, or students.

Key
Points

- The most effective institutions incorporate significant flexibility into their budgets. Recognizing that plans will not always achieve the desired outcomes, they remain prepared to adapt and change course.

- Enrollment fluctuations, revenue fluctuations, expense fluctuations, emergencies, and unforeseen opportunities all drive the need for budget flexibility.

- Building contingency into the budget is the most important strategy for enhancing flexibility.

A variety of institutional policies—not just those directly related to finances—carry financial implications. Based on the policies they adopt, for example, institutions can enhance or impair budget flexibility. While some policies are imposed on institutions, others reflect conscious decisions made by management to achieve specific objectives or for compliance reasons.

One way to influence budget decisions is to alter the policies and procedures related to resource allocation and use.

The Academic Side

Policies, procedures, and practices related to an institution's academic mission typically fall into the following categories.

Programmatic directions. The planning process that feeds into the budget process establishes priorities for academic and support programs and activities (see Chapter Six). The infrastructural plans, influenced by the strategic plan, provide the framework for allocating resources to encourage or promote selected activities. For example, if research is identified as a priority activity, departments that attract external research funding may receive increased allocations for positions and funds to allow increased faculty release time. Alternatively, if the research productivity is low because of insufficient resources within a department, the addition of a grant writer may be warranted.

If higher enrollments are the objective, academic departments that increase their enrollments may receive additional faculty positions or increased support costs per FTE faculty position. If the objective is to increase the use of instructional technology, at least two actions are likely. First, the units supporting faculty in these efforts will receive additional financial resources. Second, the individual faculty members pursuing technology in their teaching will receive enhanced staff support from the instructional technology unit (and likely go to the top of the list for upgraded personal computing). In each of these examples, the budget provides the mechanism for encouraging activities consistent with established priorities.

Programmatically, globalization has raised the need to accommodate different constituents' interests. First, study-abroad programs have risen in popularity among American students. Coordinating these programs not only requires specialized administrative systems and processes but also raises risk management concerns—all of which carry attendant costs (for example, for travel insurance, health care, and security).

At the same time, substantial numbers of international students study at American colleges and universities each year. The presence of students from many diverse cultures can strain programs and systems designed to accommodate domestic student needs and interests. For example, accommodating unique dietary restrictions in the dining hall, offering enhanced diversity within student life experiences, and recruiting faculty with the requisite experience all have budgetary implications.

As budgeters consider program priorities, they also must identify a means for measuring operational progress. The measures typically combine **quantitative indexes** (such as student-faculty ratios, student credit hours per FTE faculty position, and square footage maintained by the physical plant) and **qualitative indicators**. The latter might include the quality of a department's faculty, national reputation of a department, or service orientation of support units.

Input measures (such as the average SAT score of entering freshmen) and output measures (such as the number of students graduating) no longer provide enough information to constituents. The emphasis has shifted to outcome measures, primarily in response to the rising cost of an education. Rather than measuring the number of graduates, for instance, students and their parents want to know whether the graduates found jobs in their desired fields or gained admission to graduate school. Not all indicators lend themselves to quantification, increasing the need for professional judgment.

Each policy and procedure related to academic programming should be evaluated by three measurements:

- The extent to which the quality of the activity or program is being improved
- The extent to which the activity is responding to a change in workload or demand
- The extent to which the purpose of the activity is being altered (diminished, expanded, or redirected)

Making Changes

Four factors come into play when considering changes in a budget:

- **Increases (or decreases) resulting from inflation (or deflation).** Inflation or deflation factors reflect changes in the prices of goods and services, including cost-of-living adjustments to salaries and wages.

- **Increases or decreases related to workload.** Changes in enrollment, the demand for course offerings, the number of courses and sections taught, and the volume of sponsored activity can all lead to changes in faculty workload. Changes in administrative and staff workload mean a different level of service provided or a larger (or smaller) number of activities being undertaken.

- Improvements in, or deterioration of, the quality of a program or activity. This factor accounts for qualitative variations among programs and activities. A decision to decrease average faculty instructional workload might be made with the expectation of either enhancing the quality of instruction or improving the volume of research. Another approach might be enhancing technology to improve the instructional quality or effectiveness of faculty.

- The introduction of new or the elimination of existing programs or activities. Changes in academic programs may lead to the need to add faculty or reassign existing tenured faculty. Similarly, different types of activities may call for different administrative support services.

Considering all of these factors enables decision makers to be more discriminating when adopting budget strategies and more accurate in projecting the consequences of those strategies.

Allocation of faculty positions. Decisions about the distribution of vacant faculty positions, or which dollars to earmark for faculty hires, take on greater significance if support money automatically follows the faculty position. Before decision makers can allocate faculty positions, they must have a systematic way to establish them.

An institution can create a new position only when it has sufficient resources to cover compensation. The resources might come from tuition, endowment income, state appropriations (frequently tied to enrollment), or other sources not otherwise committed. Non-endowment gifts typically do not support a new faculty position, because the position usually represents an ongoing commitment. Unless the situation is unique (for example, a visiting scholar), most institutions require the identification of an ongoing revenue source, such as tuition or endowment income, before creating a new position. Existing faculty positions can be vacated through retirement, resignation, death, tenure denial, or a decision not to renew a nontenure-track position's contract.

Most institutions have a hierarchy of decision-making authority for the allocation of faculty positions. In one model, the chief executive or chief academic officer controls all faculty positions. All new and vacant positions are pooled, and units must submit requests with appropriate rationale if they seek additional faculty resources.

In some cases, faculty positions are controlled at the school or college level. The department heads or research directors submit requests for faculty positions to the dean of the college or school. These requests usually relate to vacancies because new positions require approval from the highest level— either the president or the provost. Occasional exceptions involve endowed chairs, but even in these cases the central administration must authorize the acceptance of the gift that provides funding for the position.

Teaching loads. Most institutions consider some measure of instructional workload when allocating resources to departments. Four of the most common indicators are student-faculty ratio, average student credit hours per FTE faculty position, faculty contact hours (weekly time spent in the classroom or lab), and number of courses taught. Departments with larger credit-hour loads have higher student-faculty ratios and generate, on average, more student credit hours per FTE faculty position. To determine the policy implications of these ratios, one also must consider the effect of the class size on teaching loads (and, more important, on learning outcomes).

Class size and instructional methodology also dictate the relationship between faculty contact hours and student-faculty ratios. The advent of more effective online instructional delivery has dramatically altered the way in which contact-hour measures and student-faculty ratios are used. The indicators generally are best used as a basis for initial analysis of the teaching/learning process, not as the sole basis for allocation decisions.

Departments that depend heavily on labor-intensive laboratory or studio instruction will have lower ratios than departments that rely on large lectures. Questions to ask include:

- Is there an opportunity to alter the mix between laboratory instruction and large lecture?

- Does the discipline require individualized instruction (as in the case of studio training for musicians)?

- Do accreditation standards mandate certain instructional methodologies?

- Is it possible to respond to increased student demand by relying more heavily on instructional technology, as opposed to adding additional faculty positions?

Individual faculty teaching loads vary widely, even within a single department. Within a given department, the following questions can be raised:

- Are faculty with lighter teaching loads given reduced loads as a matter of tradition or policy—or because they are more active and productive as scholars or more engaged in service activities?

- Are faculty teaching loads skewed by rank? For instance, are senior faculty required to teach only six courses per academic year, while assistant professors must teach seven? If so, does this practice prevent the junior faculty from competing effectively for sponsored research funding, thereby adversely affecting their likelihood of obtaining tenure?

- Do faculty members with equivalent credit-hour production actually have comparable workloads? For instance, does one individual teach large lecture sections of only two courses, while another teaches several different courses with fewer students per class?

- Do some faculty teach the same courses year after year, or are course assignments rotated throughout the department?

In addition to answering questions like these and making interdepartmental comparisons, conduct a trend analysis of departments' workload over time. An appropriate balance may have deteriorated, either because of increased demand without additional resources or reduced enrollments without a corresponding reduction in staffing.

It also is beneficial to consider a wide range of factors when making interdepartmental comparisons. Legitimate reasons may support major differences between seemingly similar departments. For instance, some disciplines enjoy an increased opportunity for sponsored support. If some faculty in those departments attract grants, their success will affect instructional ratios for the whole department.

Weighting factors for teaching loads. Faculty positions frequently are allocated based on measures of instructional load. The measures typically consist of elements weighted by level of instruction or level of student. Weighting is skewed in favor of advanced levels of instruction and students under the theory that the effort at higher levels is more time-consuming for faculty and, therefore, more expensive.

The relative difference among weights also may reflect institutional priorities regarding instruction at various levels. For instance, lower-level undergraduate courses might be weighted at 1.0, upper-level undergraduate courses at 1.5, graduate instruction at 2.0, and graduate research at 3.0. These particular weights, which may be totally arbitrary, assume that a faculty member engaged in research involving graduate students invests three times as much effort as a faculty member teaching a lower-level undergraduate course. Although instructional effort varies by discipline and even course, these variations usually are ignored, and weighting is applied uniformly across the curriculum.

If the weighting used to compute teaching load reflects institutional priorities, any revision in the weighting should result from a change in priorities. If resources are allocated based on weighted student credit hours, for example, a change in weights will lead to a change in the distribution of resources. Figure 11-1 demonstrates how a change in weighting in favor of graduate instruction and research can alter the distribution of resources.

Figure 11-1 Illustration–Faculty Staffing as Determined by Weighting Factors
(Assume 1.0 FTE faculty position carries a load of 600 weighted credit hours.)

	Credit Hours by Level of Instruction	Weighting Factor Current	Revised	Weighted Credit Hours Current	Revised	Net Increase
Department A						
Lower division	3,000	1.00	1.00	3,000	3,000	
Upper division	4,000	1.50	1.50	6,000	6,000	
Graduate instruction	1,500	2.00	2.50	3,000	3,750	
Graduate research	500	3.00	3.50	1,500	1,750	
Total	**9,000**			**13,500**	**14,500**	
Divide by full-time load # of				600	600	
FTE faculty positions				22.5	24.2	1.7
Department B						
Lower division	2,000	1.00	1.00	2,000	2,000	
Upper division	3,000	1.50	1.50	4,500	4,500	
Graduate instruction	2,500	2.00	2.50	5,000	6,250	
Graduate research	1,000	3.00	3.50	3,000	3,500	
Total	**8,500**			**14,500**	**16,250**	
Divide by full-time load # of				600	600	
FTE faculty positions				24.2	27.1	2.9

Under the existing weighting, even though Department A produces more unweighted credit hours, Department B is entitled to more faculty positions because it produces relatively more hours at the graduate level. Changing the weighting in favor of graduate effort results in an even greater disparity in the number of positions assigned to Department B. This change could be the result of a change in priority or the result of analysis indicating that the revised weighting more accurately reflects the relative effort required at the various levels.

Distribution of faculty ranks. Departments with a higher proportion of junior faculty typically are less expensive to support because salaries are lower. In addition to the fiscal implications of the distribution of faculty by years of experience and rank, there are several academic considerations:

- Is the proportion of tenured faculty low enough to provide for the periodic addition of "new blood"?
- Are the guidelines for promotion clearly established and communicated?
- Do tenure and promotion criteria differ significantly from one department to the next? How are exceptions handled when the opportunity arises to recruit a faculty "star"?
- Is the distribution of faculty expertise within a discipline or department appropriate for its instructional and research missions?
- Are vacant positions filled at the same rank as that of the former incumbent?

Even dramatic changes in policies and procedures cannot quickly change faculty demographics—especially when a substantial percentage of the faculty are tenured.

Distribution of faculty salaries. The salary distribution issue typically arises when a department seeks to fill a vacant faculty position, especially one in the senior ranks. One common strategy—filling vacant senior professorial posts from among current junior faculty—has the benefit of upward mobility, which encourages junior faculty to remain at the institution. This also enables the institution to invest salary savings elsewhere. Finally, replacing the junior faculty with an outside hire thereby introduces "new blood" into the department.

The biggest drawback to this approach is the potential for a leadership void. Unless the junior faculty member being promoted can provide the leadership lost with the senior faculty member's departure, the department may suffer. A department staffed primarily with junior faculty needs senior leadership to respond to the challenges that arise. If the person promoted cannot provide it, any benefits from salary savings or improved morale among junior faculty may be offset.

Use these questions to guide consideration of salaries:

- Does the distribution of faculty salaries correspond to faculty ranks?

- Is the distribution of faculty salaries more closely aligned with seniority or with the faculty's contributions and professional accomplishments? What incentives and disincentives result?

- How large (or small) is the gap between salaries for new hires and those with long service? What factors have influenced this gap, and what are its effects on faculty job satisfaction or the ability to recruit qualified faculty?

- Do the differences in faculty salaries across disciplines reflect market conditions?

Salary compression occurs when only a negligible difference exists between the salaries of junior and senior faculty members. The problem typically surfaces when the salaries for current employees have not kept pace with the market due to resource challenges. When new employees are hired at competitive rates, the gap between the two groups shrinks, and the premium for experience erodes. In extreme cases, salary compression can become salary inversion, which occurs when the starting salary for new hires exceeds the salaries of current employees. There is no national standard for the size of the salary-adjustment pool or the split between merit and cost-of-living adjustments. In some public institutions, the state determines the cost-of-living adjustment applied to all state employees, including faculty. Within the constraints of collective bargaining arrangements, institutions striving for improved effectiveness tend to invest more dollars in the merit pool so they can reward individual performance. Many institutions find it easier to distribute increases pro rata, thereby avoiding decisions on how to distribute merit-based increases.

When resources become available, an institution that has been unable to provide competitive salaries will attempt to remedy this situation quickly. Similarly, if an institution wants to increase its salary ranking among peer institutions, it will likely invest more in salaries than in other operating expense categories. In most cases, the merit-adjustment pool is calculated as a percentage of total salaries and distributed to each academic and administrative unit for the assignment to individual faculty and staff.

If the chief executive officer, chief academic officer, or deans reserve a portion of the total salary-adjustment pool so they can address recruitments and promotions or match offers, this necessarily reduces the merit pool. The merit pool also will shrink if used to supplement departmental allocations to remedy disparities in terms of market conditions or institutional priorities.

Use of part-time and temporary faculty. As budgets become tighter, departments and institutions stretch their dollars by hiring part-time and temporary faculty. Generally, these faculty members receive considerably less compensation and benefits than permanent faculty members. They may not be eligible for some benefits, thus increasing the institution's savings. In addition, departments can hire part-time faculty only when student demand or other factors, such as faculty sabbaticals, make the move necessary.

Excessive reliance on part-time or temporary faculty has several disadvantages. First, although many adjuncts are excellent instructors, some are not as skilled as permanent faculty. Because of the relatively low compensation they receive, they have little incentive to enhance their skills. In addition, adjuncts typically have relatively heavier course loads than permanent faculty, leaving little time for their own scholarly pursuits. Part-time faculty also tend to be less available to students and colleagues because of their other employment activities. The institution's lack of commitment often prompts part-time faculty to find the highest bidder for their services, as they jump from one temporary position to another. Finally, accreditation agencies may question the quality of instructional efforts when an institution relies heavily on part-time and temporary faculty.

Institutional policies may dictate the hiring of part-time faculty only with funds budgeted for that purpose or with savings from vacant permanent faculty positions. Or an institution may prohibit using permanent faculty position vacancy savings to hire part-time faculty. Collective bargaining agreements sometimes drive these policies, or they evolve from an institutional desire to rely on full-time faculty to the maximum extent possible.

Some states closely monitor the status of permanent employee positions at public colleges and universities. If a department attempts to maintain vacancies for the purpose of employing part-time or temporary faculty, thereby stretching the compensation budget, the state might simply eliminate the permanent position in a subsequent budget cycle.

Public institutions also may draw criticism if they appear to put dollars ahead of academic quality by hiring adjuncts. Reacting to undergraduate complaints about the overuse of part-time or temporary faculty, some states limit the number that can be employed in a given period. Other states set a cap on the overall faculty head count; hiring too many part-time faculty may cause an institution to exceed the cap.

Many policy questions relate to part-time and temporary faculty, and they include the following:

- Should departments have the latitude to hold faculty positions vacant solely to provide resources for temporary hiring?

- What is the proper balance between instruction provided by permanent full-time faculty versus temporary or part-time faculty, especially at the undergraduate level?

- How are savings from the reliance on part-time or temporary faculty used? Are they captured centrally, or do they support the department's instruction, research, or service activities?

Sabbatical leaves. Many institutions have a policy for faculty that provides one year of leave at half salary or one semester at full salary for every six to 10 years of full-time service. Some institutions award one-semester sabbaticals every seventh semester.

For one-year faculty leaves, departments use the salary savings to employ part-time instructors to cover the permanent instructor's courses or pay overload to other permanent faculty. Any surplus is used to cover other departmental needs or is captured centrally. Arrangements that allow for full pay during one-semester sabbaticals prove costly for departments because no savings are available to pay part-time faculty. Common questions related to sabbaticals include the following:

- Are sabbaticals guaranteed for all faculty meeting the minimum service requirements?

- What expectations regarding scholarly accomplishment have been established for faculty members who are granted sabbaticals?

- Are faculty expected or required to seek outside funding to cover part of the sabbatical leave?

- If one-semester sabbaticals at full pay are permitted, are the faculty member's courses canceled, or are other arrangements made (such as temporary instructors employed to teach the courses or overload payments to other permanent faculty)?

Graduate assistants. Graduate assistantships offer significant flexibility in staffing departmental responsibilities. Departments might use graduate assistants as graders, lab section coordinators, instructors of independent sections, or research assistants. Various models govern how assistantships are allocated throughout the institution and within departments. They may be based on seniority, on the percentage of teaching load represented by large lecture classes, or on scholarly or research productivity. Another approach is simply to allocate the positions across the board based solely on enrollment.

Budgetary questions related to graduate assistantships include the following:

• Is the assistantship an entitlement such that all graduate students enrolled in certain programs receive one?

• Do graduate stipends and salaries vary? If so, on what basis?

• Are assistantships limited in duration or available as long as the graduate student remains in good standing?

Academic support staff. The distribution of academic support staff—such as clerical workers, laboratory technicians, and grants specialists—may vary significantly from one department to the next. The differences may result from specific instructional methodologies, the nature and extent of research activities, instructional loads, service commitments, or historical patterns.

Increased use of technology, especially personal computers, has reduced the need for clerical support, leading to the elimination of many support positions. Once the hardware and software costs have been covered, what happens to the savings represented by the elimination of the positions? Keep in mind that the technology acquisition costs represent a one-time expense that won't be repeated for several years. The position savings, after covering the technology costs, become permanent.

Typical questions related to support staff include the following:

• Do all departments have a need for support staff?

• What is the basis for allocating support staff across departments?

• Is it possible to share staff across departmental lines due to the sporadic nature of some workloads?

The Administrative Side

The academic portion of the institutional budget cannot be understood without analyzing its relationship to the administrative and support budgets. If the academic mission (instruction, research, and service) is paramount, administrative and support budgets should facilitate activities in the academic arena. Over time, however, these activities can become ends unto themselves. For this reason, some campuses require periodic reviews of support units to ensure they continue to support the academic mission effectively.

Policies, procedures, and practices related to an institution's administrative efforts typically fall into the following categories:

Administrative support. This category includes activities, such as human resources, finance, and advancement as well as other areas that support academic activities, either directly or indirectly.

Here are relevant questions to ask about each activity:

- Is the service essential to the campus?

- Does the service provided by the support unit duplicate services available from other units?

- To what extent are new technologies (such as automated systems) or approaches (such as outsourcing and shared services) being utilized to reduce the overall cost of the service or improve its effectiveness?

- Have performance standards for the service been established? If so, are they monitored on a regular basis?

A different set of questions is appropriate for auxiliary enterprises:

- Have the activities been assessed to determine whether they should be self-operated, outsourced, or discontinued because they no longer contribute to institutional success?

- Are the activities self-supporting?

- Are they expected to pay a fair share of the institution's operating expenses, such as utilities and central administrative services (payroll, accounting, and purchasing)?

- Are the units able to generate and maintain reserves adequate to meet operating needs, including facilities maintenance as well as future program expansion?

Physical plant operations. Higher education finds itself in the unique position of being both labor-intensive and capital-intensive. Unlike other labor-intensive industries, for example, higher education invests substantially in facilities and other physical resources. Even institutions that favor online delivery of their academic mission invest heavily in technology infrastructure.

Questions relevant to physical plant operations include the following:

- Has the campus achieved all possible savings related to energy usage and efficiency?

- Do all campus facilities have a preventive maintenance plan?

- Is deferred maintenance measured regularly and assessed with respect to its appropriateness given the current operating environment?
- Does the unit have a process for determining when a facility has outlived its usefulness, given current needs and demands?
- Has the unit devoted appropriate attention to issues related to ecological sustainability?

Information technology. This category has registered explosive spending, whether for instructional technology, ERPs, wired and wireless infrastructure, networks, data warehouses, or other technological applications. Staying current with technology is challenging at best; most institutions make incremental progress.

The relevant questions for IT include the following:

- Has the institution established a strategy to guide decisions on whether to use homegrown, purchased, or outsourced applications?
- Has the institution considered pursuit of cloud-based and open-source solutions to address technology needs?
- Has the institution established policies to support the varying types of desktop technology?
- Does one unit oversee all technology, or are separate units established for academic and administrative technology?
- Has the institution established life-cycle standards for the various categories of technology to ensure that resources are not being wasted by supporting outdated or obsolete technology?

Student affairs. This administrative and support area is unique because of its direct involvement with an institution's primary constituents: the students. When reviewing student affairs, answers to the following questions may prove enlightening:

- Do on-campus housing policies support enrollment plans and contribute to auxiliary units' success? For instance, are freshmen required to live on campus and, if so, also required to purchase a campus meal plan?
- Are the offerings for student entertainment and other activities attractive enough to encourage students to stay on campus, thus avoiding potential problems with the surrounding community?
- Does the campus use residential colleges, led by faculty principals, or language houses to supplement formal instruction with extracurricular activities?

Operating expenses. Both academic departments and support units can be evaluated in terms of how effectively they use their resources to cover day-to-day operating expenses, such as travel, supplies, and services, as well as to acquire small equipment. The following questions might help assess performance in this area:

- Are units held accountable if they overspend their operating budgets?

- Does the institution enable units to carry forward unspent funds from one fiscal year to the next (to avoid creating an incentive for units to waste money late in the fiscal year rather than appear not to need it)?

- Are unit operations periodically examined to determine whether a portion of their existing budgets can be reallocated to a central pool to provide funds for higher-priority initiatives?

- Are travel funds allocated based on a clearly defined methodology?

Multiyear budgeting. The number of budget cycles influences the perspective taken during the budget process. Attention to one budget cycle focused on a single fiscal year leads to short-term thinking, primarily related to incremental changes from the current year's budget. Expanding the process to focus on multiple years encourages a more proactive approach—and has the added benefit of being recommended by some accrediting agencies.

Understandably, the out years will have fewer details, but they can still highlight shifts in priorities and broad institutional changes. For instance, an academic program being phased out over time will eventually free up resources for allocation to other units or for other purposes; the preliminary budgets for the transition years can reflect this decision.

Budget format. In most public institutions, the state dictates the format for the submission to the state. Although it may be more efficient to use the same format for internal budget purposes, the state's prescribed format may not match well with the institution's needs. For this reason, most public institutions use higher education-specific formats for internal budgeting and then aggregate the detailed information to comply with the state's prescribed format.

Both public and independent institutions should periodically assess the budget structure and the types of information it contains. As with financial statements, budgets tell different stories. A budget that has functional or programmatic expense categories, such as instruction, research, and institutional support, will not have the same structure as one that displays expenses in natural categories, such as salaries, benefits, and travel.

The combination of the two formats generally is recognized as the most beneficial for decision making. The easiest way to combine the formats is with a simple matrix: The columns present natural expense categories, and the rows present the information sorted by functional category. (See Figure 1-1 on page 7.)

Related questions about budget format address issues about all-funds budgeting versus unrestricted funds only. Undoubtedly, it is easier to focus only on the unrestricted funds when developing budgets, but this approach is distorting and tends to result in suboptimal spending and management decisions. Moreover, when restricted resources are essential to achieving the institution's aspirations, it's very misleading not to proactively manage these resources.

All-funds budgeting focuses on all resources available to support the institution's operations. It allows an institution to concentrate on the full magnitude of its operations, not just those financed through tuition and state operating appropriations. By relying on a single consolidated budget and a comprehensive process to manage and control operating resources, an institution will have the best opportunity to ensure its priorities are established effectively and funded adequately.

This approach also has the benefit of focusing on the full range of resources, allowing an institution to monitor its use of restricted resources more effectively. This can be especially important at public institutions and independent institutions with decentralized departments that manage significant levels of gift or endowment income accounts. When the resources are not budgeted and monitored centrally, departments could hoard those funds rather than deploy them in support of established priorities.

Revenue Policies

How revenues are projected, how institutional priorities are set, and what institutional policies and procedures are in place all influence the budget and the budget process. In both public and independent institutions, here are the primary determinants of revenue:

Enrollment projections. Projecting student enrollment is more art than science. The science involves determining key variables, such as acceptance rates, student retention rates, tuition levels, and the overall attractiveness of its academic programs. The art of enrollment management focuses on tasks such as recruiting students to maximize net revenue while achieving the desired student body characteristics.

National and local trends affect recruitment and enrollment as well. National high school graduate projections are projected to range from a low of 3,189,000 students expected in fiscal year 2014 to a high of 3,369,000 in 2021.[126]

Numerous other factors help determine an institution's potential applicant pool, not the least of which is the institution's character. They will shape the kinds of questions to address in this area:

- What is the target population, and what institutional characteristics help define that population?
- What information is known about the target population, and how can this information be leveraged to improve the results of student recruitment?
- Can the target population be expanded, either to grow enrollments or to enhance the quality of the student body?
- How can the institution's character be modified to make the institution more attractive to potential applicants? For instance, what new programs can be added?
- Can additional housing be built?
- Should the institution switch from Division I athletics to Division II or vice versa?

As the competition for students has increased, advertising and recruitment campaigns have become more aggressive. Although some states prohibit their public institutions from engaging in student-recruitment marketing, others recognize that attracting the best entering students may make this practice a wise investment. Relevant questions include:

- Should the institution employ its own publicity staff or contract for advertising services?
- What kind of advertising and marketing should be undertaken, and how should it be targeted?
- How can faculty, alumni, and current students become involved in recruitment efforts to enhance the overall results?
- What's the most effective way to utilize social media (for example, Twitter and Facebook) to expand on traditional recruitment methods?

Every institution has a pool of applicants that will overlap with pools of other institutions. The objective for each institution is to attract the most desirable students within that pool. Applicants are screened by the admissions office (and perhaps by a faculty committee), which evaluates each candidate according to institutional acceptance criteria.

Because many potential students apply to multiple institutions, an institution is unlikely to admit all those who are accepted. As a result, enrollment projections must be based on a firm understanding of the historical acceptance and matriculation rates—and the belief that nothing will prevent the institution from achieving similar results in the future. When major changes in institutional character occur—such as eliminating a requirement for lower-division students to live on campus or significantly revising acceptance criteria—the old acceptance and matriculation patterns may no longer hold true. Significant changes in economic conditions and shifting approaches by competitors can affect patterns as well.

Enrollment projections must be adjusted to reflect overall trends in changes in student load or persistence. Questions to consider include:

- If the number of students offered admission is too low, are admissions standards too demanding?
- If the number of students offered admission is too high, are admission standards too lax?
- To what extent will more attractive student aid packages improve acceptance and matriculation rates?
- Are life experiences appropriately credited in evaluating candidates for admission?
- What special requirements and obligations are associated with equal opportunity in the admissions process?
- Are transfer students encouraged to apply?
- Are admittance rates for transfer students adjusted to compensate for changes in the admittance rates of first-time students?
- Is sufficient effort invested in retaining current students?
- Do course availability and scheduling impede students' progress toward their degrees? For instance, is it possible to complete a four-year program within four academic years?

Admission to graduate programs is usually treated differently than admission to undergraduate programs. As a result, a different set of issues must be explored:

- Is admission to graduate programs administered by an office of graduate admissions or by individual departments?
- Does the office of graduate studies control the allocation of admissions slots by department and program? If not, are departments free to admit as many qualified students as they can attract?
- Who determines the criteria for admission to graduate programs? Who is authorized to make exceptions to the criteria?
- Are the financial aid or graduate assistantship packages attractive to prospective students?
- How are sponsored program training awards integrated with admissions policies to ensure that qualified students are admitted to take maximum advantage of such awards?

One aspect of enrollment projections is estimating the number of matriculated students who will continue at the institution through graduation. Over time, a retention history evolves to guide the projections. Students remain or depart from institutions for any number of reasons, including financial need, academic performance, family demands, employment considerations, and their relative satisfaction with the quality of their academic experience. Because it makes sense both financially and academically to retain as many students as possible, many institutions invest significantly in programs designed to enhance student retention. Budgeters should ask questions about these programs as well:

- Are the retention programs achieving the desired results?

- Is the program's success being examined in light of the program's relative cost?

- Are data being gathered for use in helping to prevent students from departing before earning a degree? Is this information shared with faculty to determine what changes might be needed in the overall approach to the delivery of academic programs?

Tuition and financial aid. A key variable in the determination of revenues is net tuition (tuition minus financial aid awarded to students). Tuition levels typically are established in close relationship with enrollment projections, expectations about nontuition revenues, and assumptions about overall expenses. In today's environment, another factor enters the mix: institutional financial aid.

Tuition usually is thought of as the published rate charged to students. In many cases—especially at independent colleges and universities—the published tuition rates bear little relationship to the amounts actually paid by students, due to the aid being awarded to attract students. This practice is referred to as tuition discounting.

With tuition discounting, institutions publish a standard tuition rate and then award institutional financial aid to reduce the net cost of attendance for the student. As a result, the process of setting tuition prices and institutional aid budgets has become an iterative one. It requires the consideration of investment returns, expectations regarding gifts available for scholarships, appropriations (for public institutions and even some independent ones), the overall budget picture, and the quality of students being recruited.

A number of institutions package aid to minimize student debt, especially for low-income students. This has been true for a number of years at elite independent institutions and, with a few notable exceptions of institutions reacting to the difficult economy, continues to be a trend. What's different is that public institutions now pursue a similar approach to enhance their competitiveness. Several public flagship institutions have begun structuring aid packages that are very attractive to low-income students and significantly enhance the diversity of the student body.

When determining tuition levels, a key consideration is the amount of net revenue that will be realized per student. This factor is particularly important for smaller institutions, where even a modest change can dramatically impact faculty and staff positions as well as basic services. Additionally, a number of independent institutions have adopted a comprehensive fee combining charges for tuition, housing, dining, and student activities. This makes the calculation of net revenue per student much easier, although it also can produce sticker shock for some prospective students. Despite the sticker shock, it is a logical approach to pricing because it's the total cost that matters—not whether it's tuition, housing, or activities.

The following questions should be asked when reviewing a potential tuition increase:

- What impact is the increase likely to have on enrollments?
- Is there a price point at which a tuition increase actually reduces net revenue?
- Is it possible that a tuition freeze or even a price reduction (with a corresponding decrease in institutional financial aid) would be more beneficial financially?
- How much should competitors' practices be considered in setting tuition rates?
- How much should federal financial aid programs be considered in setting tuition rates?
- Is variable tuition pricing an option? That is, should tuition rates vary based on the demand for particular programs, student class level, or the cost of instruction—particularly for high-cost programs?
- Assuming that a public institution has the authority to set tuition levels, how much extra, if any, should be charged to out-of-state students?
- What is the appropriate relationship between undergraduate and graduate tuition?
- How should institutional financial aid be factored into the determination of tuition?
- Should tuition be determined independent of other fees, such as housing and dining?

Fees. Most institutions set fees in combination with tuition. Setting fees for services, such as dining, housing, and parking, can be more complex than setting tuition because more factors need to be considered. Although competition and overall resource needs help determine tuition levels, the range of issues related to other fees assessed to students is much broader.

Obviously, operating costs factor into the equation. But so do working capital reserves, facilities maintenance reserves, costs of holding inventory (especially significant for bookstores and dining services), and fluctuating employment levels. Student fees are the primary revenue source for auxiliary units, which operate as self-supporting businesses. Nevertheless, the business needs of an auxiliary unit cannot be allowed to push the overall cost of attendance to levels that result in decreased enrollment.

Student fees also help fund activities, such as intramural sports, student government, student clubs, and student health and counseling centers. In some cases, fees pay for student access to intercollegiate athletics events. Other fee assessments relate more directly to academic activities, such as laboratory fees for courses taken in certain programs, technology fees, and special fees for individual music lessons or models for studio art programs.

Public institutions may have a unique opportunity when it comes to setting fees. Although it is not unusual for states to control tuition rates, they frequently do not control fees. In fact, in some states where tuition is heavily controlled and fees are not, the combined value of fees assessed to students may be significantly higher than the tuition paid.

Some public institutions that control the setting of fees, but not tuition, rely on fund transfers from auxiliary units for resources to cover some needs of academic units. This practice has been especially common since states have reduced appropriation support for campuses while preventing them from raising tuition rates.

Endowment income. The typical budgeter does not have direct involvement with endowment management. This usually is handled by the institution's treasurer, a committee of the governing board, or—in the case of many public institutions—staff at an independent fund-raising foundation affiliated with the institution.

Nevertheless, many policies related to endowments and endowment income concern budgeters:

- What are the investment objectives for the endowment? Are they focused primarily on current yield or long-term growth? (Too much emphasis on either one can be problematic. Current yield is needed to provide resources for operating expenses, but growth is essential to maintaining the endowment's purchasing power over time.)

- Is there a clearly defined asset allocation strategy?

- What is the rate of return on the portfolio? How does this rate compare with the returns for endowments of a similar size?

- What is the spending rate, and how is it calculated?

- Are procedures in place to ensure the adequate support for programs and activities, even if the endowment returns are negative in a given period?

Other policy issues relate more specifically to the income generated by the endowment:

- How is the income from unrestricted endowments used? Does it primarily support continuing operations, or is some or all of it used as seed money for new initiatives?

- How much of the endowment income is set aside to respond to contingencies?

- Is there any type of institutional matching program designed to encourage individual units to solicit new endowment gifts, under which the income will be matched by state or institutional resources?

- What portion of the endowment is restricted by donors, and how are these resources taken into consideration when unrestricted revenues are allocated throughout the institution?

Gifts. Many colleges and universities receive significantly more revenue from annual giving than from endowment income. Gifts are less predictable, however, because historical data usually determines the amount of endowment income available for spending in a given year. Nevertheless, an effective development operation can predict gift revenues with a reasonable degree of accuracy using analysis of past giving patterns and known plans for future periods. Key questions include:

- Does the institution have a process for measuring the cost of fund-raising? If yes, does the institution measure the success of fund-raising against the investment made to generate gifts?

- Does the institution pursue multiple gift strategies, including annual giving, giving societies, major gifts, planned gifts, and other methods?

- How much fund-raising effort is expected of individuals not working directly in development? For instance, are deans, department heads, and individual faculty members expected to participate in development activities?

- Does the institution maintain an alumni affairs office? If so, how closely is this office integrated with development?

- For religiously affiliated institutions, is the church a significant source of revenue?

- For public institutions, what is the relationship to the affiliated fund-raising foundation? Does the foundation determine how it will support the institution, or is this responsibility shared with institutional management?

Sponsored program funding. Sponsored support is another category that can be difficult to predict with a high degree of accuracy. Nevertheless, institutions for which sponsored programs represent a significant revenue source typically develop sophisticated models for predicting the volume of revenue to be received. In most cases, awards are received before the funding itself; this is especially true with multiyear awards, which may be for as long as five years.

With a sponsored activity, the funds are committed to a particular project and may not be used for other purposes. Accurate predictions are still important, however, because amounts funded from sponsored sources may provide budgetary relief for other unrestricted budget resources. In addition, indirect cost recoveries usually accompany such funding. In most instances, this revenue represents unrestricted funds that the institution can use for any operating purpose.

In theory, the overhead recovery funds reimburse the institution for overhead expenses incurred in support of sponsored activity. In practice, however, recoveries sometimes are used for a variety of purposes. These might include seed funding for young investigators, lab equipment, stipends for graduate assistants, supplemental funding for research libraries, and other objectives that aren't necessarily connected directly to sponsored activities.

The questions to be asked regarding sponsored support focus on two general areas. The first includes policies governing activity outside the institution—particularly those involving the federal government, the largest sponsor and the most influential participant from a regulatory standpoint. The second area includes policies related to the conduct of research and the use of overhead recoveries.

- What are the current federal research priorities?

- Are the institution's academic activities aligned with those priorities? If not, is it possible to shift priorities to compete more effectively for this funding?

- How significant is the institution's technology transfer activity, and does it lend itself to partnerships with business, industry, or governmental entities?

- Does the institution have a mechanism to support investigators' pursuit of nongovernmental sources of sponsored funding (such as foundations and corporations)?

- What are the institution's practices relative to overhead recoveries? Are they captured centrally and treated as another revenue source? Or are they allocated throughout the institution to support additional research initiatives or related activities? (For instance, some institutions routinely allocate a percentage of overhead recoveries to the principal investigator or his or her department as an incentive to stimulate additional research.)

- Does the institution allow overhead waivers to reduce the cost to sponsors when unique circumstances justify them?

Other Operational Policies and Practices

Independent institutions have more control over internal policies and procedures than public institutions, which usually must adhere to the same guidelines established for state agencies, even though their missions are dramatically different. Even with the flexibility enjoyed by independent institutions, the combination of professional standards and federal guidelines tend to mitigate most of any competitive advantage they might otherwise enjoy in these main areas.

Accounting. The complex structure of accounts used by many institutions is designed to ensure that funds can be monitored and used only for appropriate purposes. For example, colleges and universities—especially many public ones—are precluded from using funds budgeted for salaries and wages for purposes other than compensation. Other categories of operating expenses may enjoy greater spending flexibility, especially in situations that do not rely on line-item budgeting.

Accounts or funds frequently are established to ensure certain revenue sources are spent for their specified purposes. For instance, sponsored agreements have special rules related to the use of the resources. Similarly, proceeds from bond issues typically must be spent for specific capital projects. Some institutions assess special fees for activities, such as laboratory work, student activities, or technology. In such cases, the institution may require these revenues be accounted for in specific funds so they can be matched against investments in these activities.

Internal, independent, and—in some cases—federal auditors assess the degree to which faculty and staff actually comply with accounting policies and procedures. Auditors examine not only the accuracy of management reports and financial statements but also the appropriateness of expense transfers, the documentation supporting expenses, and the overall internal control structure.

Anyone with budgetary responsibility must understand several aspects of the accounting structure. Selected topics include:

- The nature of the expenses that represent appropriate charges to a specific account.
- The extent to which funds or expense charges may be transferred between accounts.
- Constraints on the use of resources imposed by the fund structure within the institution.

Financial and budgetary reporting. All institutions have financial and budgetary reporting system(s) to monitor the flow of funds and support compliance efforts. Commercially available software provides integrated applications linking modules focused on accounting, budgeting, procurement, payroll, fixed assets, and many other financial areas. This integration can reduce the amount of manual effort required to ensure compliance with regulatory requirements.

Systems such as ERPs rely on integrated databases with multiple applications accessing the same data, thereby allowing the data to be entered in the system only once. Numerous institutions have implemented data warehouses to provide some of the benefits of an ERP or to extend the ERP's capability. The data warehouse draws data from multiple operational systems and makes it available for reporting and analysis. The reliance on ERPs and data warehouses has increased management-reporting capability and created an opportunity for improved decision making and compliance.

Human resources. Because salaries and wages account for so much of an institution's budget, it is reasonable to expect that a large part of a budget's flexibility will be influenced by the institution's human resources policies and procedures. Tenure obligations represent long-term financial commitments. The manner in which faculty salary structures are established—and the ease with which adjustments can be made—strongly influence the institution's competitiveness in recruiting faculty. Similarly, support staff salary structures, whether based on market conditions, union pay scales, or statewide public employee scales, affect the ability to hire and retain qualified staff.

Contractual and tenure policies specify the lengths of probationary periods, the amount of advance notice required for termination of an appointment, schedules for performance reviews, and grievance procedures. In some states, these schedules are prescribed by regulation, and budgeting clearly depends on them.

Moreover, the policies governing the appointment of temporary and part-time personnel will determine some constraints on budget flexibility. Faculty research appointments frequently may parallel tenure-track appointments but not require a tenure commitment. This flexibility is beneficial in the area of sponsored programs when time frames may dictate quick-response hiring.

Collective bargaining. The existence of a collective bargaining agreement will restrict the actions that the administration may take during the budget process. Collective bargaining agreements usually specify salary increases, pay rates for various activities, and mandated employee benefits.

These agreements may be modified only with the consent of the designated representatives for those covered. Previously negotiated compensation increases are rarely rolled back or deferred. When this has happened, it almost always has been done to avoid the need for layoffs.

The existence of these agreements makes it somewhat easier for the administration to project compensation costs into the future. Most agreements cover multiple years and tie future salary increases to objective criteria, such as inflation, enrollment, or state appropriations. Collective bargaining agreements covering faculty employment also establish faculty workload standards. This aspect of the agreements impairs the administration's flexibility.

Agreements typically prevent the administration from increasing workloads, even when revenue shortfalls occur. Though part-time faculty are not necessarily covered under the contracts, their employment circumstances frequently are affected. For instance, an agreement may specify the circumstances under which part-time faculty can be hired as replacements for permanent faculty. Agreements also typically cover the conditions under which early-retirement programs can be implemented for faculty.

A standard feature of most collective bargaining agreements is coverage of the issue of retrenchment—major financial cutbacks. Most agreements specify the procedures to follow, the expense categories to address before making personnel cutbacks, and the levels of severance required for faculty whose positions are eliminated. All of these elements reduce the institution's flexibility in responding to a financial crisis.

Because of varying campus practices and differences in state laws, collective bargaining agreements can include a range of clauses addressing issues related to employment and factors only indirectly related to compensation. For instance, the agreements typically specify promotion and tenure criteria. Some go further to include prohibitions against tenure quotas. Others address the way in which salary adjustments will be balanced between merit and cost of living. Still others address incentives for faculty to pursue sponsored support.

Collective bargaining agreements may apply to multiple staff categories as well as faculty. For instance, one agreement might be in force for clerical personnel, another for public safety personnel, another for custodial workers, and still another for skilled trade workers in the physical plant. In each case, the agreements reduce the administration's flexibility in managing the institution.

The bottom line on collective bargaining agreements is that they are a mixed blessing for both the institution and the employees they cover. The institution gains some degree of certainty about future expenses but gives up flexibility in terms of its operational environment. As for employees, they are able to negotiate from a position of strength because they are united in their approach to the administration. The downside for some employees is that they might receive better compensation if they negotiated as individuals.

Procurement. Procurement regulations are intended to facilitate the efficient and economical acquisition of goods and services while preventing abuses or wasteful spending. As with most bureaucratic procedures, their complexity makes it hard for faculty and staff to appreciate how chaotic procurement activity would be without such a framework. Nevertheless, procurement regulations do limit flexibility.

Many institutions require all procurement activity to be processed through a single control point. Depending on staffing and the volume of transactions, this requirement can result in significant delays in the receipt of goods or services. As fiscal year-end approaches and departments attempt to spend the balances in their operating budgets, activity volumes rise, and delays become longer. If staff and faculty recognize these patterns, they can avoid the possibility of service interruptions or the loss of early-payment discounts. To improve overall results and reduce costs at the same time, many institutions have moved to more automated and decentralized procurement systems.

State regulations often govern procurement procedures in public institutions. These regulations specify ceilings above which a bid or request for proposal process is required. Depending on the nature of the procurement, the institution might have to advertise bid requests for specified periods before selecting a vendor. And in many situations, the institution must accept the lowest bid from a qualified vendor.

Occasionally, regulations allow for single-source procurements. In these cases, when there is only one vendor qualified to provide the goods or service, the institution is allowed to contract directly with the vendor without using bid procedures. Some states require preliminary state review for the procurement of certain goods or services, including costly computer systems, certain personal service contracts, and real estate.

Although the regulatory environment affecting procurement generally impairs budget flexibility, there can be advantages. Public institutions, in particular, frequently benefit from the ability to use state procurement contracts to reduce the cost of goods or services.

In addition, most institutions belong to one or more buying cooperatives, such as the Educational and Institutional Cooperative—a group purchasing organization (GPO) serving higher education and K-12 schools. GPOs enable institutions to benefit from volume discounts resulting from the combined purchasing power of higher education. They also gain access to standard contracts for many commodities.

The use of credit cards in procurement, typically referred to as purchasing cards or p-cards, contributes to flexibility as well. With p-cards, designated individuals are authorized to use a credit card issued in the institution's name to purchase allowable commodities. The companies issuing the credit cards work with the institution to identify allowable commodities and the types of vendors that deal in those commodities. Other vendors are not authorized to accept the cards.

Typical examples of allowable commodities include office supplies, scientific supplies, airlines, and hotels, but the range of allowable commodities is very extensive. Each card has an established limit to minimize the risk of inappropriate purchases. Department personnel are expected to reconcile the monthly statements with purchase receipts obtained from holders of p-cards. The accounting records then are updated to distribute the monthly charges to the appropriate accounts and expense categories.

P-cards have streamlined procurement dramatically and significantly reduced the number of purchase orders processed throughout colleges and universities.

Key Points

- Academic policies related to program direction, faculty allocations, faculty compensation, and use of part-time or temporary faculty heavily influence the approach to budgeting as well as the outcomes they produce.

- Administrative policies that affect the budget cover the gamut of support areas, including student services, facilities, IT, and auxiliary enterprises.

- Independent institutions typically can exert more control over their internal policies and procedures compared to public institutions, which usually must adhere to the same guidelines established for state agencies.

The third edition of this book closely followed institutional cutbacks triggered by the dot-com bubble burst at the turn of the millennium. This edition follows another extraordinary circumstance—the recession that began with the collapse of the U.S. subprime mortgage market in 2008 and continues to have long-lasting effects.

Higher education saw endowments shrink dramatically in 2008; the situation worsened in 2009, all because of staggering market losses triggered by the recession. At the same time, levels of state appropriations dropped dramatically, and liquidity challenges forced some institutions to issue long-term debt to finance operating expenses. The federal government attempted to jump-start the economy by providing states with so-called economic stimulus funds to close the gap created by state revenue shortfalls. Continuing shortfalls have translated into reduced state appropriations, even as higher education is expected to serve significantly more students due to enrollment spikes caused by unemployment.

Long before the 2008 recession, an institution would occasionally encounter unique problems that called for retrenchment. Typically, the institution would not have engaged in meaningful planning and, as a result, experienced a combination of factors that created financial distress. Or the institution might simply have failed to heed obvious warning signs. Sometimes an unpredictable event prompted the retrenchment—such as a physical disaster that greatly exceeded the institution's insurance protection or the sudden closing of a local manufacturing facility, which led to a dramatic enrollment reduction.

Since 2008, however, even higher education institutions employing best practices in the area of planning have had to retrench and adapt to what they refer to as "the new normal." Normal now means operating with reduced resources, coupled with increased demands for services—all under never-ending scrutiny by regulators and funders.

The broad gamut of financial distress ranges from serious—institutions that find it difficult to honor their debt service obligations—to alarming. The latter category describes institutions headed for major difficulty if they do not change their approaches, such as those operating with a structural deficit that cannot be sustained indefinitely.

A structural deficit arises when annual operating expenses exceed annual operating revenues. An institution with substantial endowment resources can operate reasonably well in this condition by using nonoperating financial gains to offset operational deficits. The vast majority of institutions, however, will not survive for long if they continue to erode reserves by incurring ongoing operating deficits.

What Exactly Is Retrenchment?

Retrenchment results from a financial crisis that, when serious enough, can threaten the institution's survival. It usually includes systematically (or, in some cases, haphazardly) eliminating major portions of an institution's programs and activities.

Because each financial crisis is unique, the elements of a retrenchment will vary from one institution to the next. Still, one action almost always accompanies retrenchment: personnel reductions. With such a large portion of institutional budgets committed to salaries and benefits, it is inconceivable that an institution can respond to a financial crisis without eliminating positions.

Though necessary for survival, personnel cutbacks have lasting negative effects on institutional culture. Any action that results in the elimination of someone's job has a devastating impact on a community—even when the position supported an activity that no longer added value for the college or university. When the cause is a financial crisis—especially one that should have been anticipated and avoided—the impact lasts for years.

Planning for circumstances that could result in retrenchment creates the opportunity to effect change that otherwise might be difficult to implement. As an example, the discussion of initiative-based budgeting in Chapter Seven includes a description of reallocation strategies. Some view reallocation as an exercise forced on an institution by external factors or organizations. In fact, it can better position an institution to respond to financial crises, possibly avoiding retrenchment in the process.

Reallocation allows an institution to systematically reduce the resources it devotes to some activities, thus freeing up resources that can be better deployed elsewhere. It is one mechanism for providing funds for initiatives that support new priorities. It has the added benefit of providing a cushion if an unexpected financial crisis arises; the institution may be able to avoid the more drastic responses that otherwise might be needed. In fact, if the reallocation enables the institution to weather the storm with only a minimal loss of faculty and staff, long-term negative cultural impact may be avoided.

Planning for Retrenchment

Planning for retrenchment may be a misnomer. The more correct phrasing is planning to *avoid* retrenchment. In reality, prior to the 2008 recession, few institutions had invested the effort in preparing for the possibility of significantly reduced resources. Admittedly, few could have anticipated the recession's magnitude. But even less pervasive cases of financial strife have caught institutions unprepared.

Just as institutions have developed disaster recovery and other emergency preparedness plans, they should develop plans to accommodate financial crises of varying proportions. In the wake of the 2008 recession, for example, several states imposed double-digit budget cuts on public colleges and universities. Some institutions could increase tuition rates to partially offset the reduction in public support, but others did not have this option because of state policies. The institutions best able to respond to the reduced resources had developed contingency plans to deal with such a severe financial challenge.

It simply is not possible to plan effectively for every contingency—especially for something of cataclysmic proportions. Nevertheless, failing to prepare the institution in any way for financial difficulties increases the likelihood of having to operate in crisis mode—at least for the short term. A lack of preparation virtually guarantees that the time needed for considered judgment will not be available once the problem surfaces.

Generally, the less time an institution has to react to a fiscal emergency, the narrower the range of options available. Rather than carefully considering their options—which could include tapping into reserves or using a budget contingency, along with unallocated initiative funds—the institution typically responds by implementing travel bans, hiring freezes, and across-the-board budget cuts. None of these actions is strategic, and each demonstrates an unwillingness or inability to protect priority activities—assuming any have been identified.

Of course, the crisis may still necessitate actions affecting travel, discretionary spending, and the filling of vacant positions, but effective planning can have a mitigating effect. For instance, the planning process already should have identified activities that will be exempt from expense controls and established the criteria for making decisions about other exceptions to necessary controls. Sponsored research programs, recent academic initiatives, patient care operations, and safety activities, for instance, might represent priority areas and, therefore, should not be subject to cutbacks.

To minimize the negative effects of financial stress, planning must focus on both mid- and long-range activities and consequences. In the short term, institutions may achieve small savings by selectively reducing nonpersonnel costs, such as travel, equipment, and supplies. But some short-term actions, such as reducing purchases of library books and periodicals, deferring maintenance and renovations, or deferring the purchase of replacement equipment, might cause severe long-term programmatic damage if they continue beyond one cycle. Although deferring a roof replacement may seem appealing in the moment, the decision may prove unwise if the roof leaks and damages expensive laboratory equipment integral to ongoing sponsored programs.

With compensation absorbing so much of their budgets, institutions cannot make large-scale reductions without eliminating faculty and staff positions—or at least resorting to furloughs. If effective planning minimizes the impact of the financial problem, normal attrition might generate enough savings to meet the reduction target. Obviously, this option is preferable to layoffs or reductions in force.

In planning their responses to fiscal crises, institutions must remain sensitive to legal constraints and external factors. Collective bargaining agreements, for example, may limit the available options. State governments have become more involved in personnel matters in public higher education; this involvement may extend from negotiating faculty contracts to controlling the number of faculty and staff positions. Under some budget formulas, adjustments to instructional methodologies or staffing patterns may affect state appropriations. For instance, an increased reliance on distance education affects student-faculty ratios and increases the need for academic support personnel, such as instructional technologists. Finally, special attention needs to be given to the resources associated with diversity programs, which sometimes represent state mandates.

A direct correlation exists between institutional size and the ability to reallocate resources and absorb deficits. Larger institutions tend to have more cushion than smaller ones, simply because the magnitude of their operations creates opportunities for flexibility. The cushion may be spread throughout programs and support services, spanning the full range of priorities. That's partly why large institutions frequently favor across-the-board cuts; the presumption is that serious negative programmatic effects will be avoided because the impact on any single activity is nominal. Unfortunately, the reality may be quite different.

Some programs operate with little or no flexibility. Even a small cut in resources may cripple them. In other cases, even a larger cut may have no discernible impact. For this reason, the planning process must identify priorities—activities that will be protected—and either explicitly, or through omission, indicate the areas that will be sacrificed should cuts become necessary.

Specific Strategies

The responses to financial hard times are as diverse as the universe of American higher education. Some cutback strategies, such as across-the-board cutting, are adopted solely because of their ease of implementation and the fact that everyone suffers together (albeit not equitably). Others reflect careful consideration of programmatic activities and prompt the institution to focus more on critical success factors.

When considering specific strategies, institutions should avoid arbitrarily cutting support areas. Understandably, an institution wants to preserve primary academic programs and activities as much as possible. On the other hand, effective delivery of primary programs requires adequate support. Even though it is much easier to eliminate staff support positions than faculty lines, this response may not be the most effective one.

In the short term, for instance, it may be more appropriate to rely on savings generated through faculty vacancies than to eliminate support positions. Another alternative may be restructuring support operations to expand the range of units served by individual academic support personnel. Rather than each academic department having one support position, a single position might support all units housed within a given building. The most effective institutions balance the need to minimize the adverse impacts on primary programs against the need to ensure those programs operate effectively.

Seven Planning Principles

When planning how to address a financial crisis, employ these general principles suggested by Robert M. O'Neil* and revised in the wake of the 2008 recession:

1. **Involve everyone in planning—especially in times of financial distress.** Boards, management, faculty, staff, and students—as well as alumni and donors—have a major stake in what happens on campus. They not only deserve to participate in meaningful deliberations and decisions but also can provide valuable insights about how resource distributions affect programs and support services.

2. **Provide participants with access to all available information.** The people responsible for planning should be sensitive to the implications of sharing information, especially when it pertains to personnel and programs. Establish confidentiality standards and emphasize the importance of adherence. Such standards facilitate access to the sensitive information needed to make informed judgments.

3. **Ensure planning does not ignore the institution's culture.** During times of financial distress, the institution may have to consider actions that run counter to its values, traditions, or operating style. Such actions, if deemed essential, should be undertaken only after extensive communication with constituencies and with acknowledgment that they represent a shift in the institution's evolution.

4. **Inform the governing board and—in a university system—central administrative staff of progress.** Educate the trustees or regents and central administration on how

---

* The principles discussed in this section originally appeared in Robert M. O'Neil's article, "A President's Perspective," *Academe* 69 (January–February 1983), 17–20.

the financial crisis response is unfolding—the first step in building support for proposed actions. Similarly, communicate changes in programmatic directions to significant friends of the institution, including alumni, donors, and local supporters.

5. Recognize the impact of the media—especially social media. Thanks to technology, constituents have nearly real-time access to information about most activities taking place on a campus—including responses to financial challenges. Members of the media are especially interested in higher education because of its community impact—and because of the controversy that frequently surrounds the range of campus activities.

Because information will likely be disseminated anyway, have a broad, consultative process when it comes to responding to financial challenges. Furthermore, proactively use various forms of technology and social media to distribute accurate information. This reduces the possibility of erroneous information being widely shared.

6. Never ignore the state legislature (if a public institution). Legislators who remain informed about planned actions tend to be more sensitive to institutional interests when setting state-level policy. Even in an environment in which the institution is granted significant autonomy, it is in the institution's best interests to remain closely connected with state government during financially challenging times.

7. Avoid unintended consequences by projecting the long-term impact of retrenchment strategies before implementing them. A simple but effective approach is to model the various strategies under multiple scenarios to determine the most likely outcomes. The administrative tools available make it possible—and easy—to predict the outcomes from various strategies with reasonable accuracy.

In addition to following these principles, consult resources available from higher education associations. NACUBO, for example, provided toolkits and other assistance to help its members respond to the financial crisis brought about by the 2008 recession.[127]

One final caution is in order. Too often, institutions immediately engage in cost shifting as a response to financial stress. *Cost shifting* refers to the practice of implementing a charge process for goods or services that previously were funded centrally or as part of a service unit's budget. It may be appropriate to require units to pay for the goods or services they consume; in fact, this may be an effective mechanism for conserving scare resources. A problem is created, however, when units that must now pay for these goods or services do not receive any additional resources.

If the decision is made to begin charging units, distribute a portion of the existing budget to the units that will be required to pay for the goods or services. Savings can be generated by not distributing the entire budget. If a good or service has been provided at no charge to the user, it's highly likely there has been some waste related to the item. By distributing only a portion of the existing budget, say 70 percent, and capturing the balance as savings, the institution will achieve the objective of reducing its expenses but without adversely affecting units that use the goods or services.

Institutional retrenchment strategies fall into one of two groups. They are either short term—spanning one to three years—or long term—beyond three years.

Short-Term Strategies

In the short term, institutions can respond to financial difficulties either by reducing expenses or by increasing revenues. Boosting revenues significantly in the short term proves problematic; it takes time to identify and pursue new revenue sources. A robust economy might make it possible to improve short-term investment returns through enhanced cash management. This scenario is unlikely with weak markets (and likely wouldn't produce material amounts of revenue anyway).

Therefore, attention usually focuses on reducing or deferring expenses. Unless institutions have been operating under severe conditions for an extended period, they usually can achieve modest savings by curtailing discretionary expenditures for supplies, travel, equipment, and minor maintenance.

Larger short-term savings can be achieved by carefully managing the number of faculty and staff. Faculty positions that become vacant may be left open, filled with lower-salaried faculty, or filled with temporary or part-time faculty. Similarly, leaving staff positions vacant or employing part-time or temporary personnel can result in savings. Fewer classes and larger sections can be scheduled while also offering fewer sections of some courses.

Without a plan focused on differential actions, short-term budget strategies invariably focus on across-the-board measures. Imposing the same burden on all units on short notice may seem more acceptable to the greatest number of people, but it fails to address the concern that priority areas could suffer serious damage.

Across-the-board actions result in high-priority activities being treated the same as those that may contribute little to no value to the institution. In addition, across-the-board philosophies carry the implicit assumption that all budgets are equally capable of responding to a modest cut. In fact, vast differences in budget adequacy may exist among programs.

Given the shortcomings of across-the-board cuts, it always will be preferable to apply cuts selectively rather than uniformly. Such cuts can be accomplished only with a clear understanding of program priorities and the level of resources needed to maintain effective programs. Selective reductions, even in accordance with an established plan, will not be well received by all constituents—especially those experiencing the disproportionately high cuts. Therefore, cutting budgets represents one of the most difficult tests for a campus administration. If the planning process is to have any credibility, however, it must guide the decisions.

Short-term strategies can generate quick savings. If the institution has not invested the effort to develop a plan, these savings can buy the time needed to undertake a more considered approach to cutting expenses. On the other hand, the amount realized through short-term strategies tends to be small compared to the overall budget. Significant reductions take considerably more effort.

In addition, short-term strategies can inflict long-term damage on programs as well as facilities (if maintenance is deferred). If temporary or part-time employees fill many vacancies resulting from the retirement or departure of experienced faculty, the institution's character can change dramatically. Programs requiring extensive involvement of senior faculty may wither, and part-time or temporary faculty may not be interested in (or capable of) student advising and counseling.

Finally, relying on attrition to achieve salary savings may mean the programs being de-emphasized may not be the ones that experience vacancies. If the vacancies occur in priority areas, the institution will need to fill the vacancies and diminish the potential savings.

Long-Term Strategies

Every institution should have infrastructural plans (see Chapter Six) that provide the context for establishing program priorities in core programmatic and essential support areas. These plans should establish the institution's priorities and identify decision-making criteria. Without the principles embodied in the plans, an institution will find it difficult to alter its allocation of resources in an intelligent manner.

Institutions faced with the prospect of implementing major budget reductions, or with the need to force significant reallocations, must review their academic programs and support activities carefully. To achieve economies and maintain or strengthen the quality of the institution, the program review must be an active process that, over time, examines all programs and activities—both primary and supporting.

Infrastructural plans provide the framework for examining the distribution of resources, while information garnered from program reviews describes how well the program array is executing the plans. A typical schedule results in a comprehensive review of each program on a five-year cycle. Programs should be reviewed with respect to their:

- Linkage to and support of the institution's mission
- Service load

- Uniqueness
- Enrollment demand (for academic programs)
- Service demand (for support programs)
- Overall effectiveness (for example, quality and productivity)
- Revenues and costs

In the absence of planning, the need for significant resource reductions or forced reallocations requires aggressive program reviews. In general, passive program shrinkage or elimination—usually through faculty and staff attrition—is insufficient to meet reduction targets. This approach may offer the least contentious way to cope with program shrinkage from a political perspective, but it typically will not achieve the objective. Faculty and staff do not limit their resignations, transfers, and retirements to low-priority, mediocre-quality, or low-demand programs and support activities. Normal attrition generally will not free up sufficient resources quickly enough to avoid retrenchment.

Large budget adjustments require changes in staffing patterns. Thus, retrenchment ultimately must focus on personnel policies and procedures. One frequent response is to provide financial incentives for early retirement, voluntary separation, or unpaid leave. As with most retrenchment strategies, the objective is to provide institutions with budget-reduction alternatives that help avoid forced terminations.

Ideally, the people opting to depart under such programs would be the least-needed or least-productive faculty and staff, but this rarely happens. In fact, the institution risks losing its most productive and valuable faculty and staff because of their marketability.

An additional concern is that the people remaining may not possess the requisite educational and research background to fulfill the commitments of those who have departed. Even faculty trained in the same discipline may not be adequately prepared to step in and teach another faculty member's courses—especially if they have not taught the content previously. A faculty member teaching in the accounting program may be well qualified to teach any accounting course, but there is no guarantee he or she has the ability to teach an auditing or tax course.

Moreover, unless used in conjunction with program review, these strategies do not earmark the programs and support activities that are the preferred candidates for contraction or elimination. The only way to avoid significant problems with incentive programs is to design them carefully and establish criteria that minimize the risk of losing the most valuable faculty and staff. Even so, the institution must prepare for the possibility of losing them.

Long-term strategies for achieving salary savings fall into these categories:

Early retirement. Faculty and staff who meet specified age and service criteria are offered a lump-sum separation allowance for agreeing to retire or resign early. In addition to the lump-sum payment, the package typically includes benefits, such as pension and health insurance.

Some public institutions are precluded from offering such programs unless they are consistent with programs available to all state employees. Still others must obtain special authorization to offer a program of any type. Another problem is the possibility that some excellent performers may choose to retire. To minimize this outcome, the program might set the severance compensation at the average salary for a particular age cohort. This criterion may discourage the best faculty from participating because they are more likely to earn well above the average salary.

Early retirement programs typically require significant front-end costs, such as a severance package and payouts in lieu of some benefits. It must be demonstrated that the program will ultimately save money and improve the overall financial picture. Nevertheless, an early retirement program may be a less expensive alternative than forced terminations that sometimes require one to two years' notice.

The current economic climate, the quality of life on campus, and the institution's general outlook play a significant role in a program's success. For instance, many programs offered in the wake of the 2008 recession failed because of the depressed stock market. Even with incentives, individual retirement portfolios had lost so much value that many feared they might not have sufficient retirement income.

Early retirement represents a big step, and employees appreciate having time to consider it carefully and consult with their advisors. Programs that require a commitment during a small window of opportunity may discourage participation. On occasion, institutions have offered programs in consecutive years with differing features and requirements. This technique usually is implemented when the financial condition continues to deteriorate or the retirement programs do not generate the level of participation needed to achieve reduction targets. Unfortunately, this practice tends to encourage potential participants to wait for what they believe to be the best possible offer.

Partial buyout. This approach enables faculty and staff to choose part-time appointments for a number of years up to an established maximum. During this period, they receive a prorated salary with full benefits; participants commonly receive a full year of retirement credit for each year in the program.

Partial buyouts tend to appeal to senior faculty and staff because their salaries are larger and they are closer to retirement. For this reason, the program can generate substantial savings with relatively low participation.

Alternative approaches. Individual campuses have employed short furloughs, which force staff to take unpaid time off; implemented modest across-the-board pay reductions; and introduced mid-career changes—a euphemism for retraining, a term sometimes found objectionable by faculty. With the latter arrangement, faculty or staff in programs targeted for reduction or elimination have the opportunity to transfer to other departments or positions to continue employment. In general, these strategies are difficult to implement unless existing policies already allow them. Otherwise, the opposition from faculty and staff can be overwhelming.

Another option involves the liberalization of the existing guidelines used to determine retirement benefits. For instance, rather than develop a specific early retirement program, an institution can elect to provide full benefits at a lower retirement age or with fewer years of service. In a traditional early retirement program with unique features, individual negotiations may take place. With liberalized guidelines, everyone qualifying under the formula receives the amount of compensation and benefits available to anyone with the same combination of age and service.

Surviving Personnel Reductions

Personnel actions are a delicate subject in the best of times. When implemented as part of retrenchment, they take on an entirely different character. Here are recommendations when contemplating personnel actions to generate savings.

Analyze the possible strategies. If offering an early retirement program, for example, ensure the savings would outweigh the implementation costs by a margin sufficient to justify the effort.

Avoid targeting specific individuals. Rather than focusing exclusively on faculty and staff assigned to a program deemed less essential, address the program itself. Singling out individuals may lead them to believe they were the victims of inappropriate discrimination.

Discrimination in and of itself is not illegal; it happens routinely and appropriately. For instance, assigning a larger reduction target to a low-demand program is a form of discrimination. On the other hand, discrimination against individuals based on age, gender, or race clearly is illegal. Follow due process with any personnel programs driven by retrenchment to ensure that employees do not feel they were coerced into making a decision and that those who choose to participate are not stigmatized.

Focus on more than the finances. Savings should not be the sole consideration when implementing new personnel policies; also consider the impact on programmatic goals and objectives.

Take care to avoid actions that faculty may perceive as a threat to tenure or academic due process. Both faculty and staff will find personnel reduction programs easier to accept if the risks associated with career transitions are minimal.

When developing personnel reduction initiatives, involve the constituent group members expected to participate in them. In addition, position and publicize the opportunities as providing benefits both for the individuals and the institution.

Termination of Faculty

Sometimes, the magnitude of the reductions needed within a short time period makes termination unavoidable. The termination of faculty is particularly difficult because most institutions maintain a strong commitment to tenure. In addition, many American colleges and universities have policies that align with the principles and guidelines established by the American Association of University Professors (AAUP).

These principles and guidelines cover academic freedom, tenure, financial exigency, and program discontinuation for reasons other than financial exigency. The AAUP guidelines, for example, oppose the dismissal of faculty or the termination of appointments before the end of specified terms, except when financial exigency occurs.

The guidelines are designed to prevent administrators from using financial exigency as a justification for capricious actions. They define financial exigency as "an imminent financial crisis that threatens the survival of the institution as a whole and that cannot be alleviated by less drastic means." While helpful, this definition can be difficult to apply due to differing interpretations of what constitutes an imminent financial crisis. It is, therefore, necessary to interpret the guidelines and adapt them to specific institutional settings when adopting the AAUP guidelines.

Views differ on whether enrollment fluctuations can be the impetus for exigency determinations. Some individuals argue that fluctuations are cyclical and should not serve as a basis for program discontinuation. Others contend that enrollment fluctuations constitute an appropriate aspect of educational policy and, therefore, should be considered.

Clearly, the quality of academic programs influences resource decisions. A program of mediocre quality with low enrollment, for example, might drain resources from higher-quality, more competitive programs. It might be necessary to respond to sagging institutional enrollments by shifting resources to make selected programs more attractive to potential students. Such action, though damaging to some programs, may be the only way to protect the financial viability of the institution as a whole.

The major issue in significant retrenchment efforts is how to handle personnel in all categories: tenured, nontenured, and staff. The AAUP guidelines address the elimination of entire academic programs. Absent financial exigency, the guidelines do not permit the termination of particular tenured faculty because of mere reduction in scope or reorganization of academic units. In a small institution with instruction as its primary mission, for example, enrollments might not justify a five-person, fully tenured art history department. If the institution wishes to reduce its commitment to art history while also adhering to institutional policies compliant with AAUP guidelines, the only alternative may be to disband the entire program. Moreover, the institution would have to justify the elimination of the art history program on academic considerations other than enrollment.

This example helps explain why some institutions have modified the AAUP guidelines or abandoned them completely in favor of other approaches. Then, in dealing with low-demand or low-quality programs, the institutions potentially could reduce the number of faculty based on enrollment.

Rather than terminating tenured faculty members, an institution might allow the size of the program faculty and staff to shrink through natural attrition. This takes time, however. Alternatively, faculty members can be reassigned or retrained to assume other duties or teach in related disciplines. When taking any such actions, institutions must be careful to honor commitments made to students currently enrolled in these programs.

Lingering effects of the 2008 recession have left multiple institutions struggling with the actual or threatened loss of accreditation due to resource shortages and related problems. Given that accreditation is a requirement for participation in federal financial aid programs, these institutions may be forced to close their doors. Certainly, such circumstances satisfy the "financial exigency" condition in the AAUP guidelines.

Other institutions may not be in such peril but still face serious financial distress due to dramatic decreases in revenue from declining enrollment, financial markets that have not recovered fully, reduced state appropriations, or other situations. If these colleges and universities have adopted the AAUP guidelines, they may struggle with how the guidelines apply as they respond to financial difficulties.

Any institution facing serious financial hardship must assess whether financial exigency—as defined in its own policies—actually exists. Because the phrase carries special meaning in the higher education community, exercise great care before invoking it. In the past, some institutions have used the phrase before initiating actions that resulted in the termination of faculty because their policies required it.

Other institutions, recognizing that the phrase can trigger other serious consequences, have attempted to address financial crises without referring specifically to financial exigency. In doing so, they hoped to avoid problems with bond rating agencies, bondholders, other creditors, and accreditation agencies. Unfortunately, failure to invoke the phrase does not guarantee that drastic measures can be avoided.

Focusing on the Long Term

Planning is a long-term continuous activity because of the complexity of the academic enterprise and the need to involve administrators, appropriate faculty bodies, and—in some institutions—students.

One option for responding to the need for structural change is program prioritization as described by Robert Dickeson.* At its core, program prioritization is undertaken to facilitate an orderly and systematic reallocation of resources, away from underperforming programs and activities, toward those existing and new activities that will contribute to enhanced institutional effectiveness and long-term success.

Relying on a broadly participative process and institution-specific criteria, representatives assess all academic programs against one another. At the same time, all administrative and support activities are assessed against one another, based on established criteria. These efforts result in all programs and activities being classified into one of four categories:

- Category I: **Enhance – Programs** that would benefit from increased investment or new programs expected to provide significant benefit to the institution

- Category II: **Maintain – Programs** that will continue without significant change

- Category III: **Reduce or Restructure – Programs** that will be contracted, consolidated with other programs, or restructured

- Category IV: **Eliminate – Programs** that will be discontinued

Once completed, the classification of programs is approved by senior leadership and submitted to the board for review and approval. After board approval, the implementation process begins.

In the absence of a comprehensive approach, such as suggested by Dickeson, a program review process typically includes at least five elements:

- The development of campus-wide or system-wide policies, procedures, and statements of priorities

- The development of an institutional mission statement

- The establishment of personnel rules

- The establishment of planning principles

- The establishment of criteria and policies and procedures for the review of new and existing programs and activities

---

* The prioritization discussion is based on Robert C. Dickeson, *Prioritizing Academic Programs and Services* (San Francisco: Jossey-Bass, 2010).

Fiscal conditions ultimately are the force behind retrenchment and any significant reallocation effort. Nevertheless, finances often are overshadowed by genuine concern for personnel policies and procedures—especially those related to faculty and staff welfare and legal rights—and the potential impact from program reviews.

Program reduction has obvious political costs and a devastating impact on morale. These costs must be compared with the net savings and other benefits, such as the ability to respond to enrollment pressures and hire quality faculty. Institutions sensitive to the well-being of those affected by program elimination will incur costs for early retirement, buyouts, external placement, or retraining.

If faculty and staff must be terminated, the institution will be responsible for severance payments. Invariably, some faculty and staff will contest their dismissals through the courts, so legal defense represents another cost to factor into the equation. The net savings from program reduction will be a function of the specific strategies employed. To the extent that the institution elects to assign faculty and staff to positions elsewhere within the institution, savings may be reduced as compared with outright terminations.

Program reduction or elimination may be a consequence of enrollment decline. These decisions will result in a loss of tuition and fee revenue and, for public institutions, possibly reduced operating appropriations. Public institutions may not be authorized to reinvest savings gained through retrenchment in other programs and activities. Instead, these institutions must return savings to the state. Finally, programs that enjoy significant external financial support may require considerable institutional support to continue. Reducing or eliminating such programs may not generate any net savings.

Other effects of retrenchment and reallocation may be more subtle and difficult to quantify. Faculty teaching in a department being downsized may find that they no longer have the job satisfaction they desire. They may elect to change jobs, potentially impairing the ability to sustain the program at the expected levels. For example, if an institution reduces the scope of a program from the doctoral to the master's level, faculty whose primary interest is doctoral training and research may not be satisfied teaching at the undergraduate and master's levels.

Taking actions that affect programs that enjoy significant support from donors may result in reduced support. Thus, it may be desirable to include external support as a criterion to consider during program reviews. Similarly, certain programs may have strong political connections. If a prominent political figure serves on a program advisory board, or the program participates in projects with important community organizations, the intangible costs of contracting or eliminating the program may far outweigh the financial benefits.

In terms of diminished public support, the institution as a whole bears the cost of reducing or eliminating such a program. Retrenchment may disrupt shared governance, unless faculty were meaningfully involved in establishing the policies that guide the retrenchment steps. Even when review criteria and related policies and procedures have been established, governance groups may struggle to specify the programs or activities to reduce or eliminate. Morale problems will assuredly arise as specific plans become known and, until they are announced, the rumor mill will be fully consumed with guessing what might happen.

Faculty, who have served the institution for a long time, may suddenly feel unwanted. If faculty terminations are decided on the basis of seniority, as is frequently the case, conflict may develop between junior and senior faculty. Retrenchment also may lead faculty and staff to pursue collective bargaining as a way to gain greater influence over the process. Adverse publicity about program reductions may exacerbate declining enrollment. Finally, situations leading to retrenchment may highlight the deficiencies within the current administration. Although the steps taken may be positive in the long run, the short-term effects can create havoc.

The economics of retrenchment require long-term plans for all programs and activities, with responsible parties held accountable for meeting plan objectives. In the academic arena, enrollments may have to be restricted to maintain the desired level of service with the available resources. Enrollment can be controlled for high-demand programs by establishing special admission requirements or implementing variable-rate tuition pricing. Long-range enrollment targets can be established for all academic programs so that planners can better gauge resource needs. Programs that fail to achieve the targets will experience consequences, which might include financial penalties (for example, reduced resources in future periods) or personnel actions (for example, demotions or dismissal).

The development of long-term enrollment targets also supports the establishment of projected staffing patterns. Institutions can project the impact of enrollment levels on decisions about promotion, tenure profile, turnover, and hiring new faculty with the objective of making future decisions in a proactive way.

Plans for program reduction also should anticipate changes in programs and activities. If an academic program is to be phased out, for example, arrangements must be made to accommodate students. Tenured faculty in the program being eliminated may need to be placed elsewhere within the institution. The elimination of a degree program will affect other programs that depend on it for courses or for students. Finally, the impact of retrenchment on diversity objectives must be considered both in terms of staffing and enrollment.

Key
Points

- Retrenchment is more than belt-tightening—it is a dramatic contraction of activities and operations, usually resulting in the elimination of positions.

- In extreme situations, retrenchment will be accompanied by a declaration of financial exigency—a statement to the internal and external communities that the institution's long-term viability will be in question if extreme actions are not taken. Beyond just eliminating positions, exigency typically entails the elimination of entire programs.

- Prioritization can help prevent retrenchment or, at the very least, deal with it effectively. This process assesses academic programs against one another and subjects administrative programs to a comparable process. The ultimate objective is to identify resources to redirect away from underperforming programs and activities toward those that contribute to institutional success.

A budget tells a story about an institution—especially if comparative information for the prior year is available. It highlights the institution's priorities because, presumably, more resources are devoted to these areas.

The budget also leaves clues about the specific model used by the institution. If all budgets in the new year reflect the same relative change from the previous year's amounts, for example, one can conclude that the institution relies on incremental budgeting rather than initiative-based budgeting or performance-based budgeting.

Budgeting is part of the larger topic of resource allocation, which is equal in importance to planning and assessment. Through the planning process, an institution decides what activities to undertake and, by omission, what activities not to pursue.

Strategic planning—the highest level of planning—usually covers a five-year period. At the other end of the spectrum is operational planning, which focuses on one fiscal year (or, possibly, two fiscal years). The strategic plan guides operational planning by providing direction for the day-to-day activities conducted throughout the year.

Because strategic plans are limited to a handful of priority areas, infrastructural plans also are developed for a two- to four-year period to address the institution's core programmatic areas (for example, academics and student engagement) and essential support areas (for example, facilities and IT), using for a two- to four-year period. Collectively, the different levels of planning should be integrated with one another and with both resource allocation and assessment. That integration puts the institution in the best position to successfully carry out its mission while moving closer to its aspirational vision.

Through the assessment process, an institution evaluates the results of its activities to determine whether changes in approach are needed. Assessment—an action-based endeavor—must have decision making as its main purpose.

The results of assessment may cause an institution to alter its plans or its resource allocation—or to intentionally keep things moving as they are. The assessment may demonstrate that the original plans were too ambitious and, therefore, expectations must be lowered. Instead of accommodating x number of participants in an advising activity, only 85 percent of x can be involved because of the time needed for students to demonstrate mastery of the relevant concepts. Alternatively, the institution might decide to add resources (for example, an additional advisor) to give students more individual attention, thereby allowing them to complete the process as originally planned.

The examples used throughout the book primarily focus on reducing expectations against plans or adding resources to meet target outcomes, although this does not have to be the case. On occasion, plans prove too conservative or resources too generous. Assessment processes should uncover either situation and lead to appropriate actions—in other words, decisions.

Here are some thoughts to keep in mind when participating in any part of the reallocation process:

Compare the budget narrative with the budget numbers. The narrative report that accompanies a budget reveals whether the institution "puts its money where its mouth is." If the narrative articulates priority areas that the quantitative tables and schedules do not reflect, it raises the issue of whether the narrative reflects reality. True institutional priorities are demonstrated through the allocation of resources, not through rhetoric.

Consider the institution's character. Planning and resource allocation approaches vary from campus to campus. What works at an older institution, with decades of established culture, probably won't work at a relatively young campus still in the development phase.

Public institutions operate differently from independent institutions, and wide variations occur even within independent institutions. Tuition-dependent religiously affiliated institutions, for example, may approach resource allocation with different values than wealthy independent institutions.

Foster internal transparency. When constituents have access to factual information, they become much less likely to fill the information void with rumors and misinformation that chip away at the institution's stability. Transparency builds trust among all levels of participants in the resource allocation process. If an open, transparent process is inconsistent with the current campus culture, the institution must acknowledge this reality and enlist the community's support in making the change.

Acknowledge external realities. While higher education has always been subjected to extensive regulation and mandates, the situation is worsening. Both public and independent institutions are regularly besieged by excessive regulation and demands for accountability. All of these measures contribute to increased operating costs, thereby reducing amounts available for programmatic purposes.

As a result of competition from other social sectors and concerns regarding tuition prices, legislators, media representatives, and the general public routinely raise questions about the value of higher education. Fortunately, ample data exist to demonstrate that investments in higher education have a significant financial return, to say nothing of the lifelong value of being an educated person.

Numerous for-profit institutions have entered the marketplace to compete directly with traditional two- and four-year institutions. Using distance offerings, rented facilities operated to meet local demand, or a combination of the two, these for-profit institutions operate in a business-like manner with a clear bottom line—increased profits.

Traditional higher education suffers from a lack of clarity about the bottom line because so many functional areas are critically important within an institution. If the institution has a medical school with a patient care mission, some would argue that the most important institutional activity is treating patients. Many working within a community college may believe meeting the workforce needs of the community represents the top priority. For others, the most important activity taking place is intercollegiate athletics because of the brand recognition, private support, and student experiences it brings. Notice that nothing has been said about educating students! In reality, traditional higher education has multiple bottom lines, which makes institutions vulnerable to competitors with the single focus of financial gain for investors.

Globalization represents another external factor that influences budgets. U.S.-based institutions have opened campuses throughout the world to extend their brand, export quality educational approaches to underserved regions, or simply gain access to new revenue streams. At the same time, U.S. institutions continue to attract record numbers of international students to their domestic campuses. Offsetting the importation of international students is an increase in American students studying abroad. Accommodating these various global experiences carries a cost—both in terms of dollars for out-of-pocket expenses and the more intangible impact on institutional systems and processes.

Consider demographics. Tuition revenues depend upon students, so the population shifts occurring within the United States will affect all institutions, particularly tuition-dependent ones.

Institutions located in the Northeast and Midwest—the regions losing students—run the risk of coming up short in the competition to fill seats. Remember, reduced enrollments do not necessarily translate into eliminated costs. On the other side of the equation, institutions located in the South and West—where student numbers are growing—may experience demand that exceeds available resources. In fact, some public institutions have been forced to cap enrollments because governmental appropriations have not kept pace with student demand.

Favor flexibility. To manage the day-to-day bumps in the road that occur throughout the year while maintaining financial equilibrium, institutions must adopt policies and procedures that contribute to budgetary flexibility.

A key aspect of flexibility is anticipating and preparing for the unexpected. This can be accomplished through contingency funds built into the expense budget to accommodate revenue shortfalls, expense overruns, or unanticipated opportunities. A good rule of thumb is to devote 3 percent of the expense budget to a contingency fund. Barring catastrophic occurrences, this should provide sufficient flexibility for the institution to make it through the year without dipping into reserves.

Of course, if conditions deteriorate markedly, protecting reserves may not be possible. This certainly will be the case if planning efforts prove ineffective or external forces create negative conditions that exceed the institution's financial capabilities. Relatively few institutions plan for catastrophes and, therefore, most experiencing them will be forced to take extreme measures if the financial situation becomes dire. Retrenchment may mean eliminating or contracting programs, which typically results in the termination of faculty and staff. As a last resort, the institution will declare financial exigency, which usually leads to large-scale program contraction.

Become actively involved. Anyone interested in participating in an institution's planning and resource allocation processes should make that interest known. If the campus climate does not prove receptive to this participation, work through the organizational structure—for example, by informing a supervisor or department head about a desire to serve on a budget committee or task force. Established forums on campus—such as the faculty senate and administrative council—offer another avenue for voicing interest. If you always adopt an institutional (versus self-interested) perspective, you should be welcomed into the process.

Key Points

- A budget tells a story about an institution and its priorities. When accompanied by a narrative expanding on the numbers, it becomes a detailed story about what matters most.

- If the financial information in the budget is supplemented with comparable information for the previous year, it is easy to identify the institution's priorities. It also becomes evident if the narrative is at odds with how the institution actually allocates resources.

- Budgeting is but one aspect of resource allocation and must be undertaken along with planning and assessment.

One need not be an accountant to understand budgets and budgeting. Although knowledge of accounting may aid the understanding of relationships between various budget elements, budgets are not subject to accounting rules.

Nevertheless, some accounting issues affect higher education budgeting. An understanding of the issues summarized below will benefit participants in the resource allocation process and help them interpret the institution's audited financial statements.

Noncash Expenses

Budgets usually focus on cash, while accounting considers cash activity as well as accruals. *Accruals* include revenues that have been earned but not collected in cash (receivables) and expenses that have been incurred but not paid for (payables).

Noncash expenses represent a different type of accrual. Unlike normal payments and payables, a noncash expense is a cost of doing business that must be recognized without a corresponding disbursement of cash. The most common example is depreciation.

Depreciation is the accounting mechanism used to spread the cost of capital assets, such as buildings and equipment, over the periods equating to their expected useful lives. Without this convention, funds expended to acquire high-cost assets would be charged entirely to the current year—automatically generating a financial loss and ignoring the reality that the assets will still be in use in the future. Therefore, the amounts invested to construct or acquire capital assets are recorded as assets rather than expenses.

The useful life for such assets is estimated and the value of the asset divided by this number, thus generating the amount representing the annual charge for using or consuming a portion of the asset. This amount represents the expense (depreciation) attributable to each period during which the asset will provide service to the organization.

In recent years, a process comparable to depreciation, amortization, has been applied to major investments in computer software, such as ERPs. Treating these costly investments as expenses attributable to one fiscal year would dramatically distort the expense totals for that year. Just as with buildings, these systems are expected to provide service for many years, so the investment is capitalized and amortized over the expected useful life. As the system updates increase the system's functionality or extend its useful life, the costs to install these enhancements are added to the unamortized cost of the system. This is comparable to what occurs with building renovations.

A key consideration related to depreciation (and amortization) is whether an attempt is made to generate revenues sufficient to offset the expense. In other words, are tuition and other revenue sources managed to cover all expenses or only cash expenses? Without generating revenues sufficient to cover both cash expenses and depreciation, the institution would operate at a financial loss or deficit. That is, expenses would exceed revenues.

Funding Depreciation

An institution that funds depreciation (or amortization) sets aside resources equal to the amount of depreciation expense recognized during that period. The funds, held in a reserve and invested, provide resources to replace the asset when its useful life has expired. Although it's possible that the investment return will not keep pace with the annual cost increases related to a replacement asset, this is a much better situation than would occur if no reserve existed.

Funding depreciation draws mixed reviews. Some accounting professionals believe it is necessary to recognize the expense of using facilities and to establish reserves to provide for their replacement. Under current accounting practices, depreciation addresses only the original cost of a facility—or the estimated market value, in the case of donated assets. Obviously, this amount falls far below what might be needed to replace the facility in 30 years. Nevertheless, recognizing depreciation and reserving the value of the expense each year generates funds that can be invested; the funds may grow enough to cover most, if not all, of the replacement cost.

Other accounting professionals argue that the institution won't likely need to generate the funds for replacing obsolete or aging facilities. They suggest donors—or, in the case of public institutions, government—will provide the necessary funds. States still recovering from the 2008 recession, however, are in no position to provide the resources needed to operate higher education, let alone finance capital asset replacement. Likewise, as facilities age or become obsolete, donors might not be willing or able to provide the resources for maintaining the physical infrastructure required by colleges and universities.

It can be helpful to compare annual depreciation expense to amounts being invested in facilities. If an institution does not invest at least as much as the annual depreciation charge, it will experience a problem over time. Essentially, the plant will become outdated. This easily calculated metric will indicate whether the institution is appropriately investing in its facilities.

Financial Aid

Some forms of financial aid represent true inflows of resources to the institution. Others merely pass through the institution's accounts en route to the students. Under accounting rules, revenues must be counted only once. If a form of financial aid is treated as revenue by the institution when it is received (for example, a gift for scholarships), the tuition for the student receiving the scholarship is reduced by the amount of the gift applied as a scholarship. The net result is that both the gift and the balance of tuition actually paid by the student are recognized as revenues.

Despite the accounting requirements, it is important to consider tuition and financial aid as separate categories in the budget—even though they likely will be addressed at the same time because of their strong connections to one another. From a management perspective, tuition and financial aid are closely linked. Therefore, it is important to focus attention on the aggregate rather than the net amounts.

Accounting Standards

Public and independent institutions follow different rules for financial reporting purposes. Independent institutions must comply with rules established by the Financial Accounting Standards Board (FASB), while public institutions are subject to rules promulgated by the Governmental Accounting Standards Board (GASB). Although the basic rules are similar, subtle differences make it difficult to compare financial reports prepared by public and independent institutions.

For instance, independent institutions have a more narrow definition of restrictions: Only donors can restrict resources. At public institutions, any external entity—including donors, governments, and even contracts—can establish restrictions. This inconsistency leads to differing accounting treatment. Public institutions treat resources derived from sponsored programs as restricted, while independent institutions consider these funds unrestricted. In addition, unrestricted net assets at independent institutions include the net investment in plant (the carrying value of facilities minus accumulated depreciation and plant debt). At public institutions, the net investment in plant is presented in a separate net asset category—invested in capital assets, net of related debt.

Other differences center on how to record certain revenues or expenses. Pell Grants offer one example of this type of difference. These are federal grants for financial aid. Public institutions include Pell Grants as nonoperating grant revenues. Independent institutions do not count Pell Grants as revenue at all. Instead, they treat grants as pass-through funds with no effect on revenues, expenses, or net assets.

Even though such differences have little impact on budgeting practices, their potential impact should be considered if one attempts to compare budgets for otherwise similar institutions.

Reconciling Budget Reporting with Accounting Reporting

Any discussion of finances on campuses is bifurcated. When discussing external financial reporting, for instance, the emphasis is on accrual-basis reporting compliant with established rules known as generally accepted accounting principles (GAAP). When discussing internal financial reporting, the focus tends to be on cash-basis budgets. This carries over to how institutions share financial information with boards—which must approve the budget and periodically review updates on the status of revenues and expenses as compared with the budget.

The final step in the budget process for a given period should be determining how well the budget predicted the revenues and expenses that would arise as the institution carried out its many day-to-day activities. In reality, however, the final budget is not shared with the board. Instead, the board sees a set of audited financial statements—a GAAP-compliant, accrual-basis series of reports that tell the story of the revenues and expenses that materialized during the year.

Two audited statements focus on the financial results for the period. The first is the activities statement, prepared on the accrual basis of accounting. Independent institutions refer to this report as the statement of activities, while public institutions call it the statement of revenues, expenses, and changes in net assets. It is difficult to compare cash-based budget reports to accrual-based activities statements. In addition to the differences caused by the basis of accounting, the formats tend to be very dissimilar.

The other audited statement provides a solution to this problem. It is referred to as the statement of cash flows by both independent and public institutions. As the name implies, this report focuses on cash rather than accruals. For this reason, it's the ideal statement to use for budgetary comparisons following the end of the fiscal year.

Relatively few institutions use the statement of cash flows in any meaningful way. Instead, they present the accrual-basis activities statement and expect the board to accept it as evidence of how well the budget worked to guide the institution's operations. But measurement and format differences make this an apples-to-oranges comparison.

Other institutions recognize that the board is better served if the statement of cash flows is reconciled to the final budget for the year. Because the final budget is in the same format that board members have seen throughout the year, they will readily understand it. This enables management to explain the variances between the original approved budget, any authorized revisions, and the final official audited financial statements for the year—a critical step in the board satisfying its fiduciary responsibilities.

Reporting Formats

Standard reporting formats do not require independent institutions to present an "operating measure"–the subtotal in a financial statement indicating whether the operating activities generated a surplus or a deficit. Although many independent institutions provide an operating measure, others elect merely to show the increase or decrease in net assets.

This addresses whether the institution is better off at the end of the year than at the beginning, but it doesn't demonstrate whether operating revenues are adequate to finance operating expenses. By their nature, nonoperating revenues are less predictable and may be less sustainable. Relying on them to offset structural deficits is a risky proposition.

Public institutions face a different problem. The prescribed reporting format requires them to present an operating measure, but from a management perspective, the measure is meaningless. Because they are precluded from treating certain revenue categories as operating revenues–even categories that support operations–public institutions are all but guaranteed to report an operating loss (deficit).

The three revenue categories that support operations, but must be reported as nonoperating, are non-endowment gifts, governmental operating appropriations, and investment income. The appropriations, in particular, represent a substantial resource used to underwrite operating expenses. Excluding this from the determination of the operating measure makes the statement of revenues, expenses, and changes in net assets grossly misleading.

Because of this situation, the vast majority of public institutions supplement their audited financial statements with analysis demonstrating whether they generated an operating surplus or deficit.

Key
Points

- Budgets are not subject to accounting rules in the same way that audited financial statements are. Budgets focus on cash, while audited financial statements are prepared using accrual accounting principles.

- Most financial aid is received by the institution and counted as one type of revenue (gifts, endowment income, or governmental grants). If applied against amounts owed by the student, the financial aid reduces the amount of tuition revenue that will be recognized.

- The accounting rules for public institutions differ from those applicable to independent institutions. Different measurement principles may lead to misleading conclusions when comparing financial information for public colleges and universities with that of their independent counterparts.

1   The College Board, *Trends in College Pricing 2011* (New York: The College Board, 2011).

2   Ibid.

3   U.S. Department of Labor, Bureau of Labor Statistics, "Consumer Price Index, All Urban Consumers – (CPI-U)," ftp://ftp.bls.gov/pub/special.requests/cpi/cpiai.txt (accessed February 6, 2012).

4   Commonfund Institute, *2011 Higher Education Price Index* (Wilton, CT: Commonfund Institute, 2011).

5   State Higher Education Executive Officers, *State Higher Education Finance FY 2010* (Boulder, CO: State Higher Education Executive Officers, 2011).

6   National Center for Education Statistics, *Digest of Education Statistics 2010*, "Table 275. Degree-granting institutions, by control and type of institution: Selected years, 1949-50 through 2009-10" (Washington, DC: National Center for Education Statistics, 2011), table 275.

7   National Center for Education Statistics, *Digest of Education Statistics 2010*, "Table 373. Expenditures of public degree-granting institutions, by purpose of expenditure and type of institutions: 2003-04 through 2008-09" (Washington, DC: National Center for Education Statistics, 2011), table 373.

8   National Center for Education Statistics, *Digest of Education Statistics 2010*, "Table 375. Expenditures of private not-for-profit degree-granting institutions, by purpose of expenditure and type of institutions: 1998-99 through 2008-09" (Washington, DC: National Center for Education Statistics, 2011), table 375.

9   National Center for Education Statistics, *Digest of Education Statistics 2010*, "Table 378. Expenditures of private for-profit degree-granting institutions, by purpose and type of institutions: 2008-09" (Washington, DC: National Center for Education Statistics, 2011), table 378.

10   Bureau of Economic Analysis, *January 27, 2012 News Release*, "Table 9.–Relation of Gross Domestic Product, Gross National Product, and National Income" (Washington, DC: National Center for Education Statistics, 2012), table 9.

11   National Center for Education Statistics, *Digest of Education Statistics 2010*, "Table 197. Total fall enrollment in degree-granting institutions, by attendance status, sex of student, and control of institutions: Selected years, 1947 through 2009" (Washington, DC: National Center for Education Statistics, 2011), table 197.

12   National Center for Education Statistics, *Digest of Education Statistics 2010*, "Table 255. Employees in degree-granting institutions, by employment status, sex, control and type of institution, and primary occupation: Fall 2009" (Washington, DC: National Center for Education Statistics, 2011), table 255.

13   Ibid.

14   Ibid.

15   Current Issues Committee "Current Issues " EDUCAUSE, http://www.educause.edu/issues (accessed February 6, 2012).

16   Babson Survey Research Group, I. Elaine Allen and Jeff Seaman, *Class Differences* (Babson Park, MA: Babson College, 2010).

17   Ibid.

18   Inside Higher Ed, *2011-12 Inside Higher Ed Survey of College & University Chief Academic Officers* (Washington, DC: Inside Higher Ed, 2012).

19   National Center for Education Statistics, *Digest of Education Statistics 2010*, "Table 275." op. cit.

20   National Center for Education Statistics, *Digest of Education Statistics 2010*, "Table 278. Degree-granting institutions that have closed their doors, by control and type of institution: 1969-70 through 2009-10" (Washington, DC: National Center for Education Statistics, 2011), table 278.

21   National Center for Education Statistics, *Digest of Education Statistics 2010*, "Table 197." op. cit.

22   Ibid.

23   National Center for Education Statistics, *Digest of Education Statistics 2010*, "Table 368. Total revenue of private for-profit degree-granting institutions, by source of funds and type of institution: Selected years, 1999-2000 through 2008-09" (Washington, DC: National Center for Education Statistics, 2011), table 368.

24   National Center for Education Statistics, *Digest of Education Statistics 20\10*, "Table 362. Revenues of public degree-granting institutions, by source of revenue and type of institution: 2005-06 through 2008-09" (Washington, DC: 2011)

25   National Center for Education Statistics, *Digest of Education Statistics 2010*, "Table 366. Total revenue of private not-for-profit degree-granting institutions, by source of funds and type of institution: Selected years, 1999-2000 through 2008-09" (Washington, DC: 2011)

26   National Center for Education Statistics, *Digest of Education Statistics 2010*, "Table 378." op. cit.

27   National Center for Education Statistics, *Digest of Education Statistics 2010*, "Table 373." op. cit.

28   National Center for Education Statistics, *Digest of Education Statistics 2010*, "Table 375." op. cit.

29   American College & University President's Climate Commitment, http://www.presidentsclimatecommitment.org/ (accessed February 6, 2012).

30   Signatories of the American College & University Presidents Climate Commitment, "Text of the American College & University Presidents' Climate Commitment," American College & University President's Climate Commitment, http://www.presidentsclimatecommitment.org/about/commitment (accessed February 6, 2012).

31 National Center for Education Statistics, *Digest of Education Statistics 2010*, "Table 21. Actual and projected numbers for total enrollment in all postsecondary degree-granting institutions, by age group, sex and attendance status: Fall 1995 through fall 2020" (Washington, DC: National Center for Education Statistics, 2011), table 21.

32 Ibid.

33 National Center for Education Statistics, *Digest of Education Statistics 2010*, "Table 197." op. cit.

34 Ibid.

35 Ibid.

36 Ibid.

37 Western Interstate Commission for Higher Education, *Knocking at the College Door* (Boulder, CO: Western Interstate Commission for Higher Education, 2008).

38 Ibid.

39 Ibid.

40 Ibid.

41 Ibid.

42 Institute of International Education, *Open Doors 2011 "Fast Facts"* http://www.iie.org/Research-and-Publications/Open-Doors/Data/~/media/Files/Corporate/Open-Doors/Fast-Facts/Fast%20Facts%202011.ashx (accessed February 6, 2012).

43 Ibid.

44 Ibid.

45 Ibid.

46 Ibid.

47 Ibid.

48 Ibid.

49 National Center for Education Statistics, *Digest of Education Statistics 2010*, "Table 380. Federal support and estimated federal tax expenditures for education, by category: Selected fiscal years, 1965 through 2010" (Washington, DC: National Center for Education Statistics, 2011), table 380.

50 Ibid.

51 Ibid.

52 National Center for Education Statistics, *Digest of Education Statistics 2010*, "Table 362." & National Center for Education Statistics, *Digest of Education Statistics 2010*, "Table 366." op. cit.

53 Ibid.

54 Ibid.

55 FAFSAOnline.com, CSS Profile, http://www.fafsa-online.com/financial-aid-application/css-profile.php (accessed on February 6, 2012).

56 National Center for Education Statistics, *Digest of Education Statistics 2010*, "Table 366." op. cit.

57 Andrea Fuller, "Endowment Returns Rise to 19%, but Trouble May Lie Ahead," *The Chronicle of Higher Education*, January 31, 2012, http://

chronicle.com/article/Endowment-Returns-Rise-to-19-/130588/ (accessed February 6, 2012).

58 Ibid.

59 Ibid.

60 National Center for Education Statistics, *Digest of Education Statistics 2010*, "Table 362." op. cit.

61 National Center for Education Statistics, *Digest of Education Statistics 2010*, "Table 366." op. cit.

62 Ibid.

63 Ibid.

64 New York State Office of Higher Education, *Aid to Independent Colleges and Universities (Bundy Aid)*, http://www.highered.nysed.gov/oris/bundy/ (accessed February 6, 2012).

65 Ibid.

66 National Center for Education Statistics, *Digest of Education Statistics 2010*, "Table 362." op. cit.

67 Ibid.

68 Ibid.

69 Ibid.

70 National Center for Education Statistics, *Digest of Education Statistics 2010*, "Table 366." op. cit.

71 National Center for Education Statistics, *Digest of Education Statistics 2010*, "Table 362." op. cit.

72 National Center for Education Statistics, *Digest of Education Statistics 2010*, "Table 366." op. cit.

73 Ibid.

74 National Center for Education Statistics, *Digest of Education Statistics 2010*, "Table 362." op. cit.

75 Ibid.

76 Association of American Medical Colleges, "About the AAMC," https://www.aamc.org/about/ (accessed February 6, 2012).

77 National Center for Education Statistics, *Digest of Education Statistics 2010*, "Table 362." & National Center for Education Statistics, *Digest of Education Statistics 2010*, "Table 366." op. cit.

78 Fuller, "Endowment Returns Rise to 19%, but Trouble May Lie Ahead," *The Chronicle of Higher Education*, January 31, 2012. op.cit.

79 Ibid.

80 NACUBO & Commonfund Institute, *NACUBO-Commonfund Endowment Study 2011*, (Washington, DC: NACUBO & Commonfund Institute, 2012).

81 Ibid.

82 Ibid.

83 Ibid.

84 National Center for Education Statistics, *Digest of Education Statistics 2010*, "Table 366." op. cit.

85 National Center for Education Statistics, *Digest of Education Statistics 2010*, "Table 362." op. cit.

86 Ibid.

87 National Center for Education Statistics, *Digest of Education Statistics 2010*, "Table 349. Percentage of undergraduates receiving aid, by type and source of aid and selected student characteristics: 2007-08" (Washington, DC: National Center for Education Statistics, 2011), table 349.

88 Ibid.

89 U.S. Department of Education, "Education Department Budget by Major Program," http://www2.ed.gov/about/overview/budget/history/edhistory.pdf (accessed February 6, 2012).

90 Student Aid on the Web, "Federal Pell Grant" http://studentaid.ed.gov/PORTALSWebApp/students/english/PellGrants.jsp (accessed February 6, 2012).

91 Department of Education, "Education Department Budget by Major Program." op. cit.

92 Ibid.

93 Ibid.

94 Ibid.

95 U.S. Department of Education, "Leveraging Educational Assistance Partnership (LEAP) Program Funding Status," http://www2.ed.gov/programs/leap/funding.html (accessed February 6, 2012).

96 Department of Education, "Special Leveraging Educational Assistance Partnership (SLEAP) Program Funding Status," http://www2.ed.gov/programs/sleap/funding.html (accessed February 6, 2012).

97 Department of Education, "Leveraging Educational Assistance Partnership (LEAP) Program Funding Status." op. cit.

98 Department of Education, "Special Leveraging Educational Assistance Partnership (SLEAP) Program Funding Status," op. cit.

99 Department of Education, "Education Department Budget by Major Program." op. cit.

100 State Higher Education Executive Officers, *State Higher Education Finance FY 2010*. op. cit.

101 National Center for Education Statistics, *Digest of Education Statistics 2010*, "Table 373." op. cit.

102 Ibid.

103 Ibid.

104 Ibid.

105 Ibid.

106 Ibid.

107 Ibid.

108 Ibid.

109 Ibid.

110 Ibid.

111 Ibid.

112 Ibid.

113 Ibid.

114 National Center for Education Statistics, *Digest of Education Statistics 2010*, "Table 375." op. cit.

115 Ibid.

116 Ibid.

117 Ibid.

118 Ibid.

119 Ibid.

120 Ibid.

121 Ibid.

122 Ibid.

123 Ibid.

124 Office of Institutional Research, "The Delaware Study of Instructional Costs and Productivity," University of Delaware, http://www.udel.edu/IR/cost/welcome.html (accessed February 6, 2012).

125 Inside Higher Ed, *2011 Inside Higher Ed Survey of College & University Business Officers* (Washington, DC: Inside Higher Ed, 2011).

126 Western Interstate Commission, *Knocking at the College Door*. op. cit.

127 Matt Hamill, "Facing the Financial Downturn: Toolkit and Resources for Colleges and Universities" NACUBO, http://www.nacubo.org/Business_and_Policy_Areas/Finance/Financial_Downturn_Toolkit_and_Resources.html (accessed February 6, 2012).

Glossary

A

Accrual
An accounting measurement method that ignores whether cash has been received or paid. Revenues are recognized and recorded when earned. Expenses are recognized and recorded when incurred and measurable.

All-funds budgeting
A budgeting model that encompasses all resources, including those that may be subject to restrictions (such as gifts or endowment income).

Amortization
The allocation of the cost of intangible assets to multiple periods. The intangible asset's cost is divided by the number of periods the asset is expected to provide benefit. The resulting amount is treated as an expense during each period.

Appropriation
Allocation of funds from a governmental entity to an institution for operating or capital purposes.

Auxiliary enterprises
Self-supporting campus-based activities that provide services to students, faculty, and staff. Examples include dining operations, residence halls, and bookstores.

B

Base budget funds
The portion of an operating budget that covers ongoing recurring activities. Also called continuing budget. Contrast with *one-time budget funds.*

Bottom up
A budgeting philosophy that involves decentralized decision making, starting at the most basic unit level.

Budget cycle
The series of scheduled events that must occur to develop a budget and complete the activities supported by the budget.

C

Capital assets
Physical resources with a cost (or fair market value, if donated) exceeding an established dollar threshold that are expected to provide service for more than a single year. Unless the resources are expected to maintain or increase their value over time, the cost of the assets is allocated to the benefiting periods through amortization or depreciation. Examples include land, buildings, equipment, and leasehold improvements.

Capital budgeting
The process used to identify and monitor resources and investments related to large-dollar projects undertaken either to acquire, construct, or improve capital assets, such as buildings.

Capitalization
The process of recording expenditures for long-term resources as assets rather than as expenses. Expenses are recognized as costs of a particular period, while capital assets' costs are recognized over time through amortization or depreciation.

Carryforward
The ability to use unspent budget resources from one fiscal period in a subsequent fiscal period. Also called carryover.

Charge-back
A process by which campus service units charge other campus units for services they receive. Examples include physical plant and information technology.

Cost center
An organizational unit that incurs expenses but does not generate revenues. Contrast with *revenue center.*

Cost shifting
The practice of forcing units to pay for goods or services, which previously were funded centrally, without providing the resources needed to pay for the goods or services.

D

Debt service
The combined principal and interest amounts paid annually to bondholders.

Deferred maintenance
The cumulative value of scheduled or routine maintenance and repairs for the built environment that an organization chooses not to undertake when originally scheduled (frequently due to financial constraints).

Depreciation
The allocation of the cost of tangible assets to multiple periods. The tangible asset's cost (or fair value, if donated) is divided by the number of periods the asset is expected to provide benefit. The resulting amount is treated as an expense during each period.

Designated funds
Unrestricted resources that the governing board or management has reserved for specific purposes. Contrast with *restricted funds.*

Direct costs
Costs that can be identified with a particular project or activity.

E

Educational and general (E&G) activities
Primary academic and related activities of a college or university. Types of E&G revenue include tuition and required fees, sales of educational services, and gifts. Types of E&G functional expenses include instruction, research, public service, academic support, student administration and services, institutional support, O&M of physical plant, and student financial aid. (The major category of activities not classified as educational and general is auxiliary enterprises.)

Endowment
A gift carrying a stipulation that the principal be invested in perpetuity, with the investment income generated by the gift being available for program support or other purposes. Income from restricted endowments supports specific programs identified by the donor, while income from unrestricted endowments may be used for any institutional purpose. True endowments are gifts of principal that may never be expended. Term endowments require that the principal be maintained and invested until a specified time passes or a specific event occurs. Quasi-endowments are resources set aside by an institution's governing board and combined with true and term endowments for investment purposes, with only the investment income available for use. Unlike the true or term endowment principal, the principal of quasi-endowments can be expended at the governing board's discretion.

Endowment income
Revenue earned by investing endowment principal, typically in stocks, bonds, and other investments. The revenue consists of dividends, interest, rents, royalties, and realized and unrealized gains from the sale of stocks, bonds, or other investments. Typically, only a portion of the earned income is made available for spending in a given fiscal year.

F

Facilities and administrative (F&A) costs
The portion of a sponsored program award that reimburses the institution for support costs incurred for the project. Also called indirect costs or overhead.

Financial exigency
An imminent financial crisis that threatens the survival of the institution as a whole and cannot be alleviated by less drastic means than the termination of faculty appointments. (Source: American Association of University Professors, *Recommended Institutional Regulations on Academic Freedom and Tenure.*)

Fiscal year
A 12-month period representing one operating cycle.

Fixed costs
Costs incurred irrespective of volume. Contrast with *semi-variable costs* and *variable costs.*

Formula budgeting
A budget strategy that relies on quantitative measures to distribute resources. Typical measures include student full-time equivalents, employee full-time equivalents, and assignable square feet.

Full-time equivalent (FTE)
A method for converting the number of part-time individuals (for example, students or faculty) into a standard equating to full-time status. For example, 30 students each taking six credit hours would equal 12 FTE students if the standard for full-time status is 15 credit hours. Contrast with *head count.*

Functional classification
A method of categorizing expenses based on their purpose rather than the nature of the expense. Examples include instruction, research, and academic support.

Furlough
Unpaid time off from work that employees are required to take as a cost-saving measure. Furloughs are usually of short duration (for example, several days or a week).

G

GAAP
Acronym for generally accepted accounting principles, the standards that must be adhered to when preparing financial statements that will be subject to an independent audit.

H

Head count
The total number of full- and part-time individuals in a given category (for example, students or faculty). Contrast with *full-time equivalent (FTE).*

Higher Education Cost Adjustment (HECA)
An inflation index maintained by the State Higher Education Executive Officers that tracks higher education cost drivers. Contrast with *Higher Education Price Index (HEPI).*

Higher Education Price Index (HEPI)
An inflation index maintained by Commonfund Institute that tracks higher education cost drivers. Contrast with *Higher Education Cost Adjustment (HECA).*

Hybrid budgeting
A budget strategy that blends elements of various discrete budget strategies (for example, responsibility center, zero based) to allocate an institution's resources.

I

Incremental budgeting
A budget strategy that focuses on percentage adjustments to the existing base budget rather than on specific priorities.

Indirect costs
Costs incurred for multiple purposes which therefore, cannot be linked to a particular project or activity.

Infrastructure
The foundational assets and resources needed to operate a college or university. Some assets are tangible (for example, roadways, steam tunnels, and computer system cables), while others are intangible (for example, systems, policies, and procedures).

Infrastructural plans
Long-term (two- to four-year) plans that guide the institution's operational activities. Such plans focus on core programmatic activities (for example, academics and student engagement) or essential campus-wide support activities (for example, facilities and IT).

Initiative-based budgeting (IBB)
A budget strategy that focuses on distributing resources to support specific priorities established during the planning process. Typically, such resources are not part of the base budget.

L

Lapsed salary
The portion of salary recaptured centrally when departments choose not to fill a vacant position or hire a replacement at a lower salary. Also called salary savings.

Line-item budgeting
A type of budgetary control under which resources are distributed in detailed categories, such as salaries, travel, and contractual services, with a requirement that funds be spent within those categories unless authorization is obtained.

M

Master plan
A depiction of the planned physical development of a campus, usually identifying existing boundaries and facilities as well as planned additions. Also called campus master plan.

Merit aid
Financial aid awarded to a student based on criteria other than demonstrated financial need. Frequently, merit aid is based on accomplishments in the classroom or on special skills or talents. Contrast with *need-based aid.*

N

Natural classification
A method of categorizing expenses by the type of expense rather than the purpose for which the expense is incurred. Examples include salaries, benefits, supplies, and travel.

Need-based aid
Financial aid awarded to a student solely on the basis of demonstrated financial need, as determined using an established methodology. Need can be met either with federal student aid programs or with institutional funds. Contrast with *merit aid.*

O

One-time budget funds
The portion of an operating budget that covers nonrecurring activities. Contrast with *base budget funds.*

Operating budget
The quantitative manifestation of an organization's (or one of its subunits') planned revenues, expenses, and contributions or withdrawals from reserves during a fiscal period (usually one year). Operating budgets typically are supported

by narrative documents identifying priorities and, in some cases, performance standards related to the various activities and programs to be supported by the budget.

Outsourcing
Contracting with a third party to provide required on-campus services. Fairly common for bookstores and dining operations, outsourcing can extend to a wide range of services, such as housekeeping, arena management, and various aspects of technology.

Overload
The additional workload of a faculty member in excess of the requirements for his or her normal full-time academic appointment. Also refers to the additional compensation provided for the additional effort.

P

Performance-based budgeting (PBB)
A budget strategy that relies on the establishment of specific institutional or unit performance objectives to justify a portion of base budget resources or incremental resources.

R

Reallocation
A process through which managers of programs and activities identify a portion of existing resources to redistribute in accordance with established priorities.

Reserves
Funds set aside as savings in accordance with organizational plans. Reserves frequently are designated for specific purposes, such as facilities maintenance and renewal, quasi-endowment, or a rainy-day fund.

Responsibility center budgeting (RCB)
A budget strategy that treats individual units and programs as revenue centers or cost centers. Revenue centers are allowed to control the revenues they generate and are responsible for financing both their direct and indirect expenses. Cost centers are supported by resources generated through charge-backs to benefiting units, assessments on the revenues generated by revenue centers, or by centrally administered allocations.

Restricted funds
Resources provided by external sources that must be retained and invested or expended in accordance with stipulations established by the provider. Under existing accounting rules, only donors can establish restrictions for independent institutions, while any external party (such as a donor, a creditor, or another government) can create restrictions for public institutions. Contrast with *designated funds* and *unrestricted funds*.

Retrenchment
Actions undertaken in response to serious financial difficulties; frequently includes the elimination or reduction of programs and activities.

Revenue center
An organizational unit with the ability to generate revenues by direct action. Contrast with *cost center.*

S

Semi-variable costs
A refinement of variable costs, semi-variable costs combine features of fixed and variable costs: They remain fixed within ranges but are affected by changes in volume. Contrast with *fixed costs* and *variable costs.*

Spending rate
The portion of resources related to each endowment fund that is made available for spending in a given fiscal year. Usually

expressed as a percentage, the amount typically includes both current investment yield (for example, dividends and interest) as well as a portion of accumulated appreciation and realized gains. Also called payout rate.

Sponsored program
An agreement between an institution and an external entity (such as a federal agency, corporation, or foundation) under which the former undertakes an activity with financial support from the latter. The agreement specifies what will be accomplished and identifies the amounts and types of costs that will be reimbursed.

Structural deficit
The amount by which operating expenses exceed operating revenues.

T

Top down
A budgeting philosophy that involves highly centralized decision making, with most direction filtering down through the organizational hierarchy from central administrative offices.

Tuition dependency
Excessive reliance on tuition and required fees to finance operations. An institution is tuition dependent if 85 percent or more of its revenue comes from tuition and required fees, especially if the tuition generated is not from diverse sources.

Tuition discounting
The practice of using institutional resources to award financial aid, thereby lowering the cost of attendance for selected students. Although the aid can address demonstrated financial need, it frequently is awarded on a merit basis.

U

Underwater endowments
Endowments with current market value that is lower than the original value of the gift(s) that established the endowment.

Unrestricted funds
Institutional resources that can be used for any purpose consistent with and supportive of the overall purpose of the organization. Contrast with *designated funds* and *restricted funds.*

Variable costs
Costs that vary directly with increases or decreases in volume. Contrast with *fixed costs* and *semi-variable costs.*

Zero-based budgeting (ZBB)
A budget strategy that requires programs and activities to rationalize their use of resources based on accomplishments.

Barr, Margaret J., and George S. McClellan. *Budgets and Financial Management in Higher Education.* San Francisco: Jossey-Bass, 2011.
The authors approach budgeting from the perspective of a budget manager. In addition to solid information directed at individuals new to the responsibilities of a budget manager, the book includes an excellent discussion of budget-related issues relevant to auxiliary enterprises and capital budgets. To illustrate many points relevant to budgeting, a case runs throughout the book.

Chabotar, Kent John. *Strategic Finance: Planning and Budgeting for Boards, Chief Executives, and Finance Officers.* Washington: Association of Governing Boards of Universities and Colleges, 2006.
Written as a high-level guide to the critical tasks of planning and budgeting, this book offers insights about how to develop strategic plans and what they should include. It highlights the importance of supporting a strategic plan with a financial plan and then linking both to the annual budgeting process. Useful charts and tables illustrate the key concepts, while a case illustrates how to apply the concepts.

Dickeson, Robert C. *Prioritizing Academic Programs and Services: Reallocating Resources to Achieve Strategic Balance.* San Francisco: Jossey-Bass, 2010.
This is the "bible" of prioritization. It describes the prioritization process from start to finish (i.e., implementation) and offers suggested criteria for prioritizing both academic and administrative programs and activities. The appendixes are particularly rich with examples and additional resources.

Ferren, Ann S., and Rick Slavings. *Investing in Quality: Tools for Improving Curricular Efficiency.* Washington: Association of American Colleges and Universities, 2000.
In this relatively short publication, the authors provide practical guidance about deconstructing the curriculum to examine how it supports or inhibits student success as a result of financial choices. It provides tools and techniques for analyzing the curriculum and then offers strategies for addressing the issues that surface.

Middaugh, Michael F. *Planning and Assessment in Higher Education: Demonstrating Institutional Effectiveness.* San Francisco: Jossey-Bass, 2010.
The reference to planning in the title is off target because the book really does not address planning. Nevertheless, it does an excellent job of explaining assessment and institutional effectiveness in terms easily understood by those not working in institutional research. In particular, Middaugh provides valuable information about communicating the results of assessment so as not to overwhelm the audience.

Snyder, Thomas D., and Sally A. Dillow. *Digest of Education Statistics, 2010* (NCES 2011-015). Washington: National Center for Education Statistics, Institute of Education Sciences, U.S. Department of Education, 2011.

This is the definitive source for data about higher education. Chapter 3, which focuses on postsecondary education, contains more than 250 pages of narrative and tables addressing a wide range of higher education issues, such as enrollment, staffing, degrees, finances, and financial aid.

Tahey, Phil, Ron Salluzzo, Fred Prager, Lou Mezzina, and Chris Cowen. *Strategic Financial Analysis for Higher Education: Identifying, Measuring & Reporting Financial Risks.* 7th ed. San Francisco: Prager, Sealy & Co., LLC, KPMG LLP, and Attain LLC, 2010.

This publication continues the series begun in 1982 by Peat, Marwick, Mitchell & Co., the predecessor firm of KPMG. It examines ratio analysis for higher education, including the Composite Financial Index (CFI) as well as other strategic financial analysis tools focused on resource allocation. The seventh edition expands the analysis of strategic financial risks and offers an extensive discussion of liquidity, including the suggestion of a ratio for measuring liquidity risk.

Reed, William S. *Financial Responsibilities of Governing Boards* Washington: Association of Governing Boards of Universities and Colleges, 2001.

Though directed at board members, this book provides a wealth of information about the finances and related processes at colleges and universities. Written for people who may not have a deep understanding of the academy, it introduces the critical issues that influence institutional success from a financial perspective. Topics include the operating budgeting, managing the endowment, capital budget considerations, and debt.

Sanaghan, Patrick. *Collaborative Strategic Planning in Higher Education.* Washington: NACUBO, 2009.

This "how-to" publication will appeal to those interested in conducting or participating in engaged, collaborative strategic planning. It offers insights about effective group interaction and describes a five-phase process for developing a strategic plan that can be implemented. Although the book focuses on *strategic* planning, the approaches and activities can apply to nearly any type of planning—whether infrastructural or operational. This is a true user's guide for effective planning.

Strauss, Jon C., and John R. Curry. *Responsibility Center Management: Lessons from 25 Years of Decentralized Management.* Washington: NACUBO, 2002.

This short publication provides a useful overview of the key issues related to responsibility center management (RCM). It discusses both planning and budgeting in an RCM environment, provides guidelines for developing and implementing resource allocation processes based on RCM principles, and—perhaps most important—offers responses to each criticism of RCM.

Whalen, Edward L. *Responsibility Center Budgeting: An Approach to Decentralized Management for Institutions of Higher Education.* Bloomington: Indiana University Press, 1991.
This book provides an in-depth examination of Indiana University's (IU) approach to developing and implementing a system of responsibility center budgeting (RCB). It provides the details of the decision-making process, summarizes the lessons learned, and offers insights that can be applied at other institutions pursuing RCB. IU may have the most complex cost allocation model in higher education, and the book includes an appendix containing a detailed explanation of its development. Additional value is provided by John Curry's afterword addressing the University of Southern California's experience with responsibility center management.

About the Author

Larry Goldstein is president of Campus Strategies, LLC, a management consulting firm providing services to colleges and universities as well as organizations serving higher education. He previously served as NACUBO's senior vice president and treasurer and as the University of Louisville's chief financial officer. His campus experience covered 20 years in financial administration, including positions with The University of Chicago, the School of the Art Institute of Chicago, and the University of Virginia.

Goldstein, a certified public accountant, earned a Bachelor of Accountancy degree from Walsh College and a Master of Science degree from the University of Virginia. He is a recipient of NACUBO's Daniel D. Robinson Accounting Award in recognition of his contributions to higher education accounting and financial reporting.